W9-AEX-328

BEING ANIMAL

Critical Perspectives on Animals: Theory, Culture, Science, and Law

CRITICAL PERSPECTIVES ON ANIMALS:
THEORY, CULTURE, SCIENCE, AND LAW

Series Editors: Gary L. Francione and Gary Steiner

The emerging interdisciplinary field of animal studies seeks to shed light on the nature of animal experience and the moral status of animals in ways that overcome the limitations of traditional approaches to animals. Recent work on animals has been characterized by an increasing recognition of the importance of crossing disciplinary boundaries and exploring the affinities as well as the differences among the approaches of fields such as philosophy, law, sociology, political theory, ethology, and literary studies to questions pertaining to animals. This recognition has brought with it an openness to a rethinking of the very terms of critical inquiry and of traditional assumptions about human being and its relationship to the animal world. The books published in this series seek to contribute to contemporary reflections on the basic terms and methods of critical inquiry, to do so by focusing on fundamental questions arising out of the relationships and confrontations between humans and nonhuman animals, and ultimately to enrich our appreciation of the nature and ethical significance of nonhuman animals by providing a forum for the interdisciplinary exploration of questions and problems that have traditionally been confined within narrowly circumscribed disciplinary boundaries.

The Animal Rights Debate: Abolition or Regulation?
Gary L. Francione and Robert Garner

Animal Rights Without Liberation: Applied Ethics and Human Obligations
Alasdair Cochrane

Animalia Americana: Animal Representations and Biopolitical Subjectivity
Colleen Glenney Boggs

Experiencing Animal Minds: An Anthology of Animal-Human Encounters
edited by Julie A. Smith and Robert W. Mitchell

BEING ANIMAL

BEASTS AND BOUNDARIES IN NATURE ETHICS

Anna L. Peterson

COLUMBIA UNIVERSITY PRESS   NEW YORK

COLUMBIA UNIVERSITY PRESS
Publishers Since 1893
NEW YORK   CHICHESTER, WEST SUSSEX
cup.columbia.edu

Copyright © 2013 Columbia University Press

All rights reserved

Library of Congress Cataloging-in-Publication Data
Peterson, Anna Lisa, 1963–
Being animal : beasts and boundaries in nature ethics / Anna L. Peterson
p.   cm.   —
(Critical perspectives on animals : theory, culture, science, and law)
Includes bibliographical references and index.
ISBN 978-0-231-16226-5 (cloth : alk. paper)   —   ISBN 978-0-231-16227-2
(pbk. : alk. paper)   —   ISBN 978-0-231-53426-0 (ebook)
1. Animal welfare—Moral and ethical aspects. 2. Animal rights.
3. Environmental protection.   I. Title.

HV4708.P478   2013
179'.3—dc23
2012039912

Columbia University Press books are printed on permanent and durable acid-free paper.
This book is printed on paper with recycled content.

Printed in the United States of America

c 10 9 8 7 6 5 4 3 2 1
p 10 9 8 7 6 5 4 3 2 1

Cover design: Jordan Wannemacher
Photo image: Hillary Kladke, Paw Prints Charming Pet Photography

References to Internet Web sites (URLs) were accurate at the time of writing.
Neither the author nor Columbia University Press is responsible for URLs that may
have expired or changed since the manuscript was prepared.

And I, a materialist who does not believe
in the starry heaven promised
to a human being,
for this dog and for every dog
I believe in heaven, yes, I believe in a heaven
that I will never enter, but he waits for me
wagging his big fan of a tail
so I, soon to arrive, will feel welcomed.

—Pablo Neruda, "Un Perro Ha Muerto"

CONTENTS

ACKNOWLEDGMENTS

It is always a pleasure to write acknowledgments, both because it means the work of writing is finished and because it is an opportunity to thank those who have made the work easier, better, or more enjoyable. I am grateful, first and always, to my family for their support and patience. My husband, Manuel Vásquez, listened to my endless worries and reflections about the issues examined in this book, even while busy with his own writing. He also tolerated and supported the huge amounts of time I have spent not only researching and writing this book but also immersed in the activist worlds of both environmental and animal advocacy. I could not do any of it without him.

There are many people in both those worlds who helped make this book possible as well. It has been a privilege and a pleasure to collaborate with smart, dedicated, and thoughtful people who care passionately about non-human nature in various forms. My own moral and political commitments, as well as my academic work, have been strengthened by my involvement with these activists. I am grateful not only to those with whom I collaborate at home in Gainesville but also to the good people from BAD RAP (Bay Area Doglovers Responsible About Pit Bulls), the Berkeley Humane Society, Maddie's Fund, and the Sierra Club, all of whom helped me think through many of the issues addressed here. I am even more grateful for the inspiration of their ongoing work.

A number of colleagues and friends also contributed to this book. In particular, I have benefited from conversations with Marc Bekoff, Laura Hobgood-Oster, Bill Jordan, LoraKim Joyner, Jessica Pierce, Katie Sieving, Sam Snyder, Dan Spencer, and Paul Thompson. I was able to present some of my early ideas about these issues at a conference at Ohio Northern University in April 2009, on the theme of "Recreate, Replace, Restore: Exploring the Intersections Between Meanings and Environments." Special thanks go to Forrest Clingerman and Mark Dixon, the organizers of that very productive and enjoyable meeting. Gretel van Wieren kindly invited me to Michigan State University when I was finishing this book and needed precisely the constructive dialogue I had there. I am also grateful for many constructive conversations with my students at the University of Florida, who have offered innovative ways to think about these issues and indulged my frequent classroom digressions about dogs.

I am indebted as well to my dog and horse trainers, Monica Body and Jessica Piazza, who probably do not realize how much they have shaped my thinking about animals, nature, and ethics. Last but certainly not least, I am grateful to my endlessly fascinating and invaluable dogs, especially Tozi, who will not stay on her side of the fence.

BEING ANIMAL

I

Introduction: Animals and Nature

Our relations with beasts lie at the centre of moral enquiry.[1]

WHO IS THIS DOG?

This book began with questions about what my dogs and my academic field, environmental ethics, might have to do with each other. According to everything I read, these two important parts of my life were entirely separate. In scholarly writing on the environment, mentions of companion animals are scarce and usually negative: domesticated animals in general are seen as human constructs separate from and opposed to wild nature. The scorn about domesticated animals is embedded within a larger lack of interest in nonhuman animals generally among environmental philosophers and other people who think seriously about nature. People who pay attention to animals, on the other hand, rarely reflect explicitly on nonhuman subjects' connections to natural places and ecological processes. While countless popular and scholarly books examine the natural environment, on the one hand, and animals, on the other, neither literature engages the other. Behind the separation between animals and nature lurks a host of unquestioned philosophical claims, beginning with an assumption that it is possible to understand the nonhuman world without serious reflection on animals, and vice versa.

I begin with the opposite claim: animals are part of nature. We cannot understand the environment or ourselves without confronting the mutually constitutive relationships that bind us to nonhuman subjects. The most intimate and complex of these relationships are with domesticated animals, liminal creatures who occupy the boundary between human society and wilderness. Their status points to the ambiguous relationship that all animals have with the environment. As active agents, they are never just part of wild landscapes. They are individual actors as well as members of biotic communities. Animals reveal the fluid and continuous character of categories like wild and domestic, nature and culture, and human and animal. Even the most domesticated creature is part of the vast realm beyond the boundaries of humanness. At the same time, even the wildest beast does not live in absolute isolation from human societies and meanings. These paradoxes organize my thinking in this book, especially the tensions between humans and animals, nature and culture, animals and nature, and domesticity and wildness. In each case, humans have constructed impassable boundaries between pairs that should be united.

The paradoxes of animals and nature are nowhere more obvious and more tantalizing than in companion species. Cats and dogs are unique among domestic animals not only because they live with us most intimately, frequently sharing not just our homes but our beds, but also because they are among the only domesticated predators. Virtually all the species domesticated for food and work are herbivores or small omnivores, like chicken and other fowl. Cows and horses are large and powerful and may trample humans or destroy our fences, but they do not hunt and eat other animals. Dogs, in particular, are capable of killing humans, and sometimes they do. For the most part, however, they behave like family members rather than powerful predators. Because they are both, they connect us to a more-than-human world that is at once familiar and mysterious.[2]

Dogs and other companion animals play unique roles in the development of *Homo sapiens* and the history of particular cultures. Many other species, wild and feral as well as domesticated, are also central in symbolic as well as practical ways to people around the world. They help us to make a living and also to make sense of the world. Wild animals represent the beauty, strangeness, and danger of a world beyond our own. Domestic animals reflect both our intimate connections to and our power over other species. While companion animals are at least partially incorporated into human families, other domesticated beasts are defined as "livestock." They are reduced to property, recognized neither as agents of their own lives nor as objects of care. The traits that define one animal as a pet and another as livestock, and indeed even that mark broader distinctions such as domestic, wild, and feral, are the result of human interpretations and practices and not of the animals' intrinsic capacities or subjectivity. This does not mean that animals do not define and shape their own worlds. Rather, it reflects the power that humans exercise over almost all members of almost all other species, from our pets to wild creatures living in wilderness thousands of miles away.

I live with four dogs, all complex and, to me, endlessly fascinating creatures. Perhaps the most paradoxical is Tozi, a brindle pit bull type dog. Tozi is the most domesticated of animals—obedient, affectionate, and sensitive to human moods and intentions. She loves children and not only tolerates but seeks out their sometimes rough attentions. She occupies the highest rung in our little pack, but she rarely enforces her rule with anything more dramatic than a sidelong glance and, in extreme cases, the glimpse of a shiny white canine tooth. People who do not generally like dogs often like her very much, because she is so calm, so gentle, so neat and polite.

Tozi is also an extraordinarily efficient predator. Her ancestors were "bull and terrier" dogs, bred in England to kill rats in cities, on farms, and in pits where men bet on the ability of dogs who killed as many rats as possible in a few minutes.[3] Tozi would have been a champion in those pits. While she has never shown aggression toward humans or other dogs, she quickly, quietly, and efficiently kills every animal her size or smaller she can reach, including not only rodents but also dragonflies, cicadas, lizards, snakes, moles, shrews, possums, and, most recently, a large adult raccoon. In order to reach them, she has climbed over, dug under, and broken through fences, as well as carving out holes in drywall.

These paradoxes pose a question: What do with do with Tozi? This is a practical question we ask in my family, as we build higher, stronger fences and supervise her every outdoor move. It is also a philosophical problem at the heart of this book. Tozi provides a lens for thinking through questions that must be answered in order to construct a nature ethic that makes sense of and values animals, ecosystems, and our own animal being.[4] What shall we make of a creature who is so tame and so wild? How can I understand this predator that kills a raccoon the same size as my child who sleeps next to her? What is the meaning of a dog who permits complete strangers to remove food from her mouth but gouges holes in the wood floor in efforts to reach the armadillo beneath the house? Who is this dog? Who am I with her, and what are we to each other? These are not rhetorical questions. Donna Haraway poses a similar non-rhetorical, deeply philosophical, question: What and whom do I touch when I touch my dog?[5] I touch family; I touch the wild. I do not touch a machine, a social construct, or a slave.

These claims run against the opinions of most environmental philosophers, few of whom seem to have met any real dogs. They suggest that I cannot and should not think about my dogs as nature. I begin with the opposite claim: it is impossible to think about nature apart from them.

MATERIALISM AND ETHICS

Thinking about animals as natural beings is difficult in environmental and animal studies because of the theoretical limitations of mainstream approaches in both fields. Even theoretical models that challenge dualistic understandings of nature and culture or body and mind still take for granted the divisions between domesticity and wildness and between individuals and wholes. In order to build a nature ethic that does justice to animals, ecosystems, and people, we need to begin with encounter and concrete engagement with nonhuman nature. To make sense of *Canis lupus familiaris* or any animal, wild or domestic, human or other, requires a theoretical approach that starts with real animals, not abstractions. More broadly, an adequate nature ethic is not just applied to or grounded in real-life practice but emerges from and always returns to actual encounter and engagement with the nonhuman world.

The most important model for this approach comes from Karl Marx, who sought a theory that does not descend "from heaven to earth" but rather ascends "from earth to heaven." Marx's philosophy does not "set out from what men say, imagine, conceive, nor from men as narrated, thought of, imagined, conceived, in order to arrive at men in the flesh."[6] Real individuals are not only the starting point of philosophy, for Marx, but its *raison d'être*. The point of philosophy, as his eleventh thesis on Feuerbach reminds us, is not merely to interpret the world but to change it.[7] Marx's interest lay only in living *human* individuals, but the power and scope of his thought makes it illuminating to apply to nonhuman subjects as well.

Some foundations for this project lie in the application of Marxian thought to the environment, a rich and growing field. One of the most prominent ecosocialist thinkers, John Bellamy Foster, contends that Marxist materialism, along with Darwinism, helped make possible contemporary ecological thought. Today, Foster argues, Marx's thinking can help us develop "a revolutionary ecological view" which "links social transformation with the transformation of the human relation with nature in ways that we now consider ecological."[8] Foster and other Marxist ecological thinkers have offered new ways of thinking about both humans and nature and the mutual shaping of individuals and structures and of nature and society. Their work shows the potential of a theoretical framework in which dualism can give way to mutual interaction. While ecosocialist thinkers have paid little attention to animals, the Marxian critique of dualistic thinking and individualistic anthropology, along with his central categories of relationship, alienation, and praxis, all offer new ways of thinking about animals and nature.[9]

Unhealthy Divisions

The separation between nature and animals is both strange and destructive. It is strange because most people readily describe animals as part of nature. Animals are, more specifically, on the "nature" side of a high, wide, and all but impassable theoretical boundary between nature and culture. (The practical boundary is usually much more porous.) It is destructive because it prevents us from understanding animals and nature as well as we might and also from protecting them as well as we should. The blocks to understanding can be considered in part as the result of several paradoxes that frame our thinking about not only nature and animals but also about what it means to be human. The divisions between thinking and concern about the environment, on the one hand, and about nonhuman animals, on the other, have developed in part because serious reflection about animals and nature would require us to confront both our own naturalness and our own complicated and often contradictory relationships to animals.

The first paradox involved in our conceptions of animals and nature is about ourselves: people are animals, yet animals are part of nature; nature is everything that is not human (or human-created); thus we cannot be animals. This is evident in the popular use of the term *animal* for all species other than *Homo sapiens*. When we stop to think about it, it becomes obvious that, as Mary Midgley puts it, "we are not just rather like animals; we *are* animals."[10] Still, we use the term as though it obviously excluded us while at the same time encompassing, unproblematically, every other living organism that moves under its own power, from gnats to lizards to coyotes to whales. Maintaining this line inviolate (at least in principle) requires defining individual creatures, species, and even qualities, habits, and capacities as one or the other: either human or animal, social or natural, intellectual or physical. The effort to keep the two sides apart leads to awkward and ultimately impossible claims that human beings are "blank slates," with no "natural" tendencies, either as individuals or as a species, because that would be "biological determinism." A more realistic view acknowledges that human beings are both natural and social at the same time, all the time.

The presumed division between the categories of human and animal is related to a series of other dualisms. The broadest of these is the divide between nature and culture (or nurture). Most Western traditions of thought, religious and philosophical, portray the two as mutually exclusive and opposed to each other. This nature-culture divide is necessary to maintain the strict split between humans and animals: we are creatures of culture and education, while they are products of biology and instinct. The opposition between nature and culture also represents a division within human beings, between our bodies and our minds or souls. It describes, further, presumed conflicts or differences between people, based on gender, ethnicity, class, national origin, or other features. In each case, certain people—women, natives, slaves—are seen as more natural, closer to animals, less cultured and civilized, than people in the other category.

Human-animal and nature-culture are familiar, if ultimately failed, paradoxes. They have been widely discussed and criticized, traced back to Plato, Thomas Aquinas, and Descartes, and blamed for all sorts of problems—or given credit for advances, depending on the writer's perspective. Well-traveled though these dualisms are, they are still worth noting and examining. They are related to another, less familiar and intuitive separation—that between animals and nature. These categories are not divided in popular attitudes as much as in scholarly and some activist thinking, from both environmentalist and animal rights perspectives. Even though animals are the most powerful and appealing aspect of nature for many people, scholarship on the environment rarely discusses animals as a distinct subject, and scholarship on animals, in turn, rarely addresses nature more broadly. This split seems unlikely, even jarring, in light of the primary opposition between humans and animals. How can animals be, on the one hand, not human and, on the other, not nature?

The conflict between animals and nature rests on the dualism between individuals and wholes, which has roots in the Enlightenment, again with a substantive contribution from the omni-culpable Descartes. Descartes and other Enlightenment thinkers, along with Protestant reformers, helped transform the Western understanding of persons from integral subordinate parts of organic collectives to rational, autonomous individuals whose liberty is ever-threatened by larger wholes. Scholars of both environmental and animal studies have failed to explore the ways this anthropology shapes attitudes about animals and nature. In particular, they have failed to question the assumption that individuals and wholes are related only in exclusionary and conflictive ways. Most, in fact, tacitly accept this assumption, insofar as they believe that it is impossible to care about both animals and the environment at the same time.

Both environmental and animal advocates assume, first, that the environment is about wholes, such as ecosystems and species, and that animal welfare is about individuals. Second, both fields presume that concern for animals necessarily conflicts with concern for ecosystems. The oppositional understanding of animals and nature is grounded in the broader conflict between individuals and wholes that pervades Western (especially U.S.) social thought, both popular and academic. Like nature and culture, individuals and collectives are seen in mutually exclusive and usually competing, rather than mutually constitutive and complementary, relationships. For example, this perspective makes government appear to threaten rather than safeguard individual liberty. This presumption of opposition means that we must choose one or the other—in our case, either animals or nature—because it is impossible to care about both.

The animal-nature split leads to a final opposition, between wild and domesticated animals. Environmental thinkers, in particular, view these two categories as absolutely separate and clearly identifiable. Wild animals are the only ones that matter for many environmentalists. They are part of nature; they belong in nature; they contribute to the health and value of ecosystems, habitats, biotic communities, and other ecological wholes. Domesticated animals, on the other hand, are by definition not wild; they were created by humans to be part of human society and fulfill our needs and desires. In the case of companion animals, they live in our homes and are often considered family members. They are border creatures, poised between the social and natural world. If they are nature, how can we— the opposite of nature—live with them so intimately? In the separation of spheres, domestic animals are double losers. On the one hand, they are reviled by environmental thinkers who see them as destructive artifacts of human design. On the other hand, within human society they are always inferior and exploited, because they can never be real persons.

If animals are Other to humans, part of the wild, the world beyond culture, then how can we understand them, and they us? What do these cross-species relationships ultimately mean? These questions can be addressed only in and through practice and encounter. Experiences with real animals are vital for understanding them as individuals, as nature, as themselves, and for understanding and challenging the theoretical categories that have been so destructive. Dualism is possible because of abstraction and reification. To challenge it, we need to make use of two categories that so far have not been central to environmental ethics—relationship and practice.

The relationships between people and animals, nature and culture, animals and the environment, and domesticity and wildness are both intimate and mutually constitutive. They emerge from and are sustained by practices of both human and nonhuman agents. These relationships, conventionally understood as dualisms, have molded our thinking about animals and nature and our ethical obligations regarding each. They also deeply influence our understandings of ourselves, both as individuals and as a species. The first challenge to these dualisms is the assertion that "nature" and "culture" are not mutually exclusive. This point has been made often and well by feminist thinkers, among others, who argue that nature and nurture are more accurately and constructively seen as mutually constitutive rather than opposed to each other.

Second, the distinction between nature and nurture does not divide humans from other animals. Nature and nurture together shape the character and lives not only of humans but also of most other animals. Individuals embody this constant interaction. All animals, including humans, are endowed by nature (courtesy of natural selection) with certain capacities and tendencies. It is foolish and destructive to ignore these innate qualities, in humans or any animal. Small children learn this when they take home a caterpillar who dies for lack of the right kind of leaves, and adults learn it all over again when their offspring have opinions, preferences, and talents that appear long before any training or social conditioning can have developed them. Nature is the first part of the equation, for humans and other animals. However, social experiences make a world of difference in what people and other animals become. The human child with innate musical talent still requires training, just as the young wolf requires instruction in order to develop her innate capacity for hunting. Recent research has shown, in fact, that many nonhuman abilities turn out to be much less "biologically determined" and more dependent on social experiences than previously thought. Not only do young predators require instruction in hunting, for example, but many songbirds cannot sing their species-characteristic songs without hearing it sung by adult conspecifics.

Nature and culture do not divide us from other animals; nor do they divide us within ourselves. We are both natural and social, human and animal, simultaneously, in all aspects of our lives. On the other side, other animals are much more complex than we usually allow, not only in their innate capacities but in their relations to various contexts. This is true for both wild and domestic animals, all of whom are both individual agents and members of various larger communities. These conclusions are not yet a universal consensus, but neither are they mere radical speculation. Careful research in both the natural and the social sciences, examining brains, behavior, socialization, and a host of other variables, points again and again to the mutual shaping of nature and nurture. All animals, including *Homo sapiens*, are the product not of "genes" or "environment" (including "culture") alone, but of the two together, even in the womb (or egg). The refusal to acknowledge the inextricable intertwining of nature and nurture, in humans and in other animals, has justified terrible cruelty and exploitation.

On both intellectual and moral grounds, we are led inevitably, though not easily or simply, to the conclusion that dualism and mutual exclusion are neither accurate nor constructive ways of understanding any beings. Challenging these dualisms is far from a novel task. The Hellenistic and Enlightenment heritage of nature-culture dualism, mind-body splits, and human exceptionalism has been mortally wounded, though not finally laid to rest. In particular, Descartes's error—the separation of mind and body that is related to the larger dualism between culture and nature—is almost too easy a target, so widely has it been attacked and discredited by environmentalists, feminists, cognitive psychologists, ethologists, neuroscientists, and many others.[11]

Of the various opposed pairs at stake here, only the dichotomy between nature and culture has received systematic attention from scholars in either environmental or animal studies. This overarching divide has provided a context for some discussion of the presumed divisions between animals and humans and also within humans, between the biological and cultural influences on behavior. The other pairs—animals and nature, wild and domestic, and individuals and wholes—have not been subject to the same critical scrutiny, at least in scholarship on the environment or on animals. It is impossible, however, to understand either nature or animals without bringing these other issues to light. Like nature and culture and body and mind, these other pairs are intimately related and mutually influential.

THINKING WITH ANIMALS

Animals' complex and often mysterious ways of being inspire endless human efforts to grasp what and who they are and what they mean for humans. This fascination is inspired by the paradoxes of animal being. They are like us and radically Other, part of the wild yet shaped by intricate social interactions with members of their own and other species. In imagination and in concrete interactions, animals provide our most powerful connections to nature in general. At the same time, they are inextricably part of human social, cultural, and personal histories, as individuals and as a species.

Animals are good to think with, as the French social anthropologist Claude Lévi-Strauss famously asserted, and not just good to eat.[12] Lévi-Strauss was pointing to the fact that people need animals not only for utilitarian purposes but also to categorize, interpret, and respond to their worlds. The truth of Lévi-Strauss's insight is reflected in the rapid growth of the interdisciplinary study of nonhuman animals in recent decades. Animals have proven good to think about (if not always with) for a large number of scholars, working from literary, historical, sociological, psychological, ethical, and scientific perspectives. Animal studies, also called human-animal studies, seeks to understand animals' places in human cultures and lives, as well as animals' own experiences and behavior. While animals have been the subject of human curiosity for all of recorded history (and before that, to judge from prehistoric cave paintings), the field has been systematized and expanded rapidly in the past decade or two. Several journals and book series have emerged, as well as regular meetings focused on different aspects of animal life and human-animal relationships.[13] Animal studies scholars have a vast data set, since animals have been ubiquitous in the myth, art, and ritual of almost every human culture, as well as in the more mundane tasks of making a living.

Thinking with animals is not only culturally valuable but perhaps even necessary for humans. Human brains evolved to think with and about other animals, to communicate with them, categorize them, and evaluate them as potential predators, prey, competition, and collaborators. Even today, thinking with animals is a special and probably necessary kind of mental and emotional activity. Research shows that children who live with companion animals develop important social and cognitive skills: they are better at decoding human nonverbal emotional cues and are perceived more favorably by peers.[14] The work of animals in diverse types of physical and psychological therapy shows that even people who do not live with animals benefit from their presence. In addition to well-documented positive effects on heart rate, blood pressure, and other physiological facts, animals can reduce social distance and facilitate positive encounters, helping to bring isolated individuals into society.[15]

Perhaps because animals are so good for us and so integral to our evolutionary and cultural history, people love to observe them, from their own pets to more exotic creatures in zoos, circuses, and safari parks. At any given time, most best-seller lists include at least a few books focused on animals, including nonfiction titles on animal behavior or training as well as novels in which animals play central roles. Dog books are especially popular, and recent best-seller lists include training guides by Cesar Millan and others; memoirs such as *Marley and Me*; studies of dog cognition and behavior, like *Inside of a Dog: What Dogs See, Smell, and Know*; and true-life stories such as *Scent of the Missing: Love and Partnership with a Search-and-Rescue Dog* or *The Lost Dogs: Michael Vick's Dogs and Their Tale of Rescue and Redemption*. However, people also read books about almost every kind of animal on almost every topic imaginable, ranging from animal emotions (*When Elephants Weep*) to novels with animals as central characters (mystery-solving cats are especially popular) to hard-to-pigeonhole best sellers like *Animals in Translation: Using the Mysteries of Autism to Decode Animal Behavior* by Temple Grandin. In addition to books, animals are the stars of television shows from *The Adventures of Rin Tin Tin*, *Lassie*, *Wild Kingdom*, and *Flipper* to the entire Animal Planet channel, as well as films featuring Willy the orca, Babe the pig, Benji the dog, and many others.

People need animals and value them—at least sometimes. People also threaten and harm animals daily by abandoning and neglecting them, destroying countless acres of wild habitat, and, of course, eating them in astounding and ever-growing quantities. Our paradoxical relationship to animals is captured in the title of a recent book—"some we love, some we hate, some we eat."[16] Serious reflection on attitudes and uses of animals in different societies must confront these paradoxes. This requires not simply acknowledging the complexity of animals' roles in human societies and their potency as symbols and aids to thought but also examining animals' own capacities, interests, and experiences.

Nonhuman behavior, especially in relation to evolutionary processes, is the subject of ethology. Although ethology as a distinct discipline traces its roots back to the work of pioneering European scientists such as Konrad Lorenz and Niko Tinbergen in the first half of the twentieth century, the field has expanded rapidly in the past few decades. Most recently, ethologists have incorporated approaches from cognitive science, which originated as an exploration of the evolutionary and adaptive dimensions of human behavior. Cognitive ethology has helped reveal both the diversity and complexity of animal behavior and the connections between some human and nonhuman behaviors and traits.[17]

Ethology shows that many animals think for themselves as fully as people think about them. Animals not only have meaning as objects of human scrutiny but also make their own meanings, as agents with distinctive interests and perspectives. They are individuals and at the same time active members of various communities, which include local habitats, larger ecosystems, populations, and often human homes, farms, or neighborhoods as well. They are all these things simultaneously. No less than humans, most nonhuman animals are both objects of larger forces and active shapers of their own lives and environments, relational beings who interact in diverse ways with the diverse other beings who share their home places. Also like humans, other animals are sometimes victims who require our help, and sometimes they can be dangerous threats from whom we need protection.

ANIMALS IN NATURE

Understanding nature and its meaning for humans is the task of environmental studies, an interdisciplinary field that emerged in the mid-twentieth century out of diverse streams, including "nature writing" and natural history, advocacy, and the emerging scientific field of ecology. Since its origins, environmental studies has had a strong though sometimes ambivalent relationship to environmental movements, and divisions within the scholarly field have often paralleled those among environmental advocates. Among scholars and activists, for example, there are diverse views on how to value nature—for its intrinsic value or its usefulness to humans—and about how best to protect it. Today environmental studies encompasses diverse disciplinary perspectives, from the humanities, social sciences, and natural sciences, as well as law and policy studies, and also myriad political perspectives, ranging from the deliberately detached to the passionately partisan.

Within environmental studies, the intertwined subfields of environmental philosophy and environmental ethics are especially relevant for this book because they focus on the meanings and values that humans find in nonhuman nature. Environmental ethics makes explicit two important principles that are broadly shared in other environmental scholarship. First, nature has intrinsic value, and second, this value resides in ecological wholes rather than individual natural entities. Together, these two principles form an ecocentric holism that underlies most theories of environmental value, from moderate to more radical streams. The dominance of ecocentric holism has contributed to the theoretical and practical gap between concern for nature in general, on the one hand, and for animals in particular, on the other. This is related to the division of animals into two categories, wild and domestic, which appear to have little if anything to do with each other. Wild animals are part of nature, while domestic animals are extensions of human society, degraded creatures who invade and harm wilderness.

The almost complete subordination of animals to ecological holism in environmental ethics is inverted in philosophical reflections on animals, which usually treat animals as isolated individuals whose ecological histories and contexts are irrelevant to their moral status. Animal ethicists prize, almost exclusively, individual qualities such as sentience or capacity for suffering. They are especially concerned about suffering caused by human actions, particularly toward animals for whom humans are responsible, such as domestic animals and those living in captivity. While animal ethics has been vital for both philosophical and practical discussions of human relations with animals, it often takes the form of abstract reflections on human duty rather than attention to concrete interspecies encounters.

In addition to the splits between animal and environmental advocates, both groups are internally divided on a number of issues, including different valuations of subgroups such as native and exotic wild animals or farm and companion domesticated animals. Disagreements about these issues reveal not only the fault lines between environmentalists and animal advocates but also, perhaps more important, different ways of thinking about problems in moral theory, including the significance of emotions and relationships and the relationship between ethics and practice.

The importance of both emotional connections and practical experiences is highlighted when we consider the fact that the theoretical divide between animals and the environment often does not translate into practice. A large number of people who see themselves as "animal lovers" also consider themselves "nature lovers."[18] Most self-described animal lovers, further, embrace both wild and domestic creatures, and for the same reasons: a felt connection to nonhuman subjects and a conviction that animals are parts of a larger community with which people are, and want to be, connected. While this sense of relationship encompasses wild animals, it finds its most concrete expression in regard to domestic animals, especially companion species such as dogs, cats, and horses. These species connect nature and human social worlds. Because of this status, they deserve much greater and more positive attention than they have received from either environmentalist thinkers or environmental activists. Felt connections and real encounters with the oppressed Other are necessary for both better knowledge and effective social change.

The mutually transformative encounters among active subjects are what make animals, and our relationships with them, different from "the environment" in general and from inanimate parts of nature. Interactions with animals are part of our experience of the nonhuman natural world, but they are also mutually transformative encounters between active subjects. This distinguishes human relations with animals from our experiences in "the environment" more generally. People often have deep love for, and powerful experiences in, natural places and entities, such as forests, rivers, mountains, even individual trees or boulders. There is, indeed, an entire genre of "nature writing" exploring these experiences in a wide variety of places, from the desert to the sea to the rainforest. However, encounters with animals challenge us and move us in different ways. They are creative social actors, sentient individuals, ecological shapers.

Thinking about animals in this way can transform understandings both of nature in general and of environmental practice. It may also contribute to a greater public relevance for environmental philosophy and ethics. A number of environmental thinkers have bemoaned their scholarship's lack of impact on policy and public opinion, finding its contributions "bleak," in the words of Bryan Norton.[19] Not all scholars believe that the lack of obvious practical applicability is a problem, but many do want their research and writing to influence public discussions about how to value and care for nonhuman nature. The lack of practical impact stems in part from the failure of environmental studies to consider nature as most people conceive it, including the central role of all sorts of animals. Environmental scholars are isolated from public discussions partly because of their own failure to think seriously about how animals are part of nature, how our concerns for animals and for the environment are connected, and how, in practical terms, we must consider both together in order to address a number of ecological and social problems.

Some scholars not only misunderstand how people think about animals but deride it. Despite the deep-seated and widespread human attraction to other species, many environmental philosophers and scientists view attachment to animals as evidence of wrong-headed attitudes toward nature. Even those who differ on most issues agree on the moral irrelevance of individual nonhuman animals. For example, a major division in contemporary environmentalism is between wilderness advocates and their critics. The advocates argue that nature is valuable in its own right and that preserving wilderness areas should be a priority for environmental advocacy. For critics of this perspective, wilderness is a social construct, produced by human imagination and culture. They see the idea of wilderness apart from human civilization as a destructive fiction. Despite deep differences, both sides of the wilderness debate describe attention to individual animals as sentimental and unscientific. Both sides also accuse the other of misreading humans' proper relationship to nature. There may be a connection between these two problems. Perhaps the difficulty of sorting out our relations to the nonhuman world is linked to the fact that environmental thought has shut out nonhuman animals.

We cannot be connected to nature without animals. The ability of environmentalists to influence public debates and policy regarding nature will be limited if we do not deal explicitly with the sentient, animate creatures who populate it. This is especially true of domestic animals, considered in environmental thought rarely and almost never positively. Domestic animals are border creatures, linking nature and culture. They are also the part of nature that most people interact with most frequently and intensely, and in many cases they enable "the only one-on-one relationship with animals left to us."[20] We can learn a great deal about nature in general from our understandings and practices regarding domestic, especially companion, animals. We also learn from the other creatures who live near us, not always by invitation—the raccoons in the backyard, feral cats in the vacant lot, mice in the attic. These animals can help us think about key issues in environmental philosophy, including not only well-established topics such as wilderness, intrinsic value, rights, and interests but also less familiar themes such as work, relationship, and home. If we do not think seriously about nonhuman animals, including domestic ones, our understanding of nature more generally will remain inadequate.

ORGANIZATION OF THE BOOK

The book is divided into eight chapters. Following the Introduction, the next two chapters provide context for the overall argument by describing and analyzing the perspectives of scholars and advocates concerned with both the environment and nonhuman animals. Chapter 2 describes the ways that environmental thinkers, especially philosophers, have conceived of and valued nonhuman animals. The chapter highlights the dominance of ecocentric holism in environmental studies, which locates value in ecological systems and considers individual animals in relation to their larger ecological functions. Chapter 3 explores scholarly and activist concerns about the welfare and human treatment of nonhuman animals. While environmental philosophers and ethicists do not have much to say about nonhuman animals, there is a vast separate literature on animal welfare, rights, and human obligations. The arguments can be broken into various models, including theoretical frameworks articulating rights or Utilitarian approaches and new perspectives, including those drawing on care ethics.

Chapters 4 and 5 lay out the issues related to wildness and domesticity. Chapter 4 explores the significance and meaning of free-ranging wild animals for environmental politics and philosophy. Environmental scholars value wild animals mainly for their role in ecosystems, and very few engage the ever-growing literature on nonhuman sociality, cognition, and emotion. I discuss, briefly, some of the recent research that shows the complexity of wild animal behavior, including playful interactions between members of different species as well as among both young and adult individuals of the same species.

In Chapter 5, I turn to environmental thinking about domestic animals, who are usually seen either as either irrelevant or destructive in ecological terms. The latter critique emerges most often in relation to farm animals, especially those raised in industrial-style facilities. However, there are also tensions between environmentalism and pet-keeping, including the environmental impact of pets' resource consumption as well as more abstract questions about whether human relationships to companion animals are always fraught with power and dominance, reinforcing exploitative attitudes toward nature more generally.

The remainder of the book builds on the concepts and context discussed in the first five chapters to develop a synthetic, constructive argument about animals, nature, and ethics. Chapter 6 examines the tensions between ecological holism and animal advocacy. This debate plays out in theory, especially in efforts to reconcile the welfare of individual creatures (wild or domestic) and the health of larger ecosystems. The conflict also has significant practical ramifications, which are exemplified in discussions about hunting. I explore this case study as a way to illuminate some of the larger moral, philosophical, and scientific issues involved in thinking about individual animals and ecosystems. I also discuss, in this context, the ecological problems created by feral and invasive animals and the ethically and politically charged debates about ways to reduce their impact.

The last two chapters reflect on the possibilities of reconciliation, common ground, and theoretical and practical innovation. I look not only at theoretical issues but also at concrete experiences, practices, and relationships among humans and nonhumans. Chapter 7 examines some of the historical, practical, and theoretical connections between environmental and animal welfare movements. These connections have not had much impact on the contemporary scholarly literature on either animals or ecology, despite a number of efforts to reconcile concern for animals and concern for nature. The most successful of these have not remained within established theoretical frameworks but have drawn instead on more innovative approaches, especially feminist and Marxist ones, that emphasize meso-level approaches and relationships between scales.

Chapter 8 proposes a practice-based nature ethic, drawing especially on Marx's categories of relationship, alienation, and practice. In the context of environmental ethics, such a model demands that we pay more attention to domestic, and especially companion, animals, with whom we have our most important cross-species interactions. The controversies surrounding "dangerous dogs" illuminate human fears about the wildness of our closest companion animals. The chapter ends with reflections on the possibility of bridging the gaps between holistic environmental concerns and concern for individual animals, grounded in lived practice.

2

Animals in Environmental Perspective

Nature means mountains, swamps, oceans, and the night sky, but it also means animals of all sorts. Recognizing their symbolic and emotional power, environmental advocates often use images of wild animals in order to raise both consciousness and money. While wolves in Yellowstone serve as proud symbols of a wilderness that deserves protection, oil-soaked pelicans on Gulf Coast beaches provide concrete images of human destructiveness. However, nature also means more homely animals who live in our backyards, city parks, and even within our houses. Familiar creatures—an owl hooting in a suburban tree, deer paused on the roadside at dusk—both symbolize nature in general and attract people to it. Not insignificantly, this is how children first focus on nature also, though sometimes they are later educated to think on grander scales.[1]

People rarely think of "nature" apart from its sentient, animate subjects. In turn, few of us see animals without some awareness of wild nature. Animals lure us to encounter and explore the more-than-human world, to cross the line between nature and culture. Wild animals do this most obviously, even (or especially) in urban and suburban areas. In such settings, where wild nature often seems distant, the sight of a hawk circling overhead or a raccoon heading back home in the early morning is a reminder of a world in which humans are not the central actors. Domestic animals also point to realities beyond the species boundary. They live in human society but are never fully of it, not just because human attitudes exclude them from full citizenship but also because the animals themselves escape full incorporation. There is always an excess, a "more," that cannot be exhausted by their lives with us. Even our closest companions, the dogs and cats who live in our homes, are never fully humanized.

This does not mean they are not domesticated; it means that domestication is not identical to humanness. This counters the claims of some environmental thinkers that domesticated animals are cultural artifacts, created by humans for human ends and thus devoid of the qualities, both ecological and individual, that give wild animals value. For these thinkers, only wild animals are nature; domesticated ones are in an entirely different category. However, this division itself is a social construct. The sharp line between wild and domestic animals has no basis in evolution, anatomy, or behavior. Domesticated, wild, and feral creatures alike shape and are shaped by their environments, interact with members of their own and other species, build relationships and families, and work to fulfill both their needs and their wants. They are competent within their own worlds. In the worlds of domesticated animals, humans are usually important (though not the only) actors.

Both evolutionary history and contemporary physical and behavioral similarities suggest that the relationships between wild and domesticated species is not absolute opposition but rather a complex continuum. This shift in perspective shakes the foundations of scholarly thinking about animals, which is divided between wild animals, to be understood in holistic environmental perspectives, and domesticated ones, to be interpreted as subordinate elements of human societies. They are radically different subjects who demand radically different moral and intellectual approaches. To challenge the hard hard-and-fast dualism between domestic and wild animals requires new theoretical perspectives, grounded not in abstract categories but in the flesh-and-blood experiences of animals.

ANTHROPOCENTRISM

Thinking about animals as part of nature pushes us to specify the meaning of *nature*, an endlessly contested word. For most of Western history, attitudes toward the nonhuman realm have involved a mixture of fear, disgust, and utilitarian appreciation. Wild animals appeared as the most potent parts of the alternately frightening or useful world beyond human civilization. Human interactions with and imaginings about wild animals have both contributed to and been molded by ways of thinking about nature in general, and in particular by the dualisms discussed in chapter 1. Not only do we hold nature apart from culture, and humans apart from animals, but we also make equally polarized distinctions within these categories, between nature and individual animals and between wild and domestic animals. Equally stark subdivisions are present within the categories "human" and "culture," as well, and not infrequently certain humans, or certain cultures, are lumped with animals or nature.

The division of nature and culture justifies the exploitation of nonhuman individuals and places on the basis of innate human superiority, usually based on qualities that no nonhuman animal possesses. In religious worldviews, this trait is often an eternal soul. Biblical traditions attribute to humans a special status, often based on their creation in God's image, which entitles them to power over the rest of creation. In extreme forms, this dominion permits virtually any treatment of wild places, plants, and animals, as long as it serves presumed human interests.

The trait that counts for secular philosophers varies—it can be reason, language, tool use, or another quality presumably unique to humans. The standard has changed over time due both to shifting cultural values and to new knowledge about both human and nonhuman capacities.[2] The hyper-valuation of rationality has roots in the Scientific Revolution, which advanced a view of nature as passive, inert, and machine-like, as Carolyn Merchant describes.[3] This new model justified the exploitation and manipulation of nature and nonhuman animals. It was accompanied by philosophical reflections that celebrated reason as the defining, and most valuable, human (mainly male) quality. René Descartes remains the paradigmatic expression of this anthropocentric tradition, the philosopher that environmentalists love to hate, the poster child for mind-body dualism and the denigration of everything associated with nature and the body, including women and animals.

Human exceptionalism undergirds not only philosophical but also popular attitudes and laws regarding both natural places and animals. This is especially evident in the definition of land, plants, and domestic animals as private property. Cutting down an ancient tree, poisoning a creek, or killing a domesticated animal is an offense against the person designated as owner. Natural entities themselves, even sentient animals, lack legal standing or rights because they have no value apart from their instrumental use by humans. No harm can be done to them for their own sakes. Animal cruelty laws, for example, have long focused on offenses done against human owners, and for many years owners could not be prosecuted for cruelty against their animals. Despite some recent changes, mainly regarding companion animals, domesticated animals continue to be defined legally as property in most cases, as are wild animals living on land owned by individuals. Intrinsic value seems possible only in nature apart from human claims of use or ownership.

Challenging Anthropocentrism: The Intrinsic Value of Nature

In contrast to the anthropocentrism that dominates popular thinking about nature, many environmental scholars and activists insist that nature has value in and of itself. Human beings are not the only centers of intrinsic value, and nonhuman natural entities can be valuable regardless of human use or appreciation. Instead, as environmental philosopher Eugene Hargrove summarizes, environmental thought usually asserts that nature and natural entities constitute "a significant good in the world" on their own terms.[4] This assertion implies a moral claim: because nature is good, it deserves human respect and protection. Environmental thinkers are divided about whether belief in nature's intrinsic value is necessary for conservation. Some believe that respect comes only with acknowledgment of intrinsic worth, while others assert that human-centered theories of natural value can also provide effective grounds for environmental practice. In reality, many people appreciate nature (like most things that we value) for a variety of reasons, including both instrumental and intrinsic values.

Nonetheless, environmental philosophers share a strong (though not unanimous) consensus that nature has intrinsic value and that this assertion is important for justifying and encouraging appropriate human attitudes toward the environment. Claims of intrinsic value are usually combined with a holism according to which the basic unit of value is an ecological collective such as an ecosystem or "biotic community." Value comes from the whole, and individuals are significant because and insofar as they contribute to the well-being of the whole. The combination of intrinsic value and holism is called *ecocentrism*, which dominates contemporary environmental ethics. Within this model, the value of nonhuman animals depends mainly on their contributions to the health and functioning of ecological wholes.

The Land Ethic

The best place to begin exploring ecocentric perspectives and their significance for nonhuman animals is the foundational text of environmental ethics—Aldo Leopold's essay "The Land Ethic," published posthumously in his 1949 book *A Sand County Almanac*. Environmental thought has grown and diversified greatly in the decades since then, but Leopold's essay remains a canonical text, cited by almost all environmental theorists, even those who diverge significantly from Leopold's conclusions. Leopold established the twin principles that dominate environmental ethics today: an insistence that nature's value is not limited to its utility to humans and an identification of the ecological community as the center of value. Animals, for Leopold, are important in direct proportion to their contribution to the good of the larger ecological community.

According to Leopold, all ethical systems assert that "the individual is a member of a community of interdependent parts."[5] Further, ethical behavior represents a triumph of education and culture over basic human nature. He believed that humans' instincts incline them to compete with each other and that the function of ethics was to constrain these natural inclinations and instead encourage cooperation. He advocated a communitarian ethic not because he thought people were social animals but precisely because he accepted the dominant view of human nature as both individualistic and self-interested and the consequent dualism between individuals and wholes. Ethics are required precisely because people are selfish and autonomous. They thus need encouragement, perhaps coercion, in order to set aside self-interest for the good of larger collectives.

The innovation of the land ethic is to expand this collective obligation to include "soils, waters, plants, and animals, or collectively: the land." This "simple" expansion of community transforms "man" "from conqueror of the land-community to plain member and citizen of it. It implies respect for his fellow-members and also respect for the community as such."[6] The land, then, is to be treated like any other community in which people participate. Leopold likened this expansion of concern to previous shifts in ethical thinking, in which marginalized human groups, such as slaves and women, were gradually included as part of the moral community. This inclusion limited the freedom of action of others, who could no longer treat people in this category in solely instrumental ways. The inclusion of the land within an expanded ethic would require people to stop treating it merely as property. Leopold sought to transform the ethic guiding people's use of land from a model "governed wholly by economic self-interest" to one in which the good of the whole took precedence over individual profit. Thus Leopold summarizes his ethic: "A thing is right when it tends to preserve the integrity, stability, and beauty of the biotic community. It is wrong when it tends otherwise."[7]

The ethical obligations of membership in the biotic community differ from those of membership in social collectives in one crucial respect: unlike human individuals, individual nonhuman members of the land community do not have intrinsic value. Leopold's ecocentrism still presumes a qualitative difference between humans and other animals. Constraints on the ways in which animals, plants, or other natural entities may be treated are based not on their individual qualities but on their membership in the land community. Leopold thus condemned an instrumental treatment of nature in general while retaining a largely instrumental role for individual animals, whose status does not differ substantially from that of plants, rivers, rocks, or soil. He saw no ethical harm in hunting abundant herbivores such as deer, for example.

The impact of Leopold's work cannot be overstated: he both foreshadowed and shaped the ecocentric framework, based on ecological science and oriented toward the good of the biotic community, that continues to dominate American environmental thinking and advocacy. This model proposes a transformation in human attitudes toward nature "from conqueror of the land-community to plain member and citizen of it." While Leopold adds that this perspective implies respect not only for "the community as such" but also for our "fellow-members,"[8] neither the theoretical nor the practical implications of the land ethic prescribe significant changes in our behavior toward nonhuman animals. People may continue to treat animals in instrumental ways, only now they are instrumental to the health of the land community rather than to human profit. The standard for judgment becomes their ecological functions and context, rather than their economic roles in human societies. Any consideration of nonhuman animals as individuals, however, remains missing.

Ecocentric Ethics

Contemporary environmental philosophers read the land ethic in distinctive ways, in accordance with the emphases of their own positions. Leopold did not elaborate his philosophical system but left only the short essay titled "The Land Ethic" and some related ideas scattered in other writings, leaving room for differing interpretations by later scholars. Leopold's thought is not inconsistent, but it is far from a systematic, fully thought-out analysis of all aspects of an environmental ethic. Still, most environmental philosophers agree that the land ethic is—and environmental ethics today should be—both holistic and centered on nature's intrinsic value.

Most also agree that these twin principles invariably make nonhuman animals at best a secondary concern for environmental thought.

The most prominent proponent of a contemporary land ethic is the philosopher J. Baird Callicott, who has updated Leopold's work to take into account contemporary ecological science. According to Callicott, concern for preservation of the biotic community always trumps moral consideration for individual members. Thus the land ethic "not only has a holistic aspect; it is holistic with a vengeance."[9] This holism stems from the land ethic's reliance on the science of ecology, which is deeply holistic in both its founding assumptions and its conclusions. The relationships between organisms, Callicott explains, bind them "into a seamless fabric. The ontological primacy of objects and the ontological subordination of relationships characteristic of classical Western science is, in fact, reversed in ecology. Ecological relationships determine the nature of organisms rather than the other way around." Callicott calls this a "superorganism" model of ecology, in which "the system itself determines its component species."[10]

A more moderate holism sees ecosystems not as organisms but as communities, in which individual members retain some autonomy. These are just two of various models proposed and debated by ecological scientists and the scholars who use their work.[11] The superorganism model implies the reification of the whole and the subordination of individual members and makes it difficult to assert any sort of rights for individual plants or animals.[12] Such rights, however, may be not only unnecessary for but even opposed to a proper environmental ethic, from an ecocentric perspective, because preserving overall ecological good often demands the sacrifice of individual entities.

This model describes life in nature as an endless struggle for survival in Darwinian terms, in which "one being lives at the expense of others." Because this is "the way the system works," as Callicott asserts, it follows that "if nature as a whole is good, then pain and death are also good. Environmental ethics in general require people to play fair in the natural system."[13] Playing fair, in this view, entails leaving wild animals to live, struggle, and die without human intervention, whether destructive or helpful in intent. Pragmatist Eric Katz rejects Callicott's moral monism but agrees on the need for individual pain and sacrifice to maintain the well-being of the ecological community as a whole: "ecosystems function, develop, and survive by means of the life and death struggle of competing natural forces, competing living beings. Humans cannot act to prevent the suffering and death of all animal life and remain true to an *environmental* ethic.[14] For Katz, Callicott, and most other ecocentrists, further, people should not only allow natural suffering to unfold but sometimes participate in it. To restore natural processes, for example, people may hunt animals of an overabundant species, just as they may remove invasive nonnative plants.

Such destruction is both necessary and justified because individual "natural entities," including animals, are subordinate to the collective values inherent in the collective. As Holmes Rolston puts it, "even the most valuable of the parts is of less value than the whole. Subjects count, but they do not count so much that they can degrade or shut down the system, though they count enough to have the right to flourish within the system."[15] For Rolston, it makes no sense to think about nonhuman natural entities, including animals, outside their participation in ecological wholes: "Loving lions and hating jungles is misplaced affection. An ecologically informed society must love lions-in-jungles, organisms-in-ecosystems, or else fail in vision and courage."[16] Such a society must also accept the death of many lions and other organisms in order to preserve the greater good of jungles and other ecosystems and of the ecological evolutionary processes that continue in them.

Naturalism and Its Discontents

Rolston bases his holistic ethic on a naturalistic description of the way nature "really is." Humans do not invent but merely discover the intrinsic value of ecosystems: "An *ought* is not so much *derived* from an *is* as discovered simultaneously with it."[17] He makes explicit the naturalism that lurks beneath many other ecocentric ethics. This approach begins with the conviction that it is possible to know how nature really operates, and that it is for the most part red and tooth and claw. Further, naturalists (and crypto-naturalists) assume, an environmental ethic should be based on what nature requires to continue operating in this way. What succeeds in evolutionary terms indicates what humans should value in nature.

Naturalism, however, has been condemned for its circular logic, according to which the attribution of value in certain entities is referred back to the original description of those entities. The problem is that descriptions are never morally neutral. A different "is," implying different "oughts," emerges when we describe ecosystems as superorganisms, for example, rather than as communities of relatively autonomous individuals. The same problem is evident in descriptions of animals. If they are like machines, our moral obligations toward them are very different than if they are feeling, thinking agents. Similarly, describing some kinds of people as naturally inclined to certain pursuits such as, say, raising children, lending money, or picking cotton, can lead to problematic moral judgments. Appealing to expert or popular consensus does not resolve this problem, as history has shown that one generation's universally accepted fact can become the next generation's anathema.

Precisely because scientific worldviews are constantly evolving, it is easy to recall many widely endorsed assertions, including a flat earth and a geocentric cosmos, that were subsequently proven false. With regard to nonhuman animals, scientists are disproving widely endorsed assumptions on an almost daily basis. Some of these findings are extremely far-reaching, such as Jane Goodall's discoveries about chimpanzees' tool use and language studies involving primates, cetaceans, parrots, and most recently, dogs. Equally revolutionary findings about avian brains have led to major revisions in nomenclature as well as to new understandings of birds' ability to perform complex cognitive and social tasks previously thought to be limited to mammals.[18] Such changes make naturalism in environmental and animal ethics as problematic as it is generally assumed to be in social ethics. If we do not know what "is," or if our picture of reality is always changing, it is impossible to use that as a basis for an "ought."

For these and other reasons, most philosophers describe naturalism as a particular kind of fallacy and avoid it as a source of moral judgment.[19] Environmental philosopher Paul Taylor, for example, explicitly denies that ecological science can provide models to use in environmental ethics, precisely because this approach confuses "is" and "ought." The question of how humans fit into the order of nature and how we should act toward nonhuman entities, in this view, is not a question of biological fact but a problem of human reason and agency.[20] We can and should use knowledge from ecology and evolutionary science, as from economics, history, psychology, and other fields. This information, however, does not lead directly to moral decisions, which require additional reflection and discernment.

Ecocentric holists, however, implicitly and sometimes explicitly rely on conceptions of "the way nature really is" to justify particular ways of treating both natural systems and individual animals. Holists believe that evolution and ecology provide unbiased descriptions that generate authoritative value claims. Callicott, for example, writes that "the ever-evolving scientific worldview enjoys genuine international currency." An environmental ethic grounded in ecological and evolutionary science, he believes, can "make a claim to universality simply to the extent that its scientific foundations are universally endorsed—whether openly and enthusiastically or sub rosa."[21] A wide range of other thinkers also place evolutionary theory at the center of environmental ethics, such as Catholic ecotheologian Thomas Berry, who describes evolution as the centerpiece of "our new story of the universe."[22]

Ecocentric interpretations of ecology and evolution almost always prioritize the well-being of wholes above individuals—until we arrive at *Homo sapiens*, when the harsh attrition necessary for evolution is rejected wholesale. Naturalism gives way to the myth of absolute divisions between humans and all other animals, as between culture and nature, domesticity and wildness. Very few environmental thinkers apply ecological holism to human beings, despite the fact that most environmental problems stem from our species' blatant disregard for natural selection and ecological limits. The reluctance to apply the "greater good" logic to ourselves stems from an acknowledgment that natural selection is an often cruel and arbitrary process. Luck, rather than inherent fitness, determines the fate of many creatures. Firstborn eagle chicks often push their younger siblings out of the nest to die. This practice is harsh for the birds unlucky enough to be born second, but it makes sense in a larger picture, since eagle parents often cannot provide well for multiple chicks.

Ecocentrists do not apply this evolutionary logic outside wild nature. While accepting the arbitrary fate of the second chick, ecological naturalists recoil from any suggestion that overtaxed human parents use the same logic. There are many reasons for this reaction, including emotional ties as well as "rational" arguments about human superiority. The underlying justification, however, is the dualistic line between humans and nature. The division between wild and domestic animals creates a similar ethical split. Many environmental thinkers believe it is acceptable and even obligatory to care for premature, ailing, or elderly pets (and some farm animals), while at the same time prohibiting such interventions in wild nature.

A Deeper Holism

Despite efforts to distance themselves from biological determinism and moral naturalism, environmentalists have been regularly accused of wanting to apply evolutionary logic to human beings. Both mainstream environmentalists and popular opinion charge certain radical ecologists with a misanthropic wish that most human beings "die off" for the greater good of wild nature. The organization Earth First! is most often associated with this perspective, even though very few of its members advocate it. This image was nurtured by a 1987 article published in the *Earth First!* journal, under the pseudonym "Miss Ann Thropy," which argued that AIDS was a necessary solution to human ecological destruction.[23] Even though many radical environmentalists, including some Earth First! members, disowned the article's perspective, it reinforced the popular impression that ecological concerns could lead to disregard for human welfare and even to fascism and genocide. The article remains the most widely cited, and often the only, evidence for Earth First!'s misanthropy.

This popular perception extends to Deep Ecology, often called the philosophical expression of radical ecological movements such as Earth First! Deep Ecology began with the work of Norwegian philosopher Arne Naess in the early 1970s. In contrast to the shallow, short-range, instrumentalist, and anthropocentric approach of most mainstream environmentalists, Deep Ecology, according to Naess, is holistic and ecocentric in a more radical and thoroughgoing way than Leopold's land ethic.[24] Deep Ecology's distinctive feature is not so much its understanding of wild nature as its redefinition of human nature. According to Naess, only a rethinking of humanness, which he terms an "ecological gestalt-shift," will bring about the necessary transformation in attitudes and treatment of nature. Where this leaves nonhuman animals, however, remains unclear.

Naess's gestalt shift begins with a rejection of "the man-in-environment image" in favor of "the relational, total-field image," according to which "a thing's essence is exhaustively determined by its relationships . . . it cannot be conceived apart from its relationships with other things."[25] In philosophical terms, this is a theory of internal relations. Most Western philosophies assume that individuals preexist their relationships with others and thus can enter into voluntary exchanges that do not affect their essential identities. Contract theory exemplifies this perspective. If relations are internal, however, there is no autonomous individual who can choose (or not) to interact with others. We are related, social creatures from the very start, and our connections with others—chosen and not—make us who we are. While internal relatedness is foreign to the Enlightenment-based theories that dominate Western social thought, it is an important principle in some alternative streams, including Marxism and perhaps Roman Catholicism, as well as in many Asian and indigenous religious traditions.

Deep Ecology's second main principle is "biospherical egalitarianism," according to which all life forms are equal in principle. This principle, even more than the assertion of interconnectedness, is the main link between the philosophy of Deep Ecology and environmental movements such as Earth First! If all species are equal, then human beings cannot justify the destruction of others—from redwood trees to phytoplankton to whales—

for their own benefit. (Very few Deep Ecologists, other than Miss Ann Thropy, actually advocate the destruction of some human beings for the greater ecological good.) This theoretical commitment to species equality is shared by many animal ethicists and a few environmental ethicists, notably Paul Taylor.

Despite the subversive implications of its core principles, Deep Ecology is more anthropocentric than either critics or supporters believe. The assertion that all beings are equal, Naess explains, is "not some kind of unconditional *isolatable* norm to treat everything the same way," but rather is "only a fragment of a total view." This total view is the goal of finding "a form of togetherness with nature which is to our own greatest benefit." Naess clarifies this by noting that "our own benefit" means "that which serves the great Self" and not just individual ego or human societies. However, human beings will find "some killing, exploitation, and suppression" necessary, precisely for this greater good.[26] The good of the human "ecological self" and that of the ecological "great Self" are thus linked in a unique way, which justifies a prioritizing of human well-being. Naess's assertion of biospherical egalitarianism coexists with the claims that humans are biologically and culturally unique and also that we have greater obligation to beings closer to us. Both these principles can justify killing or injuring nonhumans.[27] Thus even though Deep Ecology appears to be a more radical form of ecocentric holism, in the end it makes the familiar exceptions for human beings, who alone cannot be sacrificed for the greater good.

Deep Ecology paradoxically denies differences between humans and nature, on the one hand, and reaffirms human uniqueness, on the other. The "ecological self" becomes a way of encompassing nature's good within human self-interest, as ecofeminist philosopher Val Plumwood notes. The expanded self, she argues, "is not the result of a critique of egoism. Rather, it is an enlargement and an extension of egoism," which may colonize and absorb, rather than respect, natural others.[28] Plumwood's critique of Deep Ecology is especially relevant for human attitudes toward nonhuman animals, whose absorption into larger wholes has frequently justified exploitation and cruelty. From the perspective of the ones who are sacrificed, it may not matter if this larger whole is the biotic community, the ecological self, human society, or the kingdom of God. No less than anthropocentric philosophies, Deep Ecology fails to distinguish between "nature in general" and sentient, subjective creatures other than human beings. It lumps all animals on the other side of the species line into an undifferentiated "nature." Even while rejecting dualism between humans and animals in theory, even the most radical ecocentrists accept, or at least fail to question, human exceptionalism in practice.

VALUING ANIMALS IN WHOLES

In holistic philosophies such as the land ethic and Deep Ecology, individual nonhuman animals have value only because, and to the extent that, they contribute to the healthy functioning of larger ecological systems. In order for the system to continue, many individual animals and plants must suffer and die prematurely. In some species, the vast majority will die before reaching reproductive age. Because this attrition is necessary for both evolutionary and ecological reasons, there are no grounds for criticizing it within ecological holism. Ecocentrists thus condemn efforts to mitigate the suffering of wild animals or to save their lives from natural processes such as predation, starvation, or accidents. These criticisms are central to the common environmentalist dismissal of animal advocacy. However, such efforts are almost nonexistent in practice, and even philosophical justifications of such intervention in wild nature are so few and far between that the criticisms seem at the least misinformed and at worst deliberately misleading. The animal activist trying to save deer from wolves is a straw man.

Still, most animal ethicists do value individuals based on characteristics such as sentience, intelligence, or sociability, none of which are especially significant to overall ecological health. For ecocentrists, such attitudes are nonscientific, because they are not based on ecological principles; they are shallow, because they appreciate animals for human reasons; and they are sentimental, because they mistake emotional appeal for actual value. Environmentalists often criticize attention to "charismatic megafauna" such as lions, wolves, orangutans, or whales, especially when less attractive but more ecologically important natural entities are ignored or devalued. The preference for certain kinds of animals influences popular and governmental attitudes toward environmental problems and can undercut support for important programs that lack appealing "poster animals."

A good example is the aftermath of the April 2010 explosion of the Deepwater Horizon in the Gulf of Mexico. Popular and governmental concern focused on "cute big creatures" such as dolphins, sea turtles, and pelicans. When these animals did not appear to suffer significant mass die-offs, media and popular attention diminished, along with support for ongoing cleanup and restoration work, even though there is strong evidence that microorganisms such as coral and phytoplankton suffered major harm.[29] Many of the places and animals affected by the oil spill live in the deepest parts of the ocean and have never even been seen by humans, let alone established popular images that draw widespread affection and concern. As the scientists studying the Deepwater Horizon disaster learned, creatures such as squid and plankton do not draw much attention or concern, despite their ecological importance.

In the case of the Gulf oil spill, as in many other environmental problems, most people's attitudes toward the value of nature are mixed. People worried a great deal about the environmental damage done by the spill, but their responses rarely followed ecocentric principles. Some of the concern was anthropocentric, focused on human loss of life, destruction of jobs, and overall economic impact. Much of the concern focused on the fate of certain individual animals. This concern presumes that some natural entities are intrinsically valuable, worth protecting and saving even at great cost. The problem, in the view of many ecological scientists and advocates, is that the creatures who merit this devotion are not always, or even usually, those who are most important from a holistic perspective. Public responses to the Deepwater Horizon spill reflected a lack of ecological knowledge, insofar as the responses focused not on animals and plants who were crucial for the big picture but on those who were appealing in and of themselves.

While these attitudes are not exactly ecocentric, neither are they precisely anthropocentric. People value sea turtles, dolphins, and pelicans not because they are useful but because they inspire emotional and moral commitments. These commitments stem from different sources, including respect for their wildness and radical otherness as well as felt connections to sentient, intelligent, and sociable creatures who appear to be like us in some ways and with whom we can enter into meaningful interactions. Deep ecologists and other environmental holists criticize such attitudes as sentimental or shallow, because they are not based on the value of nature on its own terms or on a holistic understanding of the interdependence of all forms of life. The principles of intrinsic value and holism are linked in ecocentric thought because natural value resides only in the system itself. This perspective provides no grounds for valuing nonhuman animals in and of themselves. If individuals have value, it is in relation and subordinate to the greater good of the whole.

Environmental holism can thus be differentiated not only from ethics that value individual human beings (what Callicott terms "moral humanism") but also from philosophies that extend concern to individual nonhuman animals ("humane moralism"). Many environmental advocates disdain animal rights theories because of this individualism. From a holistic perspective, "humane moralism" does not challenge Enlightenment-based philosophies of human rights and liberation but merely extends them. Stepping across the species line, in this view, is not a significant shift as long as the individual remains the fundamental unit of concern. Theories of animal rights pose "no serious challenge to cherished first principles," or at least to the first principle of moral individualism, which Callicott sees as characteristic of "business-as-usual" Western ethical theory.[30] For him, the real issue is whether value resides primarily in individuals or wholes, rather than what kind of individuals (human or nonhuman) have value. Thus he argues that moral humanism and humane moralism have more in common with each other than either does with environmental ethics.

This way of framing the debate ignores several significant points. First, ecocentric ethics are not the first holistic philosophies in Western history. In fact, the dominance of individualism is fairly recent, rooted in the Protestant Reformation and the philosophical Enlightenment. Various forms of humanistic holism have thrived before and since those developments, including Marxist, Catholic, and Anabaptist social thought. In addition, numerous non-Western religions, including Buddhism, Taoism, and many indigenous cultures, offer examples of nonindividualistic moral philosophies, some of which have influenced many Western environmental thinkers. Holism was not invented by Aldo Leopold or Arne Naess.

Second, and more important for thinking about nonhuman animals, it is possible to see the great innovation of environmental philosophy not as holism but rather as the assertion of nonhuman centers of inherent value. Many environmental thinkers view intrinsic value as important only in combination with holism. A closer examination of the history of Western thinking about nature, however, suggests that finding intrinsic value in non-human nature is just as radical as finding intrinsic value in wholes rather than individuals. If this innovation is emphasized, then animal ethics and environmental ethics might stand together in direct challenge to the deep humanism of the Western tradition. More broadly, the relationship between how we think about and treat animals and how we think about and treat nature in general depends on a host of factors, including not only theories of value but also our definitions of animals, nature, and humanness.

ENVIRONMENTALISM WITHOUT ECOCENTRIC HOLISM?

Although ecocentrism is the overarching worldview of many environmental advocates and ecological scientists, it enters unevenly into popular attitudes about nature and animals, as responses to the Deepwater Horizon spill revealed. Most people's values are mainly anthropocentric, which means that nature is important primarily insofar as it is useful or appealing to humans. However, this utilitarian strain is often combined, in the same person or same culture, with a strong appreciation for the intrinsic value of some natural entities, especially certain individual animals or species and also certain kinds of ecosystems. Both these priorities bother ecological holists, for whom whales are arguably less important than plankton and apparently barren ecosystems such as deserts or deep oceans matter just as much as savannahs, rainforests, or alpine meadows filled with large, beautiful animals.

Ecological holism encourages people to see the value of natural entities, places, and process that they do not personally appreciate. Holists correctly assert that without this larger picture, environmental policies would be based only on human priorities and thus would fail to protect much of nonhuman nature. On the other hand, ecological holists may dismiss people's preferences too thoroughly. Terms like "charismatic megafauna" suggest that felt connections to certain animals are inevitably shallow and misguided. To dismiss these bonds is to fail to understand how people think about and value nature and to lose the opportunity to build more effective movements to protect the more-than-human world in all its complexity. Ecocentric holism is an important way to value nature but not the only way. Alternative models, which highlight holism without intrinsic value or assert intrinsic value without holism, both reveal gaps in the dominant approaches and underline enduring obstacles to an ethic that considers animals, including human ones, as both active subjects and parts of nature.

Holism Without Intrinsic Value: Anthropocentric Environmental Ethics

Many environmentalists criticize human-centered ethics as inevitably destructive of the natural world. If human goods are the priority, they assert, the environment will always lose. It is true that locating value only in humans and human goods often leads to exploitation and abuse of nonhuman nature, including animals. However, some environmental thinkers believe that it is possible to develop more positive visions of nature from an anthropocentric perspective. Such models, they argue, have greater popular appeal and thus greater potential for practical impact.

A number of anthropocentric environmental ethics are based on a commitment to preserving nature for future human generations. The liberal philosopher Avner de-Shalit, for example, has developed a secular environmental ethic based on the concept of a transgenerational community, extending into the future, which creates specific obligations to future generations.[31] In more practical terms, the influential concept of sustainability is grounded on this principle: environmental protection, balanced with economic development and social equity, should be guided by the goal of preserving resources without significant depletion or contamination for future generations into the foreseeable future. Sustainability has largely replaced environmentalism as the "generative metaphor" in public discussion about human obligations toward nature, especially since the 1987 Brundtland Commission report *Our Common Future* and the 1992 Earth Summit in Rio de Janeiro.[32] Theories of sustainability view nature primarily in human-centered terms, as a resource for meeting human needs. These models hold a mixed promise for nonhuman animals, diminishing their moral status in principle while sometimes making possible stronger practical and legal protection.

Some anthropocentric environmental ethics are religious in origin. Many of these emphasize the principle of stewardship. This model is rooted in theological worldviews, in relation to human responsibilities to be good stewards of God's creation. In contrast to the "anything goes" approach of dominion models, stewardship limits human treatment of nonhuman nature, including animals. Humans are to protect and preserve wild places, and to treat animals kindly, as expressions of respect for the Creator, manifestations of their own moral commitments, and consideration for future human generations. In a stewardship ethic, the conviction that "the land is God's" sets guidelines for human moderation and humility.[33] For religious believers, this ethic can be a strong motivator, because it grounds care for nature in a larger moral framework.

Another influential contemporary environmental philosophy, pragmatism, is also often anthropocentric in tone. Environmental pragmatism, building on the work of American philosophers John Dewey and Charles S. Peirce, rejects the metaphysical concerns of ecocentrists and constructs a holistic ethic on very different grounds. One prominent environmental pragmatist, Bryan Norton, agrees with ecocentrists that "an environmental ethic must support the holistic functioning of an ongoing system."[34] For Norton, however, this holism stems from a variety of values, not simply the greater good of the biotic community. He describes Aldo Leopold as "a moral pluralist who struggled to integrate multiple values rather than an axiomatic deducer of applications from some universal principle." According to Norton, Leopold was interested less in what people should value in nature than in what, in practical terms, they should protect through environmental management.[35] This focus on functionality defines environmental pragmatism, which aims to solve problems rather than debate metaphysics.

Echoing pragmatist themes, Don Marietta advocates an explicitly holistic and anthropocentric environmental ethic. He argues that environmental policies must be grounded in an understanding of humans as fully integrated into natural systems. "The environment that makes life possible for humans also enables all other organisms, great and small, to live, and we can see that our human lives are depending on those other lives."[36] While this view attributes some value to natural entities and places, overall Marietta argues for a "holistic anthropocentrism," centered on human goods but also placed in a larger ecological context. The value of this ethic comes from a recognition that "concern for humanity might offer a better approach to environmental ethics than has been recognized by many environmental philosophers," particularly ecocentrists such as Callicott and Naess.[37] A number of other prominent environmental philosophers, including Ben Minteer and Andrew Light, advocate a "pragmatic holism" that emphasizes practical conflict resolution over theory and at the same time is holistic in its focus on "the *entire* problematic situation."[38]

Anthropocentric environmental ethics do not challenge the notion that the world was intended primarily for human use and thus that nature's value is instrumental to human welfare. In practice, such ethics can be powerful motivations for efforts to appreciate, protect, and restore nature. People need clean air and water, safe ways to produce food, and sustainable sources of energy, and they want the same for their children and grandchildren. In a major study of American environmental attitudes in the 1990s, 85 percent of respondents cited their children or future generations in general as a justification for environmental protection, even though this issue was not listed by the researchers. This high proportion is unusual for an open-ended question, the authors note, and "in fact, concern for the future of children and descendants emerged as one of the strongest values in the interviews."[39] The same study found that few respondents held "biocentric" attitudes toward nature, according to which ecological communities and wholes are the center of value.[40] This research suggests that anthropocentric valuations of nature, combined with concern for particular species and even individual animals, characterize most Americans' environmental attitudes and can be a powerful motivation for stronger environmental laws and policies.

Pragmatist criticism can redirect environmental ethics away from the question of who has intrinsic value and toward the issue of what difference it makes to attribute intrinsic value to any nonhuman entity or whole. If the defining feature of environmental ethics is concern for nonhuman nature in any form, individuals or wholes, then environmental ethics can be connected to animal ethics in an integral way. However, pragmatism also runs into problems when important goals come into conflict: without clear philosophical grounds for choosing among different values, how are environmentalists to know what is the right decision? Both pragmatism, according to which a moral claim has value because most people accept it, and naturalism, according to which a moral claim is right because "that is the way things are," ultimately run into the same problem: they provide no grounds for choosing in difficult dilemmas. The problem with "ethical eclecticism," as Callicott notes, is that "it leads, it would seem inevitably, to moral incommensurability in hard cases."[41]

This dilemma is especially relevant to the position of nonhuman animals in environmental thought. Because of its consensus-building approach and its rejection of absolute moral claims, pragmatism generally supports moderate positions regarding animals. This means that the interests of both wild and domestic animals usually take second (or third or fourth) place to other things that humans value more. Like ecocentric holists, most environmental pragmatists support hunting and fishing in at least some circumstances, including for the control of feral and invasive species, positions that most animal welfare advocates reject. More generally, environmental pragmatism tends toward an anthropocentrism that cannot safeguard either ecological wholes or nonhuman animals when these appear to conflict with human interests or desires.[42]

Intrinsic Value Without Holism

In most versions, environmental pragmatism is a kind of anthropocentric holism that rejects the usual link between holism and intrinsic value. The other exception to this pairing is biocentric individualism, in which nature has intrinsic value, but this resides in individual entities rather than ecological wholes. This perspective is common among animal ethicists, who insist that individual animals have value regardless of their usefulness to humans and that this value restricts the ways humans may treat animals. As I discuss in the next chapter, this basic argument takes many different forms within the larger field of animal ethics, including rights,

Utilitarian, and care-based perspectives. Individualism is much less common among environmental philosophers. A major exception is the work of Paul Taylor, whose ethic of "respect for nature" locates intrinsic value in the individual entity as a "teleological center of life." For Taylor, individual plants and animals "have a good of their own. They can be benefitted or harmed." This is true even if they are not conscious of the harm or good being done to them. This value, inherent in their very nature, should protect them from deliberate harm and other forms of instrumental treatment by humans.[43]

Although Taylor writes as an environmental philosopher, he shares the methodological and ethical individualism of animal ethicists, who generally insist that intrinsic value lies in individuals rather than wholes. Taylor casts a broader net than most animal ethicists, for whom consciousness or sentience is the foundation for intrinsic value. For Taylor, all living organisms, including plants, are "teleological centers of life in the sense that each is a unique individual pursuing its own good in its own way."[44] It is no more justifiable, in this perspective, to harm animals who are common or ecologically insignificant than to harm those who are endangered. The inherent qualities of individual creatures, and not just their contribution to the good of the whole, determine moral behavior. In this perspective, collective harms are simply the sum of the individual harms that are done; the ecological community as a whole is not the focus. "It is true that a greater wrong is done when a whole species-population or biotic community is harmed," Taylor admits, but "this is not because the group as *such* has a greater claim-to-be-respected than the individual, but because harming the group necessarily involves harming many individuals." From this perspective, further, healthy ecosystems are important because they enable individuals to thrive, but systems have no value beyond this.[45] Taylor thus challenges the holism of the land ethic and other biocentric models while retaining their insistence that nonhuman nature possesses value independent of its usefulness to humans.

ECOFEMINISM

Ecofeminist thought provides an alternative and a challenge to both holistic and individualistic models. Ecofeminism begins with the claim that women have a distinctive and morally significant relationship to nonhuman nature and that gender is a significant factor in determining how people think about and treat nature. Attitudes toward nature, as Carolyn

Merchant writes, "can be seen as a projection of human perceptions of self and society onto the cosmos. Conversely, theories about nature have historically been interpreted as containing implications about the way individuals or social groups behave or ought to behave."[46] Such theories often portray nature as female and women as more "natural" (and less cultured) than men. These associations have helped justify the exploitation of both women and nonhuman natural entities, including forests, land, and animals.

Ecofeminists rethink the relationship between women and nature in order to provide grounds both for valuing nature and for rethinking gender identity. This entails a rejection of the dualisms not only between nature and culture and between humans and animals but also between women and men. Ecofeminists reject what Karen Warren calls "the logic of domination," which conceives of difference as inequality, creating "value-hierarchical thinking." Such thinking views hierarchies as dualisms, so that the terms in pairs such as nature-culture, women-men, or animal-human are seen as opposed and mutually exclusive rather than complementary. The "logic of domination" justifies the subordination of the "lower" term in each pair.[47] This logic not only justifies exploitation of subordinate categories but also links those categories together, associating women with nature and animals.

Some ecofeminists, often called "essentialist," accept the connection between women and nature and elevate these traditionally denigrated categories.[48] Others reject the dualisms altogether because, as Plumwood explains, women and men alike are equally part of nature and culture.[49] Both versions of ecofeminism challenge central assumptions of mainstream Western philosophy, most fundamentally the definition of human beings as autonomous, rational, and radically other than nonhuman nature. In place of this view of human nature, Plumwood proposes an "ecological self" which is more relational and which links its own well-being to the flourishing of nonhuman nature.[50] This is not the "Self" of Deep Ecology, which Plumwood criticizes for extending the (male) Ego to incorporate nonhuman nature, rather than respecting nature's relative autonomy. Ecofeminism provides an alternative to both holistic and individualistic environmental philosophies. This alternative is grounded in the "self-in-relationship," a model of humanness that recognizes individual integrity as well as interdependence, relationship, and continuity. This differs from both the indistinguishability of Deep Ecology and the atomism of the Cartesian tradition, because it rejects their shared presumption of conflict between individuals and wholes.[51]

While religion has contributed to mainstream thinking about nature, it also provides some important alternatives. Religiously based environmental ethics are often more anthropocentric than secular environmental philosophies, especially those that draw heavily on ecological science. Western monotheistic traditions, in particular, have been reluctant to agree with Leopold's assertion that people are just "plain members and citizens" of larger ecological communities. Many religious thinkers combine concern for overall ecological well-being with continued assertion of humans' special status and power. One such model is stewardship ethics, according to which humans have a unique role among God's creatures, resting on their creation in God's image. Humans cannot exercise simple "dominion" over nature but rather must treat it with restraint and respect, as God's stewards on earth.

Stewardship is grounded in theories about creation, one of the most persistent and important themes in religious views of nature. Because creation stories are central to many different religions, they can provide a common language for thinking about human responsibilities to nature. Even many nonreligious people find creation evocative, as Max Oelschlaeger asserts: "Religious discourse may help Americans come together as a nation and move toward sustainability because it converges, through the diversity of faith, on a common center of caring for creation."[52] This thesis received support from research on American attitudes toward the environment, which found that even individuals who do not invoke God in other contexts do so in order to talk about the meaning and value of nonhuman nature. The ubiquity of talk about God and creation, even among unbelievers, may be due to the fact that "divine creation is the closest concept American culture provides to express the sacredness of nature. Regardless of whether one actually believes in biblical Creation, it is the best vehicle we have to express this value."[53]

The power of religion both to express the value of nature and to provide a common language for environmental advocacy has attracted some secular environmental advocates and philosophers. Like Oelschlaeger, Baird Callicott argues that purely secular environmental programs may be ineffective without the justification and inspiration provided by traditional religious worldviews.[54] These thinkers acknowledge that secular, scientifically based environmental ethics may not appeal to a wider public. This reflects a major shift from attitudes of a few decades ago, when many environmentalists joined scientists in considering religious attitudes largely destructive or dismissive of ecological concerns. Similarly, a number of environmental advocacy organizations have in recent years publicized the work of religiously based activists and, in some cases, sought alliances with them. This has proven especially important in relation to environmental justice concerns among working-class and minority communities. The nation's largest environmental organization, the Sierra Club, has made religious communities central to its environmental justice work, recognizing both the growth in religiously motivated environmental activism and the fact that "lasting social change rarely takes place without the active engagement of communities of faith."[55]

While human-oriented ethics are the dominant religious approach to environmental protection, they are not the only kind. Protestant theologian James Gustafson defends a theocentric ethic, centered on God's power. In this perspective, the value of nature rests neither in the good of ecological wholes nor in the well-being of humans. Rather, Gustafson explains, nature's good comes from God and is separate from, and sometimes even opposed to, human welfare. "If God saw that the diversity God created was good, it was not *necessarily* good for humans and for all aspects of nature."[56] This approach can coexist with ecological views insofar as humans do not have special status. God is the source of human good but does not guarantee it, and while nature is not the enemy of human well-being, neither is it always a friend.[57] Theocentric environmental ethics such as Gustafson's have received little serious attention from environmental philosophers or even mainstream ecotheologians, perhaps because they appear limited in their popular appeal. Environmental advocates, however, often overestimate the appeal of ecocentrism, on the one hand, and underestimate the public influence of religion, on the other.

Even for thinkers who do not accept the religious underpinnings of theocentric ethics, such models offer alternative perspectives on some entrenched dilemmas of mainstream environmentalism. In particular, theocentrism challenges the dualisms between intrinsic and instrumental value, nature and culture, and even individuals and wholes that both ecocentric and anthropocentric thinkers have failed to overcome. A theocentric model puts all these dualisms in the context of a larger divine purpose, which both encompasses and transcends human and ecological goods. Theocentrism demonstrates that the dualism between ecocentrism and anthropocentrism does not exhaust ways of thinking about nature's value and human obligations. It dethrones humans by placing them on the subordinate side of the key divide, which is no longer between nature and culture but between God and creation.

Challenges to established Western models of thinking can also be found in Asian traditions such as Buddhism, Taoism, and Hinduism, as well as in indigenous traditions from the Americas, Africa, and Australia. In their readings of Asian traditions, environmental philosophers in the West have highlighted interdependence, which is especially prominent in Buddhism and Taoism. The Buddhist notion of dependent co-origination, in particular, resonates with the ecological conception of systems as composed of mutually dependent parts rather than isolated, autonomous individuals. In this view, "no differentiated being can exist by itself. It can only exist because it is a member of a bonded community which has evolved totally interdependently."[58] This theme is echoed repeatedly in both Buddhist thinking about nature and environmental philosophy in search of "conceptual resources" from outside the West.[59] A number of prominent Deep Ecologists, including Arne Naess, Gary Snyder, and Joanna Macy, have drawn heavily on Buddhist thought in developing their own views about ecology, human nature, and the relations between the two.

In addition, many Western environmental advocates and thinkers have found inspiration in Native American cultures, and especially in indigenous understandings of nonhuman agency, attachment to place, and constraints on consumption. Native peoples, in this view, exist in active, participatory, and respectful relationships with nonhuman entities and the land itself, and these relationships ground moral codes that enable indigenous societies to live "lightly" in wild places.[60] These themes are exemplified in Richard Nelson's ethnography of the Alaskan Koyukon people, who exist in such harmony with their environment, according to Nelson, that "despite continuous and intensive human activity, the[ir] country remains essentially pristine."[61] He contrasts this with dominant North American ways of relating to nature: "The fact that Westerners identify this remote country as wilderness reflects their inability to conceive of occupying and utilizing an environment without fundamentally altering its natural state. But the Koyukon and their ancestors have done precisely this over a protracted span of time."[62]

In many indigenous traditions, animals are active agents and participants in multispecies communities. In myth, animals such as ravens, coyotes, wolves, and deer play central roles in the creation of human cultures. A number of rituals, especially those related to hunting, trapping, and fishing, emphasize both the agency and intelligence of nonhuman animals and the importance of expressing appropriate gratitude toward prey animals. If people do not follow the proper hunting etiquette, not only will their efforts likely fail, but they may also cause larger repercussions for their own families and entire cultures. These themes of restraint, humility, and gratitude appeal to many ecocentric environmentalists.

Western environmentalists often view the traditional practices and ideas of Native Americans as models for more ecologically sound ways of living. Indigenous cultures, like Asian traditions of thought, also question the entrenched individualism of mainstream Western ways of thinking about nature, if only by showing that radically different alternatives exist. In the United States and other industrialized Western societies, however, neither indigenous nor Asian traditions have the public influence wielded by major Western systems of thought, especially Enlightenment-based liberalism and Protestant Christianity. Even environmentalists who admire non-Western attitudes toward nature acknowledge the need to engage mainstream traditions. Further, there are practical, political, and moral difficulties inherent in the appropriation of concepts from one tradition into a vastly different cultural context. Many Native American activists, for example, object to the adoption of indigenous practices, such as sweat lodges, by white environmentalists.

Despite important differences between secular and religiously based environmental ethics, the latter do not pay significantly more attention to animals than the former. In religious thinking, as in secular models, moral reflections on animals and on the environment are kept largely separate. This separation of animals and nature depends on dualisms between humans and animals and also between wildness and domesticity. The next chapter explores the animal side of this contrast.

3

Animal Ethics

VALUING ANIMALS

Although animals receive little attention in environmental thought, a growing literature addresses the moral status of nonhuman animals. Like environmental philosophy, animal ethics encompasses diverse theoretical models, including not only rights-based but also Utilitarian, virtue, feminist, and religious frameworks. Animal ethics also identifies a wide range of qualities as the source of value in nonhuman animals, from life itself to sentience, intelligence, sociability, or relations with humans. Almost all animal ethicists, however, agree that nonhuman animals have intrinsic value and should be protected on that basis.

The assertion of intrinsic value and the concomitant conviction that humans have failed to respect that value appear to provide common ground between animal and environmental advocates. However, animal and environmental ethics part ways decisively on the question of scale. The individualistic consensus of animal ethics is, if anything, more widespread than the holism of environmental thought. Both perspectives, further, view individuals and wholes in dualistic terms, meaning that people must choose between valuing individual animals and valuing nature in general, in practice if not in theory. Just as this assumption leads most environmental philosophers to dismiss concerns for animal welfare, it persuades many animal ethicists to believe that their concerns conflict with broad ecological agendas.

Utilitarianism

The first philosophical model to take animals seriously, in the West, was Utilitarianism, which emerged in the late 1700s with the work of Jeremy Bentham (1748–1832) and his student, John Stuart Mill (1806–1873). In setting out the foundations of Utilitarianism, Bentham claimed that the ultimate goal of ethics should be to create the greatest possible good for the greatest number of people, providing a shorthand phrase that continues to define Utilitarianism in popular thought. More generally, the classical Utilitarianism developed by Bentham and Mill claims that an action's utility is determined by whether it produces more benefit or harm to the overall good. As a form of consequentialist ethics, Utilitarianism makes the ends or goals more important than intentions in determining the moral quality of an act. Pain should be alleviated, regardless of whether it is caused deliberately or as an unintended effect of practices meant to achieve another goal. What matters is that a sentient individual is suffering, and the moral obligation is to alleviate this suffering rather than worry about causes or intentions.

Early Utilitarians challenged inequitable economic and political structures through their support of women's suffrage, the abolition of slavery, reforms in labor laws, and other efforts to improve human well-being. Many also advocated for animal welfare. Systematic Utilitarian thinking about animals began with Bentham, who explicitly rejected the Cartesian argument that rationality determines moral status. In his most famous reflection on animal welfare, Bentham compared the treatment of nonhuman animals to the treatment of certain categories of humans:

> The French have already discovered that the blackness of the skin is no reason a human being should be abandoned without redress to the caprice of a tormentor. It may one day come to be recognised that the number of the legs, the villosity of the skin, or the termination of the os sacrum are reasons equally insufficient for abandoning a sensitive being to the same fate. What else is it that should trace the insuperable line? Is it the faculty of reason or perhaps the faculty of discourse? But a full-grown horse or dog is beyond comparison a more rational, as well as a more conversable animal, than an infant of a day or a week or

even a month, old. But suppose the case were otherwise, what would it avail? The question is not, Can they reason? nor, Can they talk? but, Can they suffer?[1]

Like most advocates of animal welfare since his time, Bentham links moral status to the ability to experience pain. Utilitarians connect this capacity to the notion of "interests," which they find more philosophically defensible than "natural" or "human" rights. While rights confuse desired status with present status, interests speak to actual and potential capacities. Bentham famously dismissed the notion of natural rights as "rhetorical nonsense —nonsense upon stilts."[2] While rejecting philosophical rights, many Utilitarians favor the establishment and enforcement of specific legal rights as important instruments for improving the welfare of humans and nonhuman animals.

Following in the tradition established by Bentham, the most prominent theorist of animal welfare is Utilitarian philosopher Peter Singer, whose 1975 book *Animal Liberation* helped launch the contemporary animal welfare movement. Singer's argument rested on the Utilitarian principle of equal consideration, expressed by Bentham in the well-known phrase: "Each to count for one and none for more than one."[3] This equality is not a description of actual conditions, Singer explains, but rather a prescription for how we ought to treat others. The duty to treat animals equally is based on sentience and especially the capacity to suffer. Elaborating on Bentham's famous question, "Can they suffer," Singer explains the significance of sentience:

> The capacity for suffering—or more strictly, for suffering and/or enjoyment or happiness—is not just another characteristic like the capacity for language or higher mathematics. . . . By saying that we must consider the interests of all beings with the capacity for suffering or enjoyment Bentham does not arbitrarily exclude from consideration any interests at all—as those who draw the line with reference to the possession of reason or language do. The capacity for suffering and enjoyment is *a prerequisite for having interests at all*, a condition that must be satisfied before we can speak of interests in a meaningful way.[4]

It is meaningless to say that it is not in the interests of a stone to be kicked along the road, because a stone will not suffer. However, it is not nonsense to say that being kicked is not in the interests of a mouse.

Sentience provides a simple criterion that distinguishes whether or not a being has interests, irrelevant of any other abilities or qualities that being possesses. Different sentient beings have different interests, depending on various factors, including age, species, and cognitive and social capacities. The principle of equal consideration does not require identical treatment, and in fact to take a being's interests into account requires attention to his or her specific needs and capacities. For example, Singer explains that "concern for the well-being of children growing up in America would require that we teach them to read; concern for the well-being of pigs may require no more than that we leave them with other pigs in a place where there is adequate food and room to run freely. But the basic element—the taking into account of the interests of the being, whatever those interests may be—must, according to the principle of equality, be extended to all beings, black or white, masculine or feminine, human or nonhuman."[5] Species, like race or gender, is irrelevant to an individual's interest in avoiding suffering.

Singer famously used the term "speciesism," originally coined by Richard Ryder, to describe the use of species as a guideline to moral status and human obligation without regard for the actual interests of individuals. Most people are speciesist, Singer believes, because they treat equally sentient and thus morally equivalent beings different on the basis of species alone. Species is irrelevant to suffering, he writes, because "pain is pain whatever other capacities, beyond the capacity to feel pain, the being may have."[6] However, species is not irrelevant to all questions about the treatment of different animals. This is especially true in regard to the question of whether it can be acceptable to kill an animal without inflicting physical or mental pain. Here Singer nuances his position, explaining that "a rejection of speciesism does not mean that all lives are of equal worth." Species might be relevant to the question of taking life, insofar as species is related to qualities, including "self-awareness, the capacity to think ahead and have hopes and aspirations for the future, the capacity for meaningful relationships with others and so on."[7] The issue of taking life, however, is less important to Singer than the principle of minimizing suffering. Even his criticisms of the meat industry and his advocacy of vegetarianism, he explains, stem from the suffering imposed on animals during their lives rather than the fact that they are killed prematurely. This focus on suffering is widespread in both animal welfare activism and animal ethics theory.

Rights

The fact that Singer is often called an "animal rights" thinker reflects the widespread use of rights as a shorthand for ethical concern about nonhuman creatures. However, rights have a specific meaning that is important in both the animal ethics literature and broader philosophical discussions. Rights theories are a form of deontological ethics, meaning that they define morality in terms of following rules or principles, without thought for the consequences of such actions. In deontological models, the moral actor's intentions, as well as his or her adherence to the proper rules, determine whether an act is moral or not, regardless of the result. The father of deontological ethics is Immanuel Kant, who framed his moral theory in terms of "categorical imperatives," moral statements that are objectively and universally true because of their intrinsic qualities rather than their source or consequences. The most famous articulation of Kant's categorical imperative is this: "Always act according to that maxim whose universality as a law you can at the same time will."[8] From this perspective, an action is ethical only if it can be made universal. If it is not good for all people to act in this way, it is not good for a single actor to act in this way. While there are countless critiques of Kant's approach, his emphases on rationality, consistency, and universality remain highly influential in Western philosophical ethics.

Kant's thought has strongly shaped theories about rights, one of the most important concepts not only in thinking about animals but in modern political and social ethics generally. Rights are moral claims that certain categories of persons can make on other persons who are, in turn, duty bound to respect those claims. The notion of rights has theoretical roots in Kant's insistence that morality requires treating other persons as ends in themselves and never simply as means to other ends. Kant argues that persons have an intrinsic value that is independent of their instrumental usefulness to others. This is sometimes called a "natural rights" theory, because it links the possession of rights to humans' natural state rather than to specific political institutions or laws. Sometimes a particular quality, such as rationality or a soul, is cited to justify the assertion of rights, while in other cases no specific justification is given.

Many religious ethics ground rights on the creation of humans by God with intrinsic dignity and worth. Without a divine creator, however, the source of intrinsic value becomes unclear. This metaphysical vagueness invites criticism such as that made by Jeremy Bentham, who called natural rights "nonsense upon stilts." According to Bentham, theories of natural rights confuse a desirable moral status (an "ought") with an inherent natural quality (an "is"). Peter Singer addresses this issue as well, noting that the equality of which Utilitarians speak is a guideline for practice, not an actual condition. Another criticism comes from feminist thinkers, who argue that rights theories, with their emphases on justice, rationality, and equal treatment, ignore or distort important dimensions of human moral experiences and commitments. This critique has been developed systematically in care ethics, discussed below, in which emotions and relationships take center stage.

Despite the philosophical debates, rights theories have been central to a number of major political movements, beginning with the American and French Revolutions of the late eighteenth century. Since then, rights have continued to play central roles in movements to improve the conditions of specific human groups. "Rights" has in fact become shorthand for broader terms such as reform and welfare, regardless of any use of philosophical rights arguments. Thus the movement for racial equality in the United States continues to be described in terms of "civil rights," even though citizenship rights are no longer the only, or even most important, issue for most activists. Similarly, animal rights is used as a blanket term for all movements and theories about animal welfare, even in relation to thinkers who explicitly reject philosophical rights arguments. Despite the philosophical ambiguities, rights language remains compelling because rights are claims that do not depend on the whims or preferences of others.

In addition to their practical uses, rights are also applied to animals in the more limited philosophical sense. The most systematic and influential treatment is Tom Regan's 1983 book *The Case for Animal Rights*. Regan begins with the claim that "some nonhuman animals resemble normal humans in morally relevant ways. In particular, they bring the mystery of a unified psychological presence to the world." This unified self includes diverse cognitive, emotional, social, and sensory capacities, creating what Regan calls "subjects-of-a-life" who possess intrinsic value and natural rights. While Regan agrees with Singer that the capacity for pain is important, he also finds many other qualities morally relevant and believes that they justify the attribution of rights to at least some nonhuman animals. Scientific research into the cognitive and other capacities of nonhuman animals provide grounds for describing members of many different species as subjects for whom "what happens to them matters to them," as Regan puts it.[9]

Rights protect individual animals not just from physical suffering but, more broadly, from being "treated as if they exist as a resource for others; in particular, harms intentionally done to any one subject cannot be justified by aggregating benefits derived by others." While this argument rests on Kantian grounds, Regan takes issue with Kant's assertion that only "moral agents" should be treated as ends-in-themselves. In contrast, Regan recognizes "the equal inherent value of all subjects-of-a-life, including those who lack the capacities necessary for moral agency. These moral patients (as I call them) have the same equal right to respectful treatment as do moral agents."[10] Thus even creatures that lack the "richness" of capacity and experience available to (normal adult) humans have the right to respectful treatment.

If every individual animal has the right not to be treated as an instrument for human ends, then, Regan concludes, "morally, abolition is required." Like most animal rights advocates, he opposes hunting, trapping, most forms of animal agriculture, and the use of animals in zoos and circuses. The moral problem with such activities, from a rights perspective, is not just that they cause harm but that they treat animals instrumentally. Animals "have value apart from human interests, and their value is not reducible to their utility relative to our interests. To make a sport of hunting or trapping them is to do what is wrong because it is to fail to treat them with the respect they are due as a matter of strict justice." This position also leads Regan to oppose most scientific research on animals, other than that which can be performed without violating individual rights. "If that means there are some things we cannot learn, then so be it. There are also some things we cannot learn by using humans, if we respect their rights. The rights view merely requires moral consistency in this regard."[11] This position has sparked criticism from moderate animal welfare advocates who believe that it is morally acceptable for people to use animals for human benefit, as long as the animals are treated with kindness and physical and psychological suffering is minimized.

Regan also has critics among activists who believe he does not go far enough. Legal scholar Gary Francione, for example, focuses on the fact that nonhuman animals are legally property (an argument with relevance primarily to domestic animals). He finds Regan's theory inadequate because it does not directly challenge this status. Because animals are considered property, even laws to protect them do not "transcend that level of protection that facilitates the most economically efficient exploitation of the animal," according to Francione. The result is that in policy, law, and practical decisions, "animals almost never prevail, irrespective of what might be the relatively trivial human interest at stake and the relatively weighty animal interest involved in the particular case."[12]

Francione's point is important: when human and nonhuman interests are compared, the latter usually lose. However, the legal designation of animals as property may be more a symptom than a cause of this subordination. Wild and feral animals, most of whom are not considered property in law or popular opinion, do not fare better than domesticated ones when their well-being is weighed against that of people. This hierarchy influences many animal ethicists, and even those who claim to be "abolitionists" fall short of absolute egalitarianism. For example, Tom Regan attracted criticism for his claim that if humans and dogs were stranded together in a lifeboat that could not hold all of them, a dog should be thrown overboard instead of a human, because death is a greater loss for human. The difference, he adds, is absolute, so that numbers make no difference: one human life is worth more than ten, a hundred, or a million, canine lives.[13] Some critics see this as evidence, in the words of Gary Steiner, "that Regan advocates abandoning the principle of equal inherent worth whenever acting on that principle would compromise the welfare of human beings. To do so is to undermine completely the prospect of appealing to a rights-based theory as a basis for protecting the interests of animals."[14]

Regan's inconsistency is not unique. The line between humans and all other species becomes relevant, and often definitive, at some point for almost all animal ethicists, including those who advocate species equality in theory. Utilitarians, for example, also adhere to a hierarchy of values according to which human lives matter more than animal lives. This hierarchy is crystallized in John Stuart Mill's well-known assertion that "it is better to be a human being dissatisfied than a pig satisfied; better to be Socrates dissatisfied than a fool satisfied."[15] Even Jeremy Bentham, a strong advocate of animal welfare, believed that nonhuman suffering counted less than human suffering because animals lack certain cognitive capacities, including the power to contemplate the distant future. Peter Singer, similarly, qualifies his declaration of species equality: "A rejection of speciesism does not mean that all lives are of equal worth. While self-awareness, the capacity to think ahead and have hopes and aspirations for the future, the capacity for meaningful relationships with others, and so on are not relevant to the question of inflicting pain—since pain is pain whatever other capacities, beyond the capacity to feel pain, the being may have—these capacities are relevant to the question of taking life."[16]

Humans should not inflict physical suffering on any sentient animal, Singer insists, but beyond physical pain, value ranking is acceptable. This is especially true in relation to premature death. It is worse, he asserts, to take the life of a being who has been hoping and planning for a future goal than that of a being whose mental level is "below the level needed to grasp that one is a being with a future."[17] Usually, Singer explains, this principle means that it is worse to take the life of a human than of another animal, but there are exceptions, such as when the person in question does not have the cognitive capacities of "normal" human beings. This position has earned Singer notoriety among disabled rights activists.

Despite their assertion of moral equality, both rights and Utilitarian models permit hierarchies of value, especially in regard to the question of taking life. Singer in particular insists that this issue is separate from the question of inflicting suffering, on which all sentient creatures are equal regardless of species. Still, both Singer and Regan assert that in the end, at least in extreme cases, human life is worth more than nonhuman life. They are willing, as critics point out, to engage in a balancing act in which animals usually lose. This presents a problem for ethics based on rights, which gain their intellectual and moral power precisely from their claims to be absolute, objective, and universal. A theory of animal rights asserts that because (at least some) nonhuman animals have intrinsic value, we should not treat them differently from humans who also possess these qualities. In practice, however, Regan advocates very different kinds of treatment, to the extent that he would throw any and all dogs to their death before sacrificing a single human being. That is a worst-case scenario, and it arises primarily when basic human interests (such as survival) are concerned. Still, Regan's lifeboat scenario indicates that animal rights theories are less absolute than either critics or advocates often suggest. The presumed strength of rights theories, their adherence to basic principles regardless of the circumstances, thus turn out not to characterize the major applications of rights to nonhuman animals.

The frequency with which animal advocates prioritize human interests parallels the unacknowledged, perhaps unrecognized, anthropocentrism of much Deep Ecology. Perhaps because there is no other standard, human interests continue to be the deciding factor in hard cases even for people who, in theory, believe that all species are equal and that humans are "plain members and citizens" of a larger ecological community.

Religious Theories of Animal Rights

Religiously based animal ethics, like environmental ethics, have certain advantages over their secular counterparts. The conviction that meaning and value come from a god or other divine force provides the possibility, at least, of relativizing human interests and providing less biased grounds for weighing nonhuman welfare. In religious ethics the source of intrinsic worth is a divine "disinterested valuer," who provides objective grounds for valuing natural entities or wholes.[18] Some religious arguments about animal ethics resemble environmental stewardship ethics, in which animals, like all of creation, belong to God, and humans must treat them with respect because we are not their creators or masters. Others attribute intrinsic value to animals because God created them as centers of value prior to and apart from human use. Thus humans must not treat them in instrumental or exploitative ways. Some of these ethics refer explicitly to rights, while others prefer a different language of value and obligation.

The best-known religiously based animal rights ethic, developed by Christian theologian Andrew Linzey, resembles Regan's in many respects. Their systems diverge, as Linzey explains, "where Regan's system makes no use of the concept of God as the upholder and sustainer of value." For Regan, "being a subject-of-a-life is itself a sufficient criterion for the possession of rights." In Linzey's theological model, however, "what sustains subjective individuals as holders of rights is the objective right of God in creation."[19] This provides the grounding that many secular models lack: a force outside human history and culture, even outside ecological processes, which endows animals and nature itself with value that transcends human judgments or preferences.

While Linzey uses rights language, he acknowledges that it is not the only theory of moral obligation that Christians should use, nor is it comprehensive. "In fighting for the positive good of animals and humans," he asserts, "Christians will need to utilize a varied vocabulary. All that is claimed here is that rights language should be part of the necessary armoury."[20] Further, rights discourse, like all discussions of value and obligation, is part of a larger God-centered framework. Animals' intrinsic value is not mediated or exhausted by human interpretations or interests, and animals' rights are "objectively owed to animals as a matter of justice by virtue of their Creator's right. Animals can be wronged because their creator can be wronged in his creation."[21] Linzey's animal ethic is theocentric in the same way as James Gustafson's environmental ethic: in both, human and nonhuman interests are subordinate to a larger divine will, which does not always coincide with human interest. In principle, this theological foundation provides no ground for prioritizing human interests over nonhuman ones.

Another Christian animal ethicist, Stephen Webb, believes that Christians should reject rights because they "presuppose a society at war with itself, wherein individuals need protection from each other."[22] Webb echoes Mary Midgley's comment that rights is a "desperate" word, which presumes a fundamental opposition of individual interests and a need for protection from other people and society in general.[23] Behind this presumption of conflict is a belief that humans are atomistic, rational, and self-sufficient. Webb rejects both individual autonomy and the inevitable conflict assumed by rights theory. He proposes, instead, an ethic based on relationality and dependence, among people and between people and nonhuman animals.[24] Webb's relational model resembles the approach of feminist care ethicists, for whom value and obligation also stem from relationships, not abstract principles.

Animal ethics has been developed most systematically within Christianity, but some approaches also exist within other religious traditions, mostly embedded in discussions of religious attitudes toward nonhuman nature more generally. South Asian traditions such as Buddhism, Hinduism, and Jainism share an emphasis on the principle of nonviolence (*ahimsa*), which a number of environmental and animal ethicists see as an important resource for thinking not just about interhuman ethics but also about human treatment of animals. Jainism includes a long tradition of interpreting *ahimsa* as a mandate to avoid causing harm to any nonhuman animals, which leads many Jains to wear scarves over their mouths to avoid inhaling tiny insects. Some Buddhist thinkers incorporate *ahimsa* into a larger ethic of compassion toward other life forms, often relating it specifically to the duty to avoid harming. The concept of karma and the associated theory of rebirth are also important in South Asian reflections on appropriate treatment of nonhuman animals. The possibility of being reborn into another species can provide grounds for kind treatment of animals. As some Buddhist and Hindu vegetarians put it, a hamburger may be their great-grandmother. In Buddhism, further, the *jatakas*—stories of the Buddha's previous lives—show him incarnated as different nonhuman animals and demonstrating compassion to a wide range of creatures.[25]

Religiously based animal and environmental ethics have strong appeal for adherents but also face a number of limitations. The most obvious is the fact that since only believers find references to God's will or religious narrative persuasive, the audience for such arguments is limited. Secular ethicists and advocates sometimes exaggerate the limits, however, forgetting that a majority of Americans identify themselves as religious. An equally significant obstacle may be the fact that many people within every tradition reject pro-animal or pro-environment arguments as misreadings of their faith. On animal welfare, as on other contemporary social issues, many different readings are possible in almost every religion. This is especially true for Western traditions, which have been strongly anthropocentric for most of their histories. This history poses a theoretical and practical challenge for animal activists, no less than for environmental advocates.

Rights-based models and Utilitarian ethics determine appropriate treatment for animals based on their intrinsic qualities and capacities, such as the ability to feel pain or the cognitive complexity that makes an individual the "subject-of-a life." While different thinkers define varied capacities as most important, they agree that once the morally relevant qualities are identified, all individuals with those capacities should be treated alike. The principle of equality does not respect boundaries of species any more than it respects boundaries of race, gender, or religion among humans.[26] This principle has emotional as well as intellectual power, which is reflected in the strategies of many animal welfare groups. This approach is especially prominent in morally oriented vegetarian organizations and people advocating for better treatment for animals labeled "livestock," who are subject to few of the protections afforded to animals called "pets." The U.S.-based Farm Sanctuary summarizes this argument in its slogan: "If you love animals called pets, why do you eat animals called dinner?"[27] The same sentiment is expressed in more detail in a flyer produced by a group called Bay Area Vegetarians:

> Most Americans would cringe at the thought of eating a dog, and would label such a practice disgusting, cruel, and perhaps immoral, yet accept and participate in eating the flesh of cows, chickens, pigs, turkeys, and other animals. However, there is no ethical basis for such a distinction, no ethical basis for designating certain animals as existing to feed us, no moral basis for the often used excuse, "That's what they're raised for." Farmed animals are individual beings just as capable of feeling pain or experiencing pleasure as are our familiar companions, cats and dogs.[28]

The Vegetarian Society in Great Britain uses this comparison to powerful effect in their "Butcher's Cat" campaign, which asks, "Why do we make pets out of some animals, and mincemeat out of others?" The campaign uses striking images, such as a cat divided into segments resembling the traditional butcher's cuts of meat and a jar of "Kitty Tikka." The campaign argues that the distinction between "pets" such as cats and dogs and "livestock" such as pigs and cows is based on "the same kind of thinking that can view some people as humans and others as much less."[29] This echoes Singer's concept of speciesism, according to which species is as morally irrelevant as race and should not be used to justify different treatment, though it does not go as far as Singer in asserting that the line between humans and nonhuman species is equally arbitrary.

Despite their differences, in most animal ethics the primary reason that humans should change their treatment of animals is to eliminate suffering. "The capacity for suffering—or more strictly, for suffering and/or enjoyment or happiness—is not just another characteristic like the capacity for language or higher mathematics," in Singer's words. "The capacity for suffering and enjoyment is *a prerequisite for having interests at all*, a condition that must be satisfied before we can speak of interests in a meaningful way."[30] Regan points to other capacities, including intellectual and social complexity, but for him also the capacity to feel pain is foundational, as it is for most care ethicists.

Physical suffering is also a prominent theme in many animal advocacy movements, ranging from moderate welfarism to abolitionism. Because of this focus on suffering, animal welfare activists usually target practices and institutions that cause obvious physical pain, from the mistreatment of draft horses in the United States and England in the nineteenth century to the use of animals in research laboratories and the meat industry today. As just one example, People for the Ethical Treatment of Animals (PETA) explains its priorities in terms of a focus "on the four areas in which the largest numbers of animals suffer the most intensely for the longest periods of time: on factory farms, in the clothing trade, in laboratories, and in the entertainment industry."[31] Physical suffering is the key measure of welfare, not only for PETA but for the large majority of animal activists. Animals' positive capacities for pleasure, joy, and relationships receive much less attention from both theoretical and practical advocates of animal welfare. This may be because physical pain appears to be objective and universal, while positive experiences and feelings may be more varied, fluid, and subjective.

Contextual Ethics

The emphasis on suffering reflects the fact that individual qualities are the basis for animal rights and human duties in most animal ethics theories. An alternative approach, however, emphasizes context and relationships as at least partial grounds for valuing nonhuman animals. This approach has been developed most fully by Clare Palmer. Individual capacity is not irrelevant, Palmer asserts, but it is also necessary to "focus on the different relations humans have with animals." In particular, "relational states such as dependence and vulnerability and certain causal relations (when human actions have been important in shaping both animals' natures and situations) are of moral significance."[32] Palmer elaborates this approach in relation to the question of assistance. In some cases, she explains, people are morally obligated to assist nonhuman animals, especially in regard to domesticated animals who depend on human care. We are also obligated to help animals whom we hurt directly, for example in a road accident. When a wild animal has been harmed by a natural accident or the unintentional action of another person, we are permitted but not absolutely obliged to offer assistance, as in the case of a baby bird who falls from the nest. In still other cases, such as predation in the wild, people are prohibited from helping. At all times, we are obligated not to cause intentional harm to any animals, in any setting.

The core of Palmer's ethic is a "laissez-faire intuition" regarding wild animals, to whom our primary obligation is to leave them alone. In this regard she echoes Tom Regan's position regarding wild animals: let them be.[33] For domestic animals, in contrast, Palmer writes that, "When humans create sentient animals that are vulnerable or dependent, special obligations to care for or to assist these animals are generated."[34] Further, we often have duties to help animals living in what she calls the "contact zone," which includes feral animals and many wild animals who live in close proximity to humans. These different obligations rest on the varied relationships we have with different animals. Palmer's contextual ethic provides an important revision of the capacities-based approach of both Utilitarian and rights models, neither of which attend to the histories, contexts, and relationships in which people and animals are entwined. Even greater attention to relationship emerges in feminist care ethics, one of the most important theoretical approaches in contemporary animal ethics.

Feminist Care Ethics

Even more than environmental ethics, most animal ethics are dominated by emphases on universality and rationality. This is especially evident in the work of rights-based thinkers such as Regan, but many Utilitarian thinkers also insist that emotion has no place in moral theory. As Singer complains, "the portrayal of those who protest against cruelty to animals as sentimental, emotional 'animal lovers' has had the effect of excluding the entire issue of our treatment of nonhumans from serious political and moral discussion."[35] Singer and other rationalist animal ethicists also point out that an emphasis on emotions and relationships can define animals in terms of their capacity to be loved by and respond to humans. If this is the case, then care ethics, no less than other animal ethics, are relevant only to certain kinds of interactions with certain kinds of animals. Ecocentrists criticize such models as fundamentally anthropocentric, while reason-based animal ethicists such as Regan and Singer find them incapable of doing justice to the intrinsic value of all sorts of nonhuman animals.

Against the common dismissal of emotions and personal relationships, ecofeminists criticize the hyper-rationalism of both environmentalist and animal ethicists for its abstraction and lack of concern for concrete individuals.[36] Some have turned to feminist care ethics, which places emotion and relationship at the heart of moral theory, for an alternative approach to valuing animals and nature together.

The origins of care ethics lie in empirical findings that women and men make ethical decisions very differently. While boys and men often think about ethical decisions in terms of abstract principles such as rights and justice, girls and women tend to describe moral dilemmas in the context of relationships, personal experiences, and emotional commitments. As Carol Gilligan wrote, women more often view moral actors not as "opponents in a contest of rights" but rather as people with a common interest in the continuation of the network of relationships on which they all depend.[37] Ethical decision-making thus is less a process of following absolute principles than of conversation, compromise, and consensus. Gilligan calls this typically (though not universally or exclusively) female approach a "care ethic," in contrast to the rights-centered "justice" model.

Gilligan distinguishes the two approaches in terms of priority and emphasis rather than absolute opposition or mutual exclusion. "From a justice perspective," she explains, "the self as moral agent stands as the figure against a ground of social relationships, judging the conflicting claims of self and others against a standard of equality or equal respect. . . . From a care perspective, the relationship becomes the figure, defining self and others."[38] These shifting emphases lead to different moral questions and different ways of answering them. In the care perspective, the central issue is not "What is just?" but rather "how to respond?"[39] This response depends on a variety of factors, including personal loyalties and relationships, the particular situation of different actors, and overall context, rather than on objective, abstract, and universal criteria such as moral rules or rights.

For Gilligan, rights and care are complementary. Other feminist thinkers, however, see care as a comprehensive model that supplants justice and other Kantian approaches. Nel Noddings, for example, insists that morally significant relations must involve face-to-face contact and reciprocity. Love, or "natural caring," is the root of "ethical caring," which rests on an "evaluation of the caring relation as good, as better than, superior to, other forms of relatedness."[40] For Noddings, moral obligations are limited to people with whom we have intimate personal relationships: "We cannot care for everyone. Caring itself is reduced to mere talk about caring when we attempt to do so."[41] Thus, moral obligations exclude nature in general and nonhuman animals in particular, as well as humans with whom we do not have direct exchanges. Even some feminist thinkers find this approach too narrow, and Noddings has since addressed the charge of parochialism. The intensity of interpersonal care, she believes, can motivate people to create social conditions that nurture caring relations more generally—to bring into being a world "in which 'it is possible to be good.'" While ethical care "starts at home," therefore, it need not end there.[42]

Care ethics appeal to a number of feminist scholars seeking to develop better ethical responses to nonhuman animals. Acknowledging the moral relevance of emotions and interpersonal relationships seems to open up possibilities precluded by both rights and Utilitarian theories, which accord significance only to objective, rational decisions made on the basis of abstract, universal principles. However, emotions and relationships can also be defined in anthropocentric terms, as Noddings makes explicit: "I shall locate the very wellspring of ethical behavior in human affective response."[43] Care ethics, like rights, Utilitarian, and theocentric models, require revision when applied to nonhuman animals. However, they also make possible revisions in these dominant ethical frameworks. The emphases on relationship and context counter the individualism and rationalism of both rights-based and Utilitarian theories. A care ethics is not identical to ecofeminism, but it echoes important ecofeminist themes, including a valuation of qualities and perspectives that are denigrated in mainstream ethics, including many environmental ethics.

The work in animal ethics inspired by care ethics and ecofeminism departs from dominant approaches in several ways. First, they make gender an important lens for thinking about human attitudes toward and relationships with the nonhuman world. In addition, they make emotions, relationships, histories, and loyalties important for evaluating our obligations to nonhuman animals. Abstract principles are not enough to guide moral behavior, as Lori Gruen points out, because we relate to humans and other animals not as just exemplars of their species but in particular roles and relationships—as friend or lover, family or foe.[44] Even the notion of care must be contextualized, as Marti Kheel emphasizes, since a generic ethic of care fails to provide what particular animals need. In many cases, as Kheel notes, "the most caring thing we can do for animals is to leave them alone." Ethical interactions with animals should be guided by what she terms "appropriate or *contextualized* care," specific to the particular animals involved.[45]

Many feminist animal ethicists, like ecofeminists, emphasize the connections between women and nonhuman nature, based on shared histories of exploitation and objectification. Against the liberal inclination to reject the association of women with nature, care ethicists, like ecofeminists, embrace this link and use it as a source of moral knowledge. "Women, as themselves victims of objectification and exploitation, must not abandon other victims of such treatment in their rush to be accepted as 'persons' entitled to equal treatment," according to Carol Adams and Josephine Donovan. "Women must not deny their historical linkages with animals but rather remain faithful to them, bonded as we are not just by centuries of similar abuse but also by the knowledge that they—like us, often objectified as Other—are subjects worthy of the care, the respect, even the reverence, that the sacredness of consciousness deserves."[46] Feminist animal ethicists also criticize holistic environmental philosophers for their lack of concern for individual animals. The "interlocking systems of oppression" victimize some human groups as well as nonhuman nature, including individual animals.[47] This assertion challenges the depoliticized and "single-issue" approach of some animal ethicists.

The connections between women and animals are not only intellectual but also historic and practical, partly based on the "centuries of similar abuse" that Adams and Donovan note. A number of feminists point to evidence that domestic violence against women and children is linked to violence against animals in multiple ways.[48] Not only are women often associated with animals, especially domestic ones, but the vast majority of animal activists are women. This is true of the nineteenth-century antivivisection and anticruelty movements and also of contemporary activists, among whom 70 to 80 percent are women, according to one estimate.[49] Further, women are more likely than men to oppose biomedical research and other forms of institutionalized exploitation of animals.[50]

Despite their distinctive features, feminist approaches share with more traditional models a focus on animal suffering and the obligation to relieve it when possible.[51] This approach concentrates attention on the most urgent cases, seems to have universal and objective standards of detection and perhaps measurement, and inspires sympathy and action. However, an almost exclusive emphasis on suffering portrays animals in a one-dimensional way, denying agency in favor of a portrait of passive victimization. Animal ethics requires theoretical models that address more positive qualities, drawing on knowledge of animals' lives and capacities that are documented in ethology as well as human-animal social interactions.

Nonhuman animals, like humans, experience a variety of positive feelings and activities, which vary by species and also for individuals within the same species. Feelings of pleasure and joy emerge in play, social bonding, and other satisfying experiences. Pain is frequently a solitary experience, felt by and within an individual body, and in fact too much solitude itself can cause psychological suffering for many nonhuman animals as for humans. Well-being and pleasure, on the other hand, are often sparked by social pursuits, including play and affectionate interactions among companions. Greater attention to animals' positive experiences and feelings can help us think differently about what animal welfare means and requires, as the fulfillment of positive goals beyond the mere elimination or alleviation of pain, without denying the urgent and overwhelming animal suffering caused by humans. Thinking about animal welfare beyond suffering can also illuminate the vexing problem of value in both animal and environmental ethics. For animals as well as people, positive feelings, and not just the absence of pain, are a large part of what makes an experience, a life, or a place valuable.

INDIVIDUALISM AND HOLISM REDUX

Perhaps the most widespread point of conflict between animal ethicists and environmental philosophers is the scale at which value is located. If value inheres primarily in wholes, as ecological and ecocentric thinkers insist, then individual good is necessarily secondary and individuals must sometimes suffer or die in order to preserve the greater good. This perspective lies behind the conviction of most environmental advocates and thinkers that it is acceptable to harm individual animals for the well-being of a larger whole such as a plant or animal population, a species, or an ecosystem. This conviction rests on the belief that ecological wholes are "logically prior to their component species because the nature of the part is determined by its relationship to the whole. . . . A species has the particular characteristics that it has because those characteristics evolved by way of its adaptation to a niche in an ecosystem."[52]

The logical priority of wholes entails a moral priority as well, so that preserving the whole becomes necessary even at the cost of individual pain and death. For many ecologically oriented philosophers, pain and death are not just an unfortunate side effect but a central feature of systemic health. Thus, writes Holmes Rolston, "the world is not a jolly place . . . but one of struggling, somber beauty. The dying is the shadow side of the flourishing."[53] The somberly beautiful deaths are those of nonhuman animals and plants. Like most environmental thinkers, Rolston explicitly places human deaths outside the "painful good" of ecological health.

In contrast, many animal ethicists find it more philosophically coherent to locate intrinsic value in individual creatures, either because animals care about what happens to them or because animals are similar to humans in morally relevant ways (and since we know ourselves to be intrinsically valuable, creatures similar to ourselves in key traits must be similarly valuable). From this perspective, the interests of individual animals in avoiding pain and premature death usually trump more abstract collective goods such as ecosystem health. On the other hand, most animal ethicists reject ecocentric claims that individual suffering can be "beautiful" in light of larger ecological goods. Ecological talk of "interconnection," according to Stephen Webb, "is another word for violence, since the web of life that environmentalists celebrate makes pain and death an inherent part of growth and propagation."[54] (However, Lisa Sideris criticizes some environmental philosophers and ecotheologians for not taking seriously enough the pain and death inherent in natural selection.)[55]

Many animal advocates believe that collective goods, including the health of entire species or ecosystems, should at times be subordinated in order to preserve individual well-being. Jonathan Balcombe asserts, for example, that terms such as *species* and *population* "are not sensitive to the experiences of sentient individuals. When we refer to mountain lion 'harvest limits,' 'whaling quotas,' or 'fish stocks,' individuals cease to exist. Regarded in those terms, we may as well be talking about tons of sand."[56] Balcombe criticizes ecological management plans that sacrifice some animals in order to protect another. He cites a European example in which ducks of a more common species are killed in order to prevent their interbreeding with a rarer species: "It is a common theme of ours: we persecute the members of one species—in this case the white-headed duck—to the point of rarity, then we turn our sights on another, the ruddy duck, for its marginal impact on the first species. We may sympathize with the efforts to secure the protection of endangered species, but doing so at the expense of other animals is misguided, and hypocritical when we continue to threaten the endangered species through our own activities."[57] Balcombe does not offer alternative ways to remove the threats to white-headed ducks, but some animal advocates support projects to sterilize or relocate, rather than kill, animals who threaten ecological harm. A version of this approach (trap–neuter–release) is commonly used to address feral cat populations that threaten native songbirds and rodents. Such programs are controversial, with most environmentalists opposed despite support from many animal activists.

The division between animal and environmental ethics presumes that *either* only individuals possess the qualities or capacities that lead to intrinsic value *or* only ecosystems are valuable in and of themselves. Few of the parties to these arguments acknowledge that there may be different kinds of value, located at different scales, or that the same individual or place may be valuable in different ways. Pragmatists make this point, but they often do so in a way that implies that the only source of value is human appreciation: there are many kinds of value, and many valuable entities, because people care about many different things. Because pragmatism provides an inherently anthropocentric answer to the problem of what has value, it cannot satisfy proponents of either ecocentric or animal rights positions who believe that some value lies outside human experiences and perspectives.

Pragmatism also offers little help when we have to make hard choices, as when one species of sentient animal appears to threaten the survival of another kind of equally sentient animal. In such situations, people often resort to "lifeboat thinking," according to which unavoidable competition necessitates either-or choices. This way of thinking is inadequate and inappropriate for most situations that people (and animals) actually encounter, as Mary Midgley argues: "It often militates against generosity, justice, intelligent invention and even enlightened self-interest. It tends to generate bad faith. The point is that we are not usually in lifeboats. In a lifeboat (at least in a completely full one) there is no choice available but one."[58] In reality, however, we usually have multiple alternatives available, and it is usually possible to respect, at least to some extent, different kinds of value.

Toward this aim, Midgley offers a model that allows for multiplicity of values without reducing them to subjective human preferences. Different moral claims need not be viewed as concentric circles in which some values are more important than others. Instead, she proposes that we understand these claims as an overlapping web, in which different values sometimes take precedence without creating a permanent hierarchy.[59] It is possible and in fact normal to find value in a range of traits and entities. We do not have to choose to appreciate only a very limited number, even though we may choose to direct resources such as time or money toward one particular cause at a time.

In practice, this approach may begin with an inventory of the different values and claims involved in a given conflict, say between ruddy ducks and white-headed ducks, or between feral cats and native songbirds. Rather than insisting that only one kind of value exists—ecological integrity, or individual sentience—Midgley suggests that we acknowledge the various values involved without trying to exclude some or even to rank them hierarchically. Beginning in this way may make it possible to find solutions that maximize the well-being of different individuals as well as ecological wholes. Further, even though hard choices may still be necessary, this framework at least does not dismiss one kind of value, and it leaves open the possibility that other claims may take precedence in the future. For example, a particular feral cat population may be so large, or the threatened birds so rare, that lethal solutions seem required. This need not mean, first, that the lives of feral cats have no value at all or, second, that the value of those lives will not be taken into account in the future. In a different case, with fewer cats or more birds, nonlethal solutions may be adopted, favoring the cats but not dismissing the value of the birds.

As Midgley recognizes, people often value both individual creatures and larger natural environments, and not necessarily one for the sake of the other. This raises again the problems of scale and of sources of value. Many philosophers would have us believe that people value nature and animals for very different reasons, since both fields assume that we must choose between individual creatures and "nature" in general. The fact that so many people value both nature and animals suggests, however, that appreciation for the more-than-human world is broader than an either-or choice between individuals and ecosystemic integrity. This dualism, in fact, prevents us from perceiving both other sources of value and possible solutions to practical conflicts.

One way to think beyond dualism is to examine the ways that relationships generate value. Relationships are both valued in themselves and also mediators between different valued entities—between animals and nature, individuals and wholes, nature and culture. Neither environmental nor animal ethics has conceptual frameworks that focus on this middle, connecting level. They have not addressed either the relational character of their central categories or the significance of relationships themselves. This is related, possibly in causal ways, to their reluctance to talk directly about the categories of wildness and domesticity. Mutually exclusive, polarized definitions of both these terms are taken for granted, in animal ethics as in environmental philosophy. Treating *wild* and *domestic* as relational terms rather than absolutes can open the way toward reconceiving other aspects of natural value as well.

4

Wild Animals

The distinction between wild and domesticated animals is fundamental to both environmental and animal ethics. Philosophers in both camps often take this distinction for granted and use it as the basis for their respective evaluations of the moral status of different animals and human obligations toward them. However, few if any have reflected on the meanings of wildness and domestication or the relationship between them. They take the polarity of wild and domestic as the starting point for evaluating human duties to different animals. I approach it, instead, as a problem to be examined. From this perspective, wildness and domestication are not absolutes, but contextual, shifting, and relational qualities, relevant not only for species but also for individuals and for multispecies communities. This approach makes possible a new analysis not only of wildness and domestication but also of other established dualisms and the theories that rely upon them.

A relational model illuminates gaps in both environmental and animal ethics. Animal welfare advocates usually emphasize the capacities and qualities of individual animals. Environmental thinkers, on the other hand, highlight ecological settings and rarely pay attention to animals' individual situations and qualities. The two fields exist like sides of a coin, without interaction despite their proximity. This means that neither benefits from the arguments or the supporting research marshaled by the other camp. This is evident, for example, in the selective use of science on both sides.

While environmental philosophers often make ecological science central to their work, they rarely examine the ever-growing research about animal capacities, behaviors, and social relations. The inverse is true of many animal ethicists. Both groups thus miss a great deal of information that is relevant to understanding both individual animals and their environments. A more integrated and coherent approach would view wild and domestic animals as both individuals and embedded members of larger ecological and social communities.

In efforts to understand wild animals as individuals, ethological studies of complex behavior such as play, language, tool use, deception, and altruism are invaluable. This research reveals sophisticated intentionality, analysis, and communication. Play, in particular, provides a window into the complex emotions, intelligence, social relationships, and moral rules that are involved in wild lives. There is more going on in the more-than-human world, this research reveals, than generic terms such as *wildlife* can begin to explain. This research shows that wild animals have subjective preferences, intentions, and communication, all of which make possible not only their intricate relations with each other but also different forms of engagement with humans. Even most free-ranging native animals have some degree of interaction with humans, if only as a result of habitat and climate disruption. Just as no humans exist entirely apart from nonhuman animals, so no animals, however wild, have lives unaffected by human activities.

A relational approach muddies the distinction between wildness and domestication, revealing them not as mutually exclusive but rather as positions on a continuum. Between the two poles, further, lies a large gray area occupied by a host of creatures whose lives cannot be captured by either "wild" or "domestic." Before thinking seriously about either wild or domesticated animals, it is necessary to define not only what is included in each category but also what gaps are left. This clarification contributes not only to fuller, more adequate theoretical frameworks but also to better guidelines for human interactions with animals of all sorts.

WILD AND DOMESTIC

In the philosophical literature on animals, the terms *wild* and *domestic* are defined by their opposition to each other. It is impossible to understand what wild animals are and how they are valued without examining their relation to the counter-category of domesticated animals. Environmental advocates and theorists alike assume that the boundary between wild and domestic is clear-cut. This distinction is not only taken for granted but also foundational to many moral and political claims. It "lies at the very center of the land ethic," as Baird Callicott acknowledges.[1] It lies as well at the heart of most other philosophical thinking about nonhuman animals and nature.

Despite—or perhaps because of—its foundational status, the distinction between wild and domestic is rarely subject to careful analysis. When we do look closely at these terms, the supposedly clear and decisive line between them becomes blurry. The more attention we pay, the more scientifically, intellectually, and morally troubling the wild-domestic dichotomy becomes. The discussion makes little sense, first of all, in light of the theory that undergirds all the natural sciences—Darwin's understanding of evolution by natural selection. Not only ecological scientists but also most environmental advocates ground their worldviews in evolutionary explanations of the historical relations among and ecological adaptations of all kinds of life on earth.[2] Species, as Darwin wrote in *The Origin of Species*, are only strongly marked and permanent varieties. ("Varieties" in wild animals parallel "breeds" in domesticated species.) The distinction between variety and species is quantitative, not qualitative. Because every species first existed as a variety, Darwin notes, "no line of demarcation can be drawn between species, commonly supposed to have been produced by special acts of creation, and varieties which are acknowledged to have been produced by secondary laws."[3] Varieties within a breed can become distinctions among species, given time. Building on Darwin's intuitions, contemporary evolutionary biologists have found that the supposedly hard-and-fast lines between species are in fact fluid and porous. Studies of finches on the Galapagos Islands, for example, have shown that new species can emerge from different varieties much more quickly than previously thought, depending on the fluctuating availability of different food sources and other factors.[4]

If varieties and species differ in degree rather than kind, then domesticated animals cannot be as radically different from wild animals as most philosophers assume. The creation of new species through domestication is not qualitatively different from other forms of evolution. Darwin himself found the artificial selection of domesticated animals and plants crucial for understanding evolution by natural selection. "Why," he asked, "if man can by patience select variations most useful to himself, should nature fail in selecting variations useful, under changing conditions of life, to her living products?"[5] From this perspective, domesticated, feral, and free-ranging wild animals form a continuum of relationships rather than a series of sharply differentiated essences. Wildness and domestication are not intrinsic properties to be held fully or not at all, but relational qualities which exist on a continuum and vary depending on the context. Wildness, as Clare Palmer notes, "signifies a lack of interaction between humans and animals, in particular in terms of location and nondomestication. And wildness forms part of a spectrum of possible relations, not one side of a dualism; animals can be more or less wild and more or less wild in different ways."[6] Degrees and kinds of wildness or domestication can vary within species and within the life of any particular individual. In addition, individual animals display behaviors and personal qualities, such as tameness, aggression, shyness, or boldness, that make it harder to define any particular creature or species as fully and finally wild or domestic.

Animals add to the difficulty of defining these terms not only by their individual characteristics and behaviors but also by their relations to individuals of other species. Wild and domestic animals not only share similar behaviors and capacities but also interact socially with each other. These interactions regularly cross the lines between species and sometimes between wild and domestic. Predators and prey species, for example, frequently interact without regard for wildness or domestication. Well-fed domestic cats kill countless wild native birds and rodents, and wild predators, such as coyotes, panthers, and wolves, sometimes prey on domestic cattle, sheep, and goats.

On the other side, there are numerous well-documented stories of wild animals forming friendships with members of different species, sometimes even across the lines of predator and prey. Some of these have become well known through books, articles, and the Internet. For example, a series of popular children's books document the friendship between Owen, an infant hippo and Mzee, an Aldabra tortoise who lived in the Kenyan wildlife park where Owen was brought after being separated from his mother in the December 2004 tsunami.[7] Their bond is especially notable because reptiles such as tortoises are usually considered incapable of complex social relationships. Several well-documented friendships have developed between members of two highly social species, dogs and elephants. The connection between Tarra, an elephant at a sanctuary in Tennessee, and Bella, a dog living there, is the subject of another children's book as well as numerous news stories. At the Houston Zoo, Maximus, a formerly homeless pit bull, lives in the elephant enclosure, where he enjoys friendly interactions both with human visitors and the elephants themselves.[8]

In addition to such friendships, different species sometimes create families. Dogs and wolves, for example, can and do mate outside of human-controlled settings and produce fertile offspring, challenging not only wild-domestic divisions but also the standard definition of species. There is also strong evidence that individuals from related wild species can interbreed, creating new species that are effectively hybrids. This has occurred, for example, when members of rare wild species, such as Florida panthers and red wolves, have been reintroduced into areas where they were previously extirpated. In the absence of many members of their own species, some of these animals have apparently mated with similar animals (Texas cougars and coyotes, respectively). Such mixing creates dilemmas for the ecologists seeking to restore rare animals to their original ranges. Animals' boundary crossings also raise theoretical questions for scholars who took for granted the boundaries of key categories such as species, wildness, and domestication. The meanings of these categories are always tied up with relationships—to other animals of their species, to different species (predator, prey, or playmate), to home places, and to humans. Dualism and mutual exclusion are never helpful ways to conceive of them.

Given that the divisions between species can be elusive, it is not surprising that the line between the much broader categories of wildness and domestication becomes fuzzy upon examination. This is especially true when we consider the in-between category of feral animals, former domestics who live as wild creatures. Sometimes these animals become a distinct species, like the Australian dingo, while others, like American mustangs, are recognized as a breed (variety) within an existing species. Feral animals are especially problematic for environmental discourse and practice, precisely because they do not fit neatly into the categories that undergird key moral claims. For this reason, feral animals are also extremely helpful for thinking through the complex relations between animals and nature. They are both wild and domestic at the same time, or perhaps neither.

Feral cats are an especially illuminating, and controversial, symbol of the conflict between environmentalism and animal welfare. They are reviled by many bird lovers and ecologists because they prey on native wildlife, but at the same time they are loved and protected by some animal advocates who see them as victims of human neglect. Feral cats reveal the extent to which human values and preferences enter into ethical discussions and conflicts about nonhuman nature, including the foundational distinction between wild and domestic animals. Debates about feral cats show, further, that different individuals and social groups value animals and nature in different ways. There is no single "nature," no single kind of human relationship to it, and no single way to value it. Just as the cats themselves continually negotiate and revise their relations to both natural and social communities, so animal and environmental advocates should engage in constant reflection on the real animals they encounter, rather than letting preestablished categories determine both human attitudes and animals' fates.

Despite the tensions and ambiguities entailed in defining animals as either wild or domestic, the distinction remains important in most environmental discourse. One reason is a desire for intellectual clarity, which is difficult if we consider all animals on a broad continuum without clear divisions. Maintaining a sharp divide between wild and domestic animals makes it possible to discuss duties toward nature in general without entering the muddy minefield of domestic animal welfare. If domesticated animals are radically other than wild ones, we can separate their moral status (and real characters and experiences) from those of animals in nature, wild animals, the ones who count for environmentalists. The theoretical distinction between wild and domestic thus lies at the core of environmental thought, even though it is not often brought into the open.

Equally important, however, are morally and politically weighted reasons. Chief among these is the fact that all humans, including environmental activists and theorists, depend upon the bodies and lives of domesticated animals. Even those who do not consume or wear animal products are implicated in larger structures of agriculture, settlement, and transportation that could not survive without domesticated animals. Taking their interests into account would require unimaginable transformations not only in individual human behavior but also in the organization of entire societies, changes which many animal advocates propose but which most environmentalists find impractical and unnecessary.

ENVIRONMENTAL PERSPECTIVES ON WILD ANIMALS

In holistic environmental ethics, intrinsic value inheres in the ecological community. The value of individual animals depends on their contributions to the overall good of wild places and ecological processes. The animals that matter are free-ranging wild creatures living in their native habitats, and these matter because of their place and function in the whole ecosystems rather than any unique qualities or capacities. Nonsentient landscape features, such as trees, lakes, mountains, or rivers, possess greater value than even the most complex individual animal. Species that are rare or endangered or that play significant roles in a larger ecosystem have special status, even if they have relatively low cognitive, social, or emotional complexity. On the other hand, domesticated, feral, and nonnative ("exotic") animals have little or no intrinsic value, and some, especially those considered "invasive," are pests who should be eliminated for the good of the ecological community, regardless of their individual qualities.

Virtually all holistic environmental thinkers take this approach to wild animals, usually without reflecting on the definitions of the terms at stake. As noted earlier, Aldo Leopold, for example, saw native animals as part of a larger biotic community that also includes soils, waters, and plants, together known collectively as "the land."[9] The land is "a fountain of energy flowing through a circuit of soils, plants, and animals."[10] Animals are important in this community, but only in relationship to the larger energy flows that sustain the land overall. Human actions, Leopold famously asserted, should be judged on the basis of their contribution to the land; thus "a thing is right when it tends to preserve the integrity, stability, and beauty of the biotic community. It is wrong when it tends otherwise."[11] The same principle can be used to evaluate the role of different animals in the biotic community: those who do not contribute to its integrity, stability, and beauty are not right for that setting. Land ethicists thus justify the elimination, through hunting or other measures, of animals who are not native to the land community, whose numbers are excessive, or who otherwise fail to contribute to the ongoing good of the ecological whole.

This does not mean that Leopold was not interested in animals as such. His writings reveal him as a passionate naturalist who observed the activities of wild animals as well as other natural events and landscapes with empathy and fascination. Like many wilderness advocates, he was especially interested in "charismatic megafauna," particularly predators such as wolves and grizzly bears, the keystone species in many wild ecosystems. Leopold knew that because such animals require extensive habitats, their protection can help ensure wilderness preservation in general. Writing in the 1940s, he noted that the U.S. national park system had no wolves and that the situation of grizzlies in the parks was "precarious." In addition to destructive predator-control systems, he blamed the decline of these species on the fact that the parks were too small for far-ranging species such as wolves, who could not thrive as detached islands of population.[12] Protecting grizzly bears and wolves requires the preservation of much larger amounts of land as national parks or wilderness areas. As advocates of the Endangered Species Act (1973) also knew, setting aside the amount and type of land necessary for large predators often has the happy side effect of providing habitat for a host of other smaller and less charismatic animal and plant species. For many ecocentrists, then, large wild animals have special value based both on their ecological significance and on their practical role in the preservation of larger land communities.

Leopold valued not only the ecological but also the symbolic value of large predators. Wolves, mountain lions, and grizzlies, in particular, symbolize both valued landscapes and a proper human attitude toward nature. This attitude requires that we appreciate dangerous wild animals and allow them to live freely in their native habitats. Even though they have no utilitarian value for humans and may even harm human interests, they represent the intrinsic value of nature. In an essay called "Wilderness," Leopold wrote that, "Of the 6000 grizzlies officially reported as remaining in areas owned by the United States, 5000 are in Alaska. Only five states have any at all. There seems to be a tacit assumption that if grizzlies survive in Canada and Alaska, that is good enough. It is not good enough for me. The Alaskan bears are a distinct species. Relegating grizzlies to Alaska is about like relegating happiness to heaven; one may never get there."[13]

Leopold wanted a world with grizzly bears and wolves in it, and he appreciated the ecological importance of diverse wild species. However, he showed little interest in animals as individuals beyond their symbolic and scientific importance. He did not want to interact with them, other than perhaps through hunting and scientific observation. Most important, he did not believe that humans had any moral duties toward individual animals other than to respect their roles in the larger community. He accepted predation and other causes of suffering as ecologically necessary and healthy and did not think that people should intervene in these processes. He especially opposed efforts to reduce the number of wild carnivores, either to protect game for human hunters or to protect domesticated herbivores such as sheep or cattle. In this respect, Leopold echoed the attitudes of earlier preservationists, including John Muir, while prefiguring the approaches of contemporary ecocentric environmental advocates and thinkers.[14]

In an ecocentric perspective, the most essential and perhaps only human obligations to wild animals are, first, not to interfere in their lives and, second, to preserve the kind and amount of habitat that they need to live freely. Humans do not have any obligation to protect wild creatures from their fates and may, in fact, have permission or even a duty to "eliminate" animals who threaten overall ecological integrity. For example, native wild animals such as white-tailed deer may be seen as a threat to ecological systems if their numbers grow too great. Nonnative, feral, and domesticated animals are even more problematic. A holistic environmental perspective can justify culling such animals in order to restore or preserve a particular kind of ecological balance. Another solution would be to reintroduce large predators to wild habitats, which has been done in some cases, most famously with the reintroduction of wolves to Yellowstone National Park. Regardless of the specific proposal, the guiding criterion is the good of the whole, not of individuals.

Many ecocentrists believe that humans can hunt, fish, and perhaps trap wild animals, as long as they do not disturb the ecological balance of a given land community by, for example, killing members of endangered species. Individual features such as sentience or social complexity are irrelevant to these decisions. Nor do people have duties to assist wild animals who are suffering as a result of natural processes or even human actions. Not only do humans lack obligations to help wild animals, but, further, we would in fact do a great harm by helping them to avoid pain. Natural selection requires this "painful good."[15] To extend rights to wild animals would be in effect to domesticate them—a fate literally worse than death.[16]

ANIMAL ETHICS PERSPECTIVES ON WILD ANIMALS

Many environmental thinkers believe that "animal rights" is concerned mainly, even exclusively, with domestic species. They assume this, first, because the common description of animal ethics as about rights implies an inclusion within human societies that characterizes domestic, but not wild, animals. Rights are socially defined and protected, and they do not seem relevant, practically or philosophically, to creatures who live outside human society. If they are relevant, it is only as an extension of the principles developed for dealing with domestic animals, such as rules against causing deliberate harm. In practical terms, people affect the well-being of domestic animals most directly and frequently, and thus we have greater responsibility and obligations for them, and we can make the most difference in their lives. Ethical guidelines regarding wild animals often take shape mainly as extensions of theories (such as Utilitarianism or rights) that were initially developed for domesticated animals, just as domestic animals are dealt with in models first used in regard to people. For many environmental thinkers, such extensions cannot do justice to wild animals living in wild places.

Animal advocates do pay particular attention to domestic animals because of the direct human impact on the fates of such animals. The vulnerability of domestic animals underlines both our responsibility and our potential capacity to help. However, many animal ethicists also address human moral obligations toward free-living wild animals and those who are neither fully domesticated nor fully wild. A major concern is the use of animals in scientific research, many of which are either semidomesticated (such as the rodents who make up the vast majority of test animals) or captive wild animals, including nonhuman primates. Another important issue is the plight of wild animals kept in captivity in zoos and aquariums or raised for the fur trade. In regard to free-ranging wild animals, animal ethicists have focused on actions that have direct impacts on animals' well-being, especially hunting, trapping, and fishing. Some also address ecological dimensions of harm to animals, for example the use of toxic pesticides, habitat destruction, pollution, and climate change. Large animal welfare groups such as the Humane Society of the United States, for example, have programs addressing these issues as well as domestic and captive animals.

Related to the claim that animal advocates are concerned only with domestic animals is the charge, made by a number of environmental thinkers, that animal advocates want people to treat wild and domestic animals identically. Here environmentalists may find themselves the unlikely bedfellows of people who oppose animal welfare for explicitly anthropocentric reasons. For example, both environmentalists and their critics charge that animal activists would require humans to assist all animals in need, end predation, even eliminate prey species. For example, in his influential 1989 essay, "Animal Liberation: A Triangular Affair," Baird Callicott claimed that animal advocates wanted to "liberate" domesticated animals into the wild, which he saw as an ecological disaster.[17] It would also be "a logical impossibility," he adds, because domesticated animals have been bred to stupidity and dependency.[18] Another prominent environmental thinker, Mark Sagoff, writes that animal liberationists would, if empowered, eliminate wild animals through contraception so that fewer would suffer and die; convert wilderness areas into farms where animals could be well taken care of; and adopt starving deer as pets.[19] These claims resemble charges made by corporate and scientific interests who profit from animal experimentation. Despite (or because of) the inflammatory nature of these accusations, neither Callicott nor Sagoff cites animal advocates who have gone on the record calling for these measures.[20]

The reason for the lack of citation is not discretion but lack of evidence. Even the most radical of animal advocates do not call for the liberation of domestic animals or the protection of wild animals from predation and other natural harms. To attack "animal rights" in general on the basis of a position that is virtually absent from both academic and practical animal advocacy echo the common accusation that environmentalists hate people and prefer trees—a fallacious yet useful straw man. In fact, most animal advocates share with most environmental thinkers a conviction that humans' main obligation toward free-ranging wild animals is to leave them alone. This is the position of even the paradigmatic rights thinker Tom Regan. In the preface to the 2004 edition of *The Case for Animal Rights*, Regan explicitly rejects Callicott's charge that he wants to end predator-prey relations. Rather than intervention in affairs of wildlife, he proposes that "what we ought in general to do is . . . nothing."[21] Like most animal advocates, Regan and Singer oppose hunting and other deliberate harm to animals, but beyond this, they do not argue that people should assist or protect wild animals from the usual dangers of wild nature.

In short, most animal ethicists acknowledge the very different circumstances, characters, and capacities of wild and domesticated animals, as well as of different species within each category. Species is not an arbitrary category, as Mary Midgley points out, but matters for the well-being of different animals and the treatment they require.[22] Thus even advocates of species equality do not propose that all kinds of animals be treated identically. However, some moral principles that originated in relation to domestic animals have been extended to all animals. This is especially true of the prohibition on causing direct harm, which has different implications depending on the situation and characteristics of different animals. In regard to domesticated animals, at a minimum this principle bans physical abuse and requires the provision of adequate food, water, shelter, space, and medical care. For some animal advocates, avoiding harm means not just reform but the abolition of institutions and practices such as animal agriculture entirely. In regard to wild animals, the rule against causing direct harm usually leads animal ethicists to oppose hunting, fishing, and trapping, as well as capture or confinement for research or entertainment purposes. There are some areas of disagreement and ambiguity, but very few animal advocates call for direct human intervention in the lives of free-ranging wild animals.

That said, animal ethicists raise important questions regarding our moral obligations to wild animals. One of the most extensive and coherent recent treatments of this issue is Clare Palmer's argument for a contextual animal ethic. She outlines different guidelines for wild and domestic animals, based on the different sorts of relationships people have with them. The most appropriate ethic regarding animals will come from thinking about "certain morally relevant *relations* alongside morally relevant *capacities*."[23] Capacities are not irrelevant, and sentience is crucial to moral consideration. However, the capacities and inherent qualities of different animals cannot, by themselves, determine our duties toward them.

Few people, Palmer points out, have relationships with wild-living animals that generate "duties of assistance." However, she adds, many people do have "just this kind of assistance-generating relationship with (most) domesticated animals and also, at least on occasion, with animals (such as zoo animals or feral animals) in the 'contact zone.' . . . When humans create sentient animals that are vulnerable or dependent, special obligations to care for or to assist these animals are generated."[24] In a contextual ethic, humans have obligations toward animals in direct proportion to their impact on animals' lives. This means we have more and greater obligations toward domesticated animals and relatively few toward free-ranging wild animals, apart from the familiar injunction to leave them alone.

Some circumstances may increase human obligations to animals, wild or domestic. If an animal has been harmed, directly or indirectly, by past human actions, then humans in general and the responsible individual in particular have duties to alleviate or repair the harm if possible. Thus, according to Palmer, the person who injures a wild animal, even inadvertently, has a greater duty to relieve the animal's suffering than does an uninvolved person. The latter may help, at least in some circumstances, but is not obliged to do so. As an example of how this ethic plays out in concrete cases, Palmer asserts that a hiker who encounters an injured animal is morally permitted, though not necessarily required, to alleviate the animal's suffering by taking him or her to a veterinarian or even killing the animal as painlessly as possible, if the injuries are very severe and medical help is not available.

Palmer describes her position regarding free-ranging wild animals as a laissez-faire approach, according to which people have duties to assist wild animals only when they have directly caused harm. Absent direct responsibility for harm, people may be permitted to help, although in some situations we may be required to stay away completely, so as not to interfere in important ecological and evolutionary processes. While other animal ethicists do not make their contextual approach explicit, most share Palmer's conclusions, especially in regard to free-ranging wild animals. Thus philosophers as different as Tom Regan, Peter Singer, and Gary Francione agree with the laissez-faire approach that Palmer advocates, as do most holistic environmental philosophers.

The laissez-faire consensus reveals that few animal ethicists are consistently abolitionist. In concrete cases, most take into account varying capacities and contexts. As a result they advocate different responses in relation to free-living wild animals and captive or domesticated ones.[25] Exemplifying the transition from sweeping standards to practical distinctions is Paul Taylor who, like Regan and Singer, rejects species boundaries as arbitrary guidelines to human moral obligation. (Taylor is also one of the few philosophers who does not distinguish, at least in theory, between obligations to animals and to plants.) Taylor's ethic of "respect for nature" asserts that "all organisms are teleological centers of life in the sense that each is a unique individual pursuing its own good in its own way."[26] In practice, however, his position is far from absolutist or abolitionist. He accepts some forms of hunting for ecological reasons, and he even allows that it might be morally permissible to kill animals for food, since eating is a basic interest of humans. We are only prohibited from harming or killing nonhuman animals in pursuit of trivial interests, such as entertainment.[27] In general, however, Taylor advocates noninterference in wild nature, demonstrating again that the laissez-faire assumption has broad support across significant philosophical divides.

Despite its wide acceptance by otherwise diverse thinkers, the claim that humans should not intervene in wild nature is not unproblematic. If wildness and domestication are indeed ambiguous, fluid, and overlapping in both reality and theory, we cannot always distinguish clearly between wild and domesticated animals and thus know with certainty our moral obligations in each sphere. Such certainties presume, as Palmer puts it, "a dualistic separation of humans from the rest of nature, between the 'wild' and what is 'not wild.'"[28] While Palmer correctly identifies these problems, she does not acknowledge that the laissez-faire assumption—that humans should not interfere with "wild" animals—takes the same dualisms for granted. The laissez-faire ethic presumes that it is possible to identify, and somehow fence off, spheres of wildness apart from human influence. Anthropogenic changes, however, extend human influence into all parts of the globe, even places, such as the North and South Poles, where few people reside permanently.

Bill McKibben made precisely this point in his influential 1989 book *The End of Nature*: with climate change, human impact extends so far in both time and space that it no longer makes sense to speak of wild nature as a separate sphere.[29] If McKibben is right, then people have duties to wild animals whose opportunities to thrive are harmed by climate change and other large-scale human actions, including habitat destruction; the contamination of rivers, lakes, and even oceans; and the use of toxic chemicals in agriculture, among many other examples. To limit human obligation to cases in which direct impact is obvious thus seems less an intellectually coherent response than an effort to avoid responsibility in the face of overwhelming culpability.

This has echoes of equally problematic approaches in social ethics, such as the early form of feminist care ethics articulated by Nel Noddings, according to which our moral duties begin and end with direct, face-to-face relationships. Such a position, as Joan Tronto notes, "ignores the ways in which we are responsible for the construction of our narrow sphere."[30] Tronto argues that Noddings's willingness to help the stranger at her door but not "starving children in Africa" fails to acknowledge "the ways in which the modern world is intertwined and the ways in which hundreds of prior public and private decisions affect where we find ourselves and which strangers show up at our door."[31] This critique is even more trenchant in regard to environmental problems, which also result from global interconnections and countless public and private actions, many of which are far removed from their negative consequences. In this light, the laissez-faire consensus regarding wild animals avoids responsibility for the scope of human impact. This makes it impossible to address many of the most urgent moral, political, and scientific challenges that face humans, nonhuman animals, and ecosystems in general.

Such problems raise the more general question of how ethicists, from environmental as well as animal perspectives, should understand the relationship between the well-being of individual animals and the well-being of ecological communities. Both animal and environmental ethicists agree, first, that wild animals are vital for ecological functions, and second, that healthy ecosystems are vital for wild animals. Both have value and require protection, whether the individual or the whole is the starting point. The problems arise when the relationship between individuals and wholes appears to be one of opposition and mutual exclusion, a common assumption in both environmental and animal ethics. This assumption of duality rests on a conviction that our spheres of influence and our relationships are clearly demarcated and limited. These lines prove inaccurate, however, in light of the ecological, social, and historical complexities of human-animal interactions, on the one hand, and of the animals' own agency and capacities, on the other.

INTENTIONALITY, AGENCY, AND PLAY IN WILD ANIMALS

When environmental thinkers draw on scientific research, they usually turn to conservation biology and ecology. This literature reinforces the view of wild animals as, first and foremost, components of larger ecological wholes. From this perspective, the behavior and characteristics of individual animals are less significant than their relations with other organisms and their place in the overall biotic community. On the other hand, work in animal ethics frequently cites ethological research on nonhuman cognition, agency, sociality, and morality, but very rarely refers to research in ecology. This gap does not stem from opposition between the two scientific fields, since many ecologists are interested in the ways animals adapt to and use their environments and most ethologists recognize that individual animals' roles in larger ecosystems are crucial to understanding individual behavior. It seems the result, rather, of habit and taken-for-granted assumptions in animal and environmental ethics alike. The citation gap is not only unnecessary but unfortunate, since both environmental and animal advocates could strengthen their own work through greater engagement with diverse scientific literatures.

Much research on wild animals has been done in laboratories or other controlled settings, such as zoos. Obviously, animals' behavior is very different in such situations than in their native habitats. Equally obviously, however, it can be very difficult to study the activities and relationships of free-living wild animals in their native habitats. Despite the challenges, in the past several decades numerous rigorous studies have provided details about the lives and capacities of wild animals. These include many careful, long-term studies of particular populations, beginning with Jane Goodall's groundbreaking studies of chimpanzees in Tanzania, begun in the early 1960s. Goodall was young, female, and lacking in formal scientific training. Her methods were as unconventional as her status, and she broke many long-standing taboos for animal research, including the prohibition on naming her subjects. Despite, or perhaps because of, her unorthodox methods, Goodall's fieldwork led to remarkable findings, including the discovery that chimpanzees made and used tools, the first well-documented instance of such behavior in nonhuman animals. Western philosophers and scientists had long considered tool-making and use to be one of the markers of human uniqueness and superiority over other species. Goodall's observation of chimpanzees stripping twigs to make termite-hunting sticks made it impossible to continue asserting the specialness of *Homo faber* in that respect.[32] Subsequent research has shown that other animals, including ravens, also make and use tools.[33]

Many influential studies of wild animal behavior were, like Goodall's, focused on primates, especially great apes. Primate studies in the wild and in naturalistic captive settings have revealed extraordinary complexity in social organization, behavioral codes, emotional attachments, rivalries, playfulness, and many other areas. Primatologists are especially fascinated by behavioral similarities between nonhuman great apes and humans, and many argue that in light of such similarities, we should not draw such a hard-and-fast line between humans and closely related species. Frans de Waal, for example, asserts that we should not assume that a chimp comforting an attack victim or sharing food is acting instinctively while similar actions by humans are evidence of morality. To attribute radically different causes to similar behavior in two closely related species is less plausible and less parsimonious than to assume common processes and origins. Many traits we see as exclusively human, including emotional, moral, and social capacities, in fact precede the evolution of *Homo sapiens* and are shared, in some form, among human and nonhuman species.[34]

Among the most significant of these is the capacity for language, which, like tool use, has long been considered an exclusively human talent, perhaps the most jealously guarded of all. Many language studies have been done with captive apes who have been taught human words, most often in American Sign Language. Chimpanzees, bonobos, and gorillas in these studies have not only learned extensive vocabularies but also combine signs to create new words. They also use words in other settings, both in interactions with other chimpanzees (including those who have not learned sign language) and in solitary activities. In one of the earliest reviews of the language studies, Eugene Linden observed that sign language–trained chimpanzees "think aloud" by using signs while looking at magazine pictures. They do not, in Linden's words, use language just to please their "masters" or to receive rewards, but rather they use the new tools they have acquired for their own purposes.[35] Captive chimpanzees' facility with sign language is probably rooted in the fact that wild-living chimpanzees use many different gestures, part of an extensive communication system that remains largely uninterpreted by human observers.

Studies of communication in other species reveal further complexity. Dorothy Cheney and Robert Seyfarth found that vervet monkeys have different alarm calls for different predator species and respond differently if another monkey's warning indicates the presence of a leopard or an eagle, for example.[36] Non-primate species, including prarie dogs, also have complex alarm systems. Ethologist Con Slobodchikoff of Northern Arizona University has documented more than one hundred words used by prairie dogs, including "adjectives" that differentiate between the height or color of clothes of people observed near the colony. Prairie dogs use different sounds to describe how fast a person is moving or whether he is carrying a gun. Slobodchikoff sees ethical implications in his findings. "If animals can think, if they have self-awareness, this sort of raises an ethical question about what it is we are doing with animals and how we really should treat animals."[37] Jane Goodall has made similar arguments regarding chimpanzees and other animals for decades. Commenting on Slobodchikoff's prairie dog research, Goodall was pessimistic about how much even the most rigorous scientific research would change human attitudes: "There is a real strong need in the minds of many people to keep that line sharp between humans on the one hand and the rest of the animal kingdom on the other."[38]

Even though it may not transform popular thinking about other animals, evidence continues to mount that nonhuman animals have countless skills, activities, and emotions that were long thought to be exclusively human. Among the better-known examples is the deceit practiced by killdeers (and some other birds), who distract predators away from their nests by feigning a broken wing. Once the bird has led the predator far enough away, she flies to safety. The deliberate and intentional nature of this behavior is evident in the fact that the birds make sure they remain in the predator's line of sight and look back to check the response. If the predator does not follow, the bird often moves closer. The birds also understand the kind of threat posed by different animals: they react to nearby cattle with warning cries to direct them away from the nest and reserve the broken-wing display for predators. They also differentiate between the threats posed by individuals of the same species. In a controlled study, the birds responded more strongly to humans who previously had stared menacingly at the nest than to people who ignored it.[39] Killdeers' practice of feigning injury to deceive potential predators is clearly not blind or simplistic but rather entails high levels of intentionality, discrimination, and flexibility.

Nonhuman animals can be not only deceitful but also altruistic, meaning they set aside or even sacrifice their own interests for the sake of others. Altruistic behavior is especially fascinating to many scientists because it does not seem to benefit the individual and thus is hard to explain in terms of natural selection. The sacrifices made by parents for their offspring do not trouble evolutionary interpretations, since the parents' investment will pay off in the continuation of their genes in the next generation.[40] Evolutionary fitness is based on the number of adult offspring raised successfully, and sometimes individuals may leave more adult offspring by caring for existing children rather than protecting themselves. This means that genes that support parental care will leave more "replica genes" in the next generation than genes that encourage parental selfishness in regard to offspring.[41] The evolutionary logic behind parental sacrifice can be applied without difficulty to near relatives. From the standpoint of natural selection, William Hamilton explains, "there is nothing special about parent-offspring relationship except its close degree and a certain fundamental asymmetry. The full-sib relationship is just as close." Half-siblings are as close as grandparents and grandchildren, and so forth.[42] In other words, the selective advantage of helping siblings survive to adulthood is almost as great as is the advantage of helping offspring, and often, as Hamilton notes, there are more opportunities to help relatives of the same generation than grandchildren and further descendants.[43]

This explanation for helping behavior is known as "kin altruism." In one type, individuals who do not have their own infants help raise the offspring of close relatives, as is common among wolves and some other social carnivores. These "babysitters" are investing in the future of their own genetic line by helping their siblings and half-siblings grow to adulthood. In another common example, animals who live in large extended families give alarm calls when a predator is nearby. Discussing this practice among birds, Hamilton notes that an alarm call "probably involves a small extra risk to the individual making it by rendering it more noticeable to the approaching predator but the consequent reduction of risk to a nearby bird previously unaware of the danger must be much greater."[44] Since the tendency to give alarm calls has evolved among many different species, it must have conferred advantages that are greater than the risks run by the alarm-givers.[45] Similarly, a willingness to forgo having one's own offspring must convey proportionately greater benefits through the survival of full or half-siblings. Evolutionary explanations of helping behavior are important because they show that nature, as Darwin himself recognized, entails not only competition, struggle, and pain but also care, nurture, and sacrifice.

Some forms of altruism or helping behavior are not easily explained in terms of genetic ties between the helper and the recipient. One explanation for assistance offered to individuals who are not closely related is "reciprocal altruism" (also known to ethologists as "tit-for-tat" strategies), in which an individual helps another with the expectation that the favor will be returned in the future. This concept expands our understanding of nonhuman behavior because reciprocity seems to involve a greater degree of learning, flexibility, and conscious beliefs than parental or kinship help. Reciprocity entails a number of complex skills and relationships, including good memories and stable relationships, as well as an ability to anticipate future benefits in return for present sacrifices.[46] Reciprocal altruism has been documented in a number of species of birds and mammals, where there is good evidence that animals who were once helped by a particular animal are more likely to help that same individual later than one with whom they do not have that history. In addition, recent research suggests that altruism has strong enough benefits to have evolved on its own, even apart from kinship and reciprocal explanations.[47] This is because altruism is important to social living, which confers a strong selective advantage for the success of crucial activities such as escaping predators, locating and acquiring food, and raising young.

Altruism that first spreads because of the evolutionary benefits of caring for one's own relatives creates patterns of behavior that can then be applied in other settings, including assistance and even self-sacrifice for individuals who are not close relatives. Such an extension may explain much non-kin altruism, Mary Midgley speculates. Helping behavior, like other kinds of sociability, represents an "extension to other adults of behavior first developed between parents and young—grooming, mouth contact, embracing, protective and submissive gestures, giving food. In fact, wider sociability in its original essence simply *is* the power of adults to treat one another, mutually, as honorary parents and children."[48] Parent-child relationships, for Midgley, serve as a model and source for other types of altruistic and nurturing social interactions.

These interpretations are not mutually exclusive. No single explanation, especially one that relies on "mere instinct," can explain complex behavior such as altruism. Instead, for nonhumans as well as humans, multiple factors are usually involved in such practices. Kinship and social bonds, reciprocity, and other factors, including conscious intentionality, all contribute in different degrees. Further, once patterns of behavior are created, they frequently extend beyond the original context. This is evident in both humans and other species. For example, the desire for fatty foods was highly adaptive in the environments in which our hominid ancestors developed, because calories, protein, and other nutrients were in short supply. Applied in most modern societies, such cravings are not only nonadaptive but often positively damaging, but people still seem hard-wired to desire fat. Similar extensions are obvious in many nonhuman species, such as the stalking behavior of house cats who have neither the need nor the opportunity to catch their own food. Behaviors such as these, which appear nonfunctional (and thus not encompassed by simple evolutionary explanations), are harder to explain. This is especially evident in the case of play, which by definition excludes purely functional or utilitarian explanations.

Ethology provides a portrait of animals ranging from great apes to octopi who act with intentionality, creativity, deceitfulness, generosity, and bravery. One of the most challenging kinds of animal behavior is play, which is common in a wide variety of nonhuman species. The complexities of play emerge as soon as we attempt to define it. Gordon Burghardt, one of the preeminent scholars of animal play, explains that the first difficulty in studying play is that "we are unclear what it is, what it is good for, how it originated, and how it evolved."[49] Burghardt describes play not in terms of an exclusive definition but rather in reference to five broad criteria: play is not (merely) functional; it is an end in itself rather than a means to another end (autotelic); it differs clearly from "serious" activities; it is repeated; and it occurs in a stress-free environment.[50] This expands on other definitions, including Konrad Lorenz's description of play as skilled movements that are self-rewarding.[51] Implicit in these descriptions is an understanding that play is not random or accidental but deliberate. In this light, it is possible to understand a wide variety of activities as play. Play, as Burghardt notes, is not rare or exceptional but rather "embedded in the normal lives of animals."[52] Evidence of play behavior is widespread in both domestic and wild animals, including not just birds and mammals but also invertebrates, reptiles, and fish.

The ubiquity of play raises the question of how it evolved. Play has costs: it consumes calories, takes time and attention away from presumably more pressing tasks, such as finding food, and it may distract animals from predators or other threats. This makes it important for ethologists to understand what purposes or functions play serves that may counteract its nonadaptive aspects. Scientific interpretations of play, in nonhuman animals as well as in humans, offer a host of different explanations. Some propose largely instrumental origins for play, arguing that it develops important physical and intellectual skills necessary for survival or teaches young animals social rules. Other explanations make the adaptive dimensions less direct but still see play as instrumental to other goals. Play may encourage creativity and innovation, or it may be a respite from care or stress.[53] Burghardt resists purely functional or adaptive explanations for animal play but agrees that it has important roles, such as teaching rules, sharing, and reciprocity. Play may thus be an essential precursor to the evolution of morality.[54]

Other ethologists have developed this thesis more fully. Marc Bekoff, in particular, has conducted research showing that social play has its own special rules, including self-imposed handicaps that players use to limit the force they use when playing with smaller or weaker animals.[55] Bekoff describes this self-restraint as "a sense of fairness," which he believes is widespread among nonhuman animals because it is necessary not only for play but for survival in many social species, including humans.[56] Bekoff also describes rules that nonhuman animals develop and employ in order both to guide their actions and to communicate with others. One of the best examples is the canid play bow, which provides crucial information to participants about other interactions—"what comes next is play." Play bows are a kind of "metacommunication," or communication about communication.[57]

While evolutionary explanations are part of the picture, they cannot explain all play behavior. Play is, by definition, not instrumental; it is not, or not only, a means to another end but is self-rewarding, or autotelic—it is done for its own sake. Further, intentionality is crucial to play—actions that seem to indicate aggression (wrestling, chasing, growling) take on very different meanings when they are understood as play. Playing animals must know not only that their partner is playing but also that their partner knows that they are playing. The complexity of play, and the sophisticated agency involved, makes play hard to explain in functionalist terms, but also make it an especially rich topic for exploring agency, intentionality, and other complex aspects of animal behavior. As a kind of excess, beyond the satisfaction of basic physical needs, play reflects a level of complexity and intentionality that may be harder to perceive in reproductive, food-seeking, and protective behaviors.

Social play includes interactions between members of different species as well as among both young and adult individuals of the same species. The scientific literature is full of examples of cross-species play, including play between wild and domesticated animals. Examples include dogs playing with mountain gorillas in Rwanda, chimpanzees with young humans or baboons, foxes and gazelles, elephants and wildebeests, and many more.[58] Such interactions reveal the communication of intentions and desires across species lines. For example, members of many species, including humans, clearly recognize the play bow as an invitation to play and, even more important, a signal that the actions that follow are not a threat. Dogs play bow not only to people but to cats, horses, and other species, including polar bears. At our barn, the dogs know that not all the horses are equally playful. When the horses are being let back into their pasture after feeding time, the dogs do not invite all of them to play, but wait for the two young geldings who are most likely to respond affirmatively. The dogs then perform energetic play bows until the horses engage in a chase that seems satisfying to all parties. Because the initial play bow makes the dogs' intentions clear, the horses do not respond to their barking and running as they would to similar behavior from another predator. As a result, we see dogs running after horses but in a way that clearly differs from an aggressive, predatory chase.

Play undermines some of our most important and taken-for-granted distinctions, including not just the line between wild and domestic but also that between human and nonhuman. Play crosses those lines all the time, creating relationships that mediate and connect rather than excluding and opposing. Play raises questions about how we should respond to wild animals. For some observers, complex, intentional behaviors like play prove that certain animals are "like us" and thus worthy of interest and perhaps respect or moral consideration. For others, play reveals the radical otherness of nonhuman animals. Thus Burghardt asserts that "play is a crucial test for the power of science to understand 'mysteries,'" such as the subjective consciousness of other beings.[59] I argue that what play shows is the coexistence of similarity and otherness, which makes relationship possible. Other animals, like other people, are at once like us and not like us, and appreciating the similarities as well as differences, and relating across them, is crucial to formulating our ethical responses to all these other beings.

Beyond Laissez-faire?

The laissez-faire model that dominates both environmental and animal ethics dictates a single obligation to wild animals: "Let them be." By definition, wild animals are those with whom humans have no close interactions. We should try to maintain this situation: the best relationship is no relationship at all. For most ethicists, leaving wild animals alone is not just our primary but perhaps our only moral obligation to them. However, the notion that there are animals with whom we have no interactions is problematic in light of large-scale anthropogenic effects on almost all environments around the world, even those where no humans live permanently. Climate change, oceanic "dead zones," and acid rain affect animals far from the points of origin, so that no animal, however wild and free-roaming, is completely out of the human contact zone. While the differences among kinds and degrees of contact matter, morally as well as in other ways, it is hard to maintain that we have no responsibility to the animals, however far away, who are harmed by our consumption of energy and forests and by our contamination of land, water, and air. Simply letting animals be may mean abandoning them to slow and painful deaths. The breadth and depth of human culpability for environmental destruction demands a more proactive approach.

In addition to these negative factors, there are more positive reasons to think beyond the laissez-faire model. Environmental educators and psychologists argue that practical experiences and relationships change people's attitudes toward nature. If this is true, then environmentalists are right to be concerned that increasing numbers of people around the world have fewer experiences in wild places and contacts with nonhuman animals. Richard Louv documented and lamented humans' increasing distance from nature in his best-selling book *Last Child in the Woods: Saving Our Children from Nature-Deficit Disorder.* Short-term consequences of this deficit can may include social and emotional problems; a long-term consequence may be declining support for environmental reforms. As Louv puts it, "Lacking direct experience with nature, children begin to associate it with fear and apocalypse, not joy and wonder."[60]

Louv's book resonated with many parents and teachers, as well as conservationists, and launched a number of discussions about how to encourage children (and adults) to spend more time outdoors. President Barack Obama developed a national program based on precisely this concept, "America's Great Outdoors," launched in June 2010. Because "Americans today have become increasingly disconnected from our great outdoors," with negative consequences for people, especially children, and for natural resources and places, the program aims to increase Americans' access to and engagement in "the great outdoors."[61] The initiative includes new urban parks and community green spaces, reflecting an awareness that more than 80 percent of Americans live in cities and suburbs and visit wilderness areas infrequently, if at all.[62] Most of what we experience as nature is in intermediate spaces between human-dominated environments and wilder areas. Human-nature encounters are more common in these smaller-scale settings, what Wendell Berry calls "edges."[63]

The animals we encounter in such marginal areas can be domestic, feral, or members of wild species that have adapted to living in close proximity to humans, such as raccoons, squirrels, and sparrows. Most environmental ethicists do not count these animals as part of real nature, which leaves few ways for humans to interact with the animate dimensions of wild nature. Some ecocentrists propose that hunting and fishing can serve as models for contemporary Western relationships to nature. Animal welfare advocates, however, reject interactions that are fulfilled by the death of one party at the hands of another. Some point to other ways to relate to wild animals, such as birding, hiking, or canoeing. These are passive and transient, however. More intimate and lasting relationships with wild animals are rare and require long and patient work on the part of the human involved, as in the case of people who work in wild animal refuges or rehabilitation centers, or researchers engaged in long-term field studies. Such relationships are impossible for most contemporary urban and suburban residents. This turns our attention to the animals who accept and even welcome our attention—the domesticated species who have developed alongside humans for thousands of years. Environmental thought has failed to plumb the significance of these animals and of our relationships with them.

5

Domesticated Animals

DOMESTICATION

People have domesticated animals for a variety of reasons, including companionship, food, protection, and assistance with tasks such as hunting, farming, and pest control. Domestic animals provide stable sources of high-quality protein as well as leather, wool, horn, and fur. They are much better than humans at many tasks, such as pulling a plow, killing rats, or locating and catching fast-moving or well-hidden prey. Because of the advantages of domestication, over the past several thousand years humans have tried to domesticate hundreds of species. Most of these attempts failed, including efforts with species, such as zebras, that are closely related to animals that have been successfully domesticated. Only around fifty species of birds and mammals have been fully domesticated.

Domestication entails changes in behavior and physiology, achieved by human intervention in reproduction, mainly by controlling which individuals reproduce. Common behavioral changes associated with domestication include decreased shyness, fear, and aggression around humans and often increased playfulness. Physical changes usually include a decrease in brain size as well as a host of other developments, depending on both biology and the traits desired by humans who are influencing the animals' reproduction. Some species become smaller as a result of domestication, while others become larger; some become hairier, others less hairy. Many develop a wider variety of coat or plumage colors and patterns, often including more white markings. These changes are the result of human selection working on natural variations in behavior, color, size, coat length, feather shape, and countless other features.

Some scientists describe domestication as a kind of "neoteny," indicating the retention of juvenile characteristics into adulthood. These include behavioral traits such as sustained playfulness and submissiveness as well as physical characteristics such as large eyes and round foreheads, which are exaggerated in some breeds, such as Persian cats or Pekinese dogs. The neoteny theory is problematic both because it suggests that domesticated animals are immature versions of wild ones and because it conceives of domestication as simply a matter of human selection of desirable traits. Both biologically and historically, domestication is much more complex and less predictable than this version suggests.

Domestication involves not only physical changes but also an intense, long-term relationship between humans and nonhuman animals. The relationship is mutual, though not egalitarian. Many researchers believe that dogs and cats, in particular, played active roles in their own domestication by choosing to approach and remain near human settlements and initiate different kinds of interactions with humans. The thesis of nonhuman agency challenges traditional interpretations of domestication as a one-way process of human domination and control. Today scholars increasingly argue that human choices and ingenuity constituted only one element in domestication, and that the choices and ingenuity of nonhuman animals have been equally important.[1] In this light, domestication is an evolutionary strategy not just of humans but also of the wild animals who found life more secure with human protection and food, thus well worth the costs. "Domesticated animals chose us as much as we chose them," as Stephen Budiansky puts it. This mutual agency makes domestication "a remarkable evolutionary compact among the species" rather than simply another instance of humans' power over wild nature.[2]

The vast majority of domesticates are herbivores, such as sheep, cattle, horses, and goats, as well as some omnivores, such as chickens and ducks. Most of these herbivores are considered "livestock," while the few domesticated carnivores, mainly cats and dogs, are primarily pets. This division is central not only to popular attitudes about proper treatment but also to law and policy. Laws regulating animal cruelty, for example, often exempt food animals entirely or at best provide much less protection for the animals and much greater freedom for the "owners." Some animals in both groups are also workers, a category that is not as important in the scholarly literature as it should be. The labor of dogs and horses, above all, has had momentous effects on human societies in Europe, Asia, the Middle East, and the Americas, in particular. Archaeologists, historians, and evolutionary biologists all acknowledge that human history would not be the same without the contributions of domesticated animals.

Even when kept primarily as pets, domesticated animals are not simply "tame." Individual members of domesticated species may not be tame at all due to a lack of socialization with humans, especially during infancy. Feral animals—members of domesticated species who live outside human society—can be as wary of humans as their wild relatives. However, the infants born to feral or free-roaming domesticated animals can, if socialized early, behave similarly to the offspring of mothers living fully domestic lives. Thus while it can be very difficult to make an adult feral cat into a house pet, kittens born to feral mothers usually adapt to domesticity very well if they have positive experiences with people from a young age.

On the other hand, some individual members of wild species may be very docile and develop positive relationships with humans, usually as a result of intense care and interaction during infancy. Thus people in different cultures have long kept ravens, squirrels, deer, and other wild animals as pets. The tameness of certain individual wild animals, however, is not passed on to offspring. Maternal behavior can strongly influence infants' responses to humans, of course, but the babies born to a pet squirrel or a captive zebra are still wild animals biologically. The same is true of wild animals kept captive in zoos, aquaria, circuses, fur farms, "exotic animal" ranches, laboratories, and wildlife refuges. Captive wild animals are not domesticated, no matter how docile individual animals may become. Selective breeding for tameness is possible, but it changes the physical as well as behavioral character of the animals, as was demonstrated in a well-known case in Russia in the 1950s. The least aggressive and fearful foxes on a fur farm were selectively bred, in an effort to create fur-bearing animals that would be easier to handle. The result, within a few generations, was foxes who were indeed more tractable and friendly to humans but who also ceased to look like fur foxes. They developed many physical traits associated with domestication in dogs and other species, including piebald coats and floppy ears. This accidental experiment demonstrates, among other things, both that the physical and behavioral characteristics associated with domestication are linked together and that it is impossible to control for single traits, physical or behavioral, since they are complex characteristics with multiple genetic causes.[3]

Scholars of domestication, including biologists, archaeologists, and historians, disagree on many key issues, ranging from the mechanism by which domestication occurs to the time and place that different species were first domesticated. There is no dispute, however, that the first animal to be domesticated was the dog. The domestic dog, *Canis lupus familiaris*, emerged from wolves (*Canis lupus*) during the late Paleolithic period, at least 15,000 and perhaps more than 30,000 years ago. The wide range of possible dates stems both from the multiplicity of sites and from the different kinds of evidence used. Fossil evidence reveals the changing body shapes evident in the skeletal remains of wolves, dogs, and the various in-between species that emerged during the course of the transformation. In addition, archaeologists have discovered fossils that indicate closer relationships between humans and dogs, such as joint burial sites and footprints showing dogs and people walking close together. More recently, DNA evidence has both enriched and complicated archaeological understandings of dogs' history. An excavation in Belgium recently pushed the date for domestication back to 31,700 years ago, using both fossil and DNA analysis.[4] Not all archaeologists accept this as proof of true domestication, however; some believe that the skull found in Belgium is that of a wolf in transition to a dog, rather than an actual specimen of *Canis lupus familiaris*. While new research and new methods of interpretation will undoubtedly continue to generate disagreements about the precise timing of domestication, there is abundant and varied evidence that by at least 15,000 years ago domestic dogs had emerged from wolves and were living closely with humans in Europe and elsewhere. This is at least 5,000 years earlier than the next instances of successful domestication.

The Belgian research suggesting a much earlier time also indicates that Europe was the site of the earliest domestication, in contrast to other studies that show dogs first emerging in Asia or Africa. Recent archaeological finds in the Czech Republic add to the arguments that the earliest domestications took place in Europe and that there were multiple sites of origin for dogs during the late Paleolithic period.[5] The ambiguity about the location of domestication seems to be unique to dogs. Most domesticated animals emerged in a single place and then spread to other areas. Most experts believe that the same process occurred with dogs, but some think that wolves were domesticated in several different sites. Until humans began extirpating them from much of their native range, wolves were the most widely dispersed mammal species besides *Homo sapiens*. Wolves and humans, both social predators, would have interacted in many different settings, making it plausible that the steps toward domestication occurred more than once.

The multisite thesis and other theories about dog domestication are significant because they highlight both relationship and animal agency. Not only did wolves live near humans in many different areas (Asia, Europe, Africa, and the Middle East) prior to domestication, but wolves have distinctive traits—high sociability, intelligence, and behavioral adaptability—that facilitated the process of domestication. This process likely involved as much initiative on the part of wolves as of humans. Just as their skills at hunting and protection made dogs attractive and useful to humans, people's ability to provide a stable food supply, primarily through refuse, made them attractive and useful to wolves. Wild animals can seek relationships with people for their own purposes and on their own terms.

The occupation of North America marks a significant episode in the shared history of wolves, dogs, and humans. Both wolves and humans crossed the Bering land bridge 10,000 to 15,000 years ago. Recent research suggests that already-domesticated dogs accompanied the humans as well, providing assistance that, as one scholar argues, may "have been the reason people made it across the land bridge."[6] More generally, early humans' partnership with dogs provided a huge survival advantage: they served as lookouts and guards, pulled and carried burdens, and made it possible to hunt large game. During crucial periods of human prehistory, groups that included dogs probably endured a number of threats that destroyed dogless communities. It is possible, in fact, that "dogs were probably a big reason why early man survived and Neanderthals didn't. Neanderthals didn't have dogs."[7]

Dogs are not only the first animals domesticated but also the most widely dispersed domesticated animals in the world. They were one of the few domesticated animal species living with indigenous peoples in the Americas prior to the European colonization that began in 1492. Unlike Asian, African, European, and Middle Eastern societies, precolonial Native Americans did not have domesticated goats, sheep, cattle, pigs, or horses. As Marion Schwartz notes: "Dogs were the only animals present in the majority of Native American groups, the only animal allied with humans."[8]

EXPANDING THE MIXED COMMUNITY

Dogs are the only species whose domestication significantly predates the rise of agriculture. The emergence of *Canis lupus familiaris* was followed by the domestication of sheep, about 10,000 years ago, and by the domestication of goats, pigs, and cattle a millennium or two later. Most of these domestic species emerged in the Middle East, Near East, and Eurasia around the same time as the domestication of plants, and especially the cultivation of grains, which began in the Near East about 9,500 years ago.[9] Other farm animals emerged even more recently: chickens about 6,000 years ago, and donkeys, horses, and ducks around 4,000 to 5,000 years ago.

Cats were probably also domesticated 8,000 to 10,000 years ago, also in the Near East. Even more than dogs, cats probably largely self-domesticated, meaning that they sought out human settlements as a good source of food, especially the rodents who were attracted to the grain cultivated by early farmers.[10] Cats today differ less from their wild ancestors in appearance and behavior than do other domestic species and, as countless feral cats around the world attest, often live easily without human care. Cats may be the main exception to the rule that domestication succeeds only with social species. Most wild felids are solitary hunters, with lions the main exception, although the ancestors of domestic cats may have been more sociable than most.

Like dogs, the herbivores that were successfully domesticated all evolved from animals with flexible behavior and a willingness to scavenge new food sources. They were, in Stephen Budiansky's term, "opportunists."[11] Most domesticated animals also came from highly social species with clear methods of expressing dominance and submission, which are intelligible not only to members of their own species but also to observant humans. The same is true in reverse: with a little practice, these animals can read human signals as well as or better than we can read theirs.[12] This is abundantly clear in the formal training of dogs and horses, which can reach astonishing levels of sophistication and subtlety. In informal interactions, as well, many domesticated animals learn to interpret human body language and actions with great accuracy.

This is nowhere more evident than in the case of Clever Hans, the horse who amazed crowds in the early 1900s with his correct answers to questions about math and other intellectual problems. Early investigations showed that there was no fraud, because the horse performed just as well when his trainer was absent. Eventually, however, a psychologist determined that Hans was responding to the body language of people around him. He read clues so subtle that even his trainer believed the horse really knew the answers. The case of Clever Hans is discussed in almost every overview of research in animal behavior, although with widely different interpretations. For many scientists, the case supports the need for "a more critical attitude toward those who attributed human-like mental powers to animals," because it showed that instead of actually multiplying or dividing, Hans was reading the reactions of audience members. This approach often presents Clever Hans as evidence for the validity of Morgan's Canon, the principle that, "In no case may we interpret an action as the outcome of the exercise of a higher psychical faculty, if it can be interpreted as the outcome of one which stands lower in the psychological scale."[13] From this perspective, the ability to interpret human body language is a "lower" capacity than the ability to do math. Other interpreters find Hans's capacity to decode the tiny, involuntary movements of people around him more impressive than the ability to add or subtract.[14] From this perspective, the Clever Hans case not only underlines the sophisticated social and intellectual skills of many animals but also the intensely mutual character of domesticated animals' relations with people. Hans's ability to "read" his human interlocutors was made possible by millennia of subtle communication, as much emotional as physical, between horses and people.

Agency and Choice

The evolutionary relationship between humans and domesticated species is increasingly understood as one of mutual shaping rather than unidirectional human influence. This is especially likely in the cases of dogs and cats, powerful predators who could be incorporated into human societies only because they deliberately restrained their aggression. The boldest and most curious wolves and wildcats were the likely pioneers, seeking out easy sources of food around the settlements of human hunters. In turn, humans favored individual animals who were the most docile and easy to handle, providing them with greater care, food, and reproductive opportunities.

Domestication changed *Homo sapiens* just as much as we changed the nonhuman creatures involved. Domestic animals would not exist without us, but humans also would not be what we are without them; in Roger Caras's words: "We are the products of cultures, histories and events all made possible because there have been animals for us to eat, some to milk, still others to wear, ride and otherwise burden. They have been the constants in our cultural and intellectual evolution, surpassed in importance only by the potential of our own brains."[15] Our brains, in fact, have been profoundly influenced by our relations with nonhuman animals. This is especially true for dogs, domesticated at a time when early humans were still evolving. Recent research suggests that evolving humans' relationship with dogs altered the structure of both species' brains. One of the various physical changes wrought by domestication is a reduction in the size of the brain: 16 percent for horses, 34 percent for pigs, and 10 to 30 percent for dogs. This is because, as Temple Grandin puts it, "once humans started to take care of these animals, they no longer needed various brain functions in order to survive." Animals who were fed and protected by humans did not need many of the skills required by their wild ancestors and lost the parts of the brain related to those capacities. A similar process occurred for humans, who seem to have been domesticated by wolves. About 10,000 years ago, when the role of dogs was firmly established in most human societies, the human brain also shrank by about 10 percent. Further, Grandin explains,

> what's interesting is what *part* of the brain shrank. In all of the domestic animals the *forebrain*, which holds the frontal lobes, and the *corpus callosum*, which is the connecting tissue between the two sides of the brain, shrank. But in humans it was the *midbrain*, which handles emotions and sensory data, and the *olfactory bulbs*, which handle smell, that got smaller while the corpus callosum and the forebrain stayed pretty much the same. Dog brains and human brains specialized: humans took over the planning and organizing tasks, and dogs took over the sensory tasks.[16]

Dogs may be the only species that had such a profound influence on humans' physical evolution and early survival as a species. However, other domestic animals have joined dogs in shaping human history around the globe. Numerous animals provided concentrated protein and fat, thus helping humans survive and even thrive in otherwise resource-poor environments and making it possible for them to settle or to move about with more flexibility than that afforded to hunting and gathering societies. Horses made possible unprecedented travel, exploration, and military actions in many cultures, undoubtedly changing the course of history numerous times. (The old proverb about losing a kingdom for want of a horseshoe nail makes this point in homely form.)[17] Horses and other work animals, such as donkeys and oxen, transformed agriculture by making it possible to plow larger and more difficult tracts of land.

Beyond their economic, nutritional, and military uses, domesticated animals have been central to the religious and cultural life of countless cultures. Many activities dependent on animal resources, including cheese-making, baking, leatherwork, and spinning, have not only economic but also artistic and cultural significance. In religion, domestic animals have played a vital role as well. Most animal sacrifices have used domestic rather than wild species, and domestic animals appear in the mythology of human groups around the world. Dogs in particular connect the mundane world to more transcendent realms, by guiding people to their destination in the afterlife, in Egypt and some Native American cultures.[18] Roger Caras proposes that humans' dependence on animals served, in fact, "as the facilitators of our own cultural evolution. . . . We arrived at the human state incomplete, willing but unable to take giant steps. At each turn in our evolution as culture-makers, animals enabled us to move on to the next level."[19]

ENVIRONMENTAL PERSPECTIVES ON DOMESTICATED ANIMALS

The problem for many environmentalists is that each level of human social development seems to entail greater consumption of natural resources and destruction of wild places. They see domestic animals as so embedded in human society that they are no longer part of nature at all but rather coconspirators in humans' assault on the natural world. This is especially evident in agriculture, which some environmental thinkers identify as the beginning of the end of a healthy relationship with nature. Cultivation of domestic plants and animals enables people to live longer, have more children, and consume many more calories and resources per capita. While this is most obvious in relation to contemporary factory farming, some critics see agriculture of almost any kind as destructive.[20]

Domestic animals not only contribute to the ecological damage wrought by agriculture but have also influenced human attitudes and practices regarding nature. Paul Shepard makes this point in relation to the use of dogs in hunting, which transformed it from a kind of communion between people and prey into another instance of human domination over nature: "Before the hound, men hunted with their minds and were on holy ground. With the dog, an equilibrium was lost." The later incorporation of horses only compounded the damage: "Mounted the hunters became slavemakers, and everything was relentlessly hunted, as the two slaves became the weapons against the earth." Together dog and horse became "the means in human hands that hounded and horsepowered the earth into polluted, destabilized, and homogenized environments." Shepard's attack on horses and hounds comes in a book titled *The Others: How Animals Made Us Human*. The only animals who "made us human," in his view, are wild ones: domestic animals are perverted forms that corrupt their human masters and destroy "the Gaian sensibility—that humility and nurturing ethos which resists the pastoral exhortation to overtake, control, and contain."[21]

Shepard's approach is extreme, especially his attempt to transfer responsibility for ecological destruction from humans to hounds and horses. However, many other ecocentrists share his contempt for domestic animals. Against the notion that domestication is mutual strategy by humans and nonhumans alike, these environmentalists describe it as a straightforward process of human manipulation and exploitation. The products of this process are "perverse and dysfunctional" versions of their wild ancestors, "blunted in mind and body."[22] This contempt for domesticated animals is widespread in the environmental literature. For example, Baird Callicott asserts that domesticated animals, especially farm animals such as chickens and calves, are so far removed from their wild origins that it is impossible to speak of their "natural behavior." To see such creatures as natural is "profoundly incoherent," he writes: "It would make almost as much sense to speak of the natural behavior of tables and chairs."[23] On similar lines, Eugene Hargrove writes that the domestic dog is "pure and simply a human artifact, bred through artificial selection over hundreds of thousands [*sic*] of years. It is now a part of human history, not natural history."[24] Holmes Rolston draws an equally stark distinction between domestic and wild animals: "A gazelle is pure wild grace, but a cow is a meat factory, pure and simple."[25] Summarizing the arguments, Paul Shepard calls domesticated animals "freaks and travesties of the wild forms . . . ecological wrecks."[26] Domestication is a travesty not just because it modifies animals' behavior and appearance but because it removes animals from wild ecosystems in which the good of the whole always takes precedence over the interests of any single part.[27]

While not all environmentalists see domestic animals as "travesties," most are aware of the damage done at least by those kept in confined feeding operations and other forms of industrial agriculture. Opposition to such practices is one of the few issues, in fact, on which environmentalists and animal welfare activists routinely agree. Some people in both camps oppose not just factory farms but all forms of animal agriculture due both to the ecological harm it causes, including contamination of water and soil, excessive consumption of resources, and deforestation, and to the physical and psychological suffering of the animals involved. Others reject industrial agriculture but accept other forms of animal agriculture, especially when the farms are small-scale, diversified, and locally oriented and use organic sources. Such models are both ecologically better and less stressful for the animals involved, though still problematic for many critics.

Beyond the harm caused by animal agriculture, environmentalists frequently point to the fact that domestic and feral animals destroy native wild animals and plants. Most notably, domestic cats kill millions of songbirds annually. Many environmental groups, like many animal advocates, call on people to keep their housecats indoors, in order to protect birds and also to keep cats safe from disease, fights, cars, and predators. The issue becomes more difficult in regard to feral cats, who do not have owners to control their behavior. Many animal welfare advocates support trap–neuter–release (TNR) programs, but environmentalists often describe these programs as inadequate to deal with the scope of the problem. TNR is controversial, as Katherine Grier summarizes, "because of the continued dependence of feral cat colonies on human caregivers, the presence of feral cats as community nuisances, and the impact of feral cats on wildlife, particularly songbirds."[28] The debate about feral cats sheds light on larger conflicts between animal advocates and environmentalists, in part because it requires a hierarchy of value that determines whether cats or birds shall live. Perhaps even more revealing is the way in which TNR, in attempting "to define a place that is neither tame nor fully wild for cats in communities," muddies the all-important line between wildness and domesticity.[29] It is hard to know how to value, let alone how to treat, animals that do not fit neatly into a single category.

The marginal status of domesticated nonhumans seems to ensure the worst of both worlds. On the one hand, domestic animals do not deserve protection as integral parts of native ecosystems because they are part of human society rather than wild nature. On the other hand, because they are not human, domestic animals are not protected within human society. "Food animals," in particular, often have no more legal protection than the tables and chairs to which Callicott compares them. Many environmentalists find this unproblematic, because they believe that domestic animals are not active agents but mere artifacts of human domination. Thus according to Holmes Rolston, the "value destruction" that occurs when a sheep is eaten is far less than that in a human death, "especially since they have been bred for this purpose and would not otherwise exist."[30]

This logic is frequently used to justify exploitative practices regarding domestic animals, ranging from animals raised for meat to those kept on fur farms. However, "the problem with the 'bred for that purpose' argument," as Jonathan Balcombe explains, "is that it has no bearing on the moral object—the suffering of the animal. If being bred for the bullfight somehow meant that the animal was insensate to pain and suffering, then that could have some bearing on the rightness or wrongness of the act. But there is no evidence for this. A bull destined for the bullring, a mouse caged for a carcinogenicity study, and a salmon fattened for the angler's hook are no less sentient than those more fortunate individuals with a life of freedom."[31] Only a purely instrumental and anthropocentric ethic can justify "bred for this purpose" claims. Such arguments have echoes of the logic used by some theologians to justify human dominion over nature because "God made it for this purpose." The same argument has often been used to justify the enslavement or legal subordination of certain categories of humans. Most environmentalists dismiss dominion arguments as both self-serving and philosophically flawed. They fail to acknowledge, however, similar weaknesses in claims that human intentions can trump animals' intrinsic capacities to feel pain.

More generally, because of their focus on wild nature and ecological processes, most environmental thinkers pay little or no attention to the harms suffered by domestic animals. The one exception is intensive animal agriculture, mentioned earlier, which is of concern more because of the environmental destruction it causes rather than for the suffering of the domestic animals involved. I have found no other writings in which environmental philosophers examine the moral implications of other uses of domestic animals. A few mention the plight of captive wild animals in laboratories, circuses, aquaria, or zoos in relation to the impact on wild populations, especially when the animals involved are rare or endangered. Animal welfare advocates, in contrast, devote most of their attention to the use of animals, both wild and domestic, in precisely these situations—zoos, farms, and laboratories.

Even though most environmental thinkers believe that domestic animals have much less intrinsic value than wild animals, many agree with animal ethicists that we have duties to care for and protect domestic animals. These responsibilities stem directly from the dependence that makes domestic animals inferior to wild ones. We are obliged to leave wild animals alone because they are free and autonomous creatures who should be able to live their lives without human intervention. The duty to let them be corresponds to a general release from obligations to help them, except in situations when we have caused harm directly. Domestic animals, however, do not have free and autonomous lives and often cannot live without human assistance. Their vulnerability is a direct result of past and present human actions, which means that humans have much greater responsibilities to them than to free-living wild creatures.

An interesting paradox thus characterizes many environmentalists' attitudes toward domestic animals: they are ecologically problematic and inferior in almost every way, but their suffering concerns us in a way that the plight of altogether more pleasing wild animals cannot. While humans have responsibilities to protect some domestic animals from "unnecessary" pain, such protection is never acceptable in wild nature, where the integrity of ongoing ecological processes always trumps the well-being of individuals.[32] Thus the environmentalist values the "pure wild grace" of the gazelle whose suffering he will not relieve, at the same time denigrating the cow to whom he offers help. In the wild, pain is never unnecessary; even when it is not in the interests of the suffering individual, it serves some larger ecological and evolutionary interest.

This categorical distinction between human responsibilities toward wild and domestic animals is justified not by the animals' differential capacities but by their relations to human beings. The dualistic ethic adopted by these environmental thinkers thus resembles Clare Palmer's contextual model. Palmer explicitly rejects a sharp division between wild and domestic, allowing for a broad contact zone and many different gradations of obligation. In the end, however, only a categorical distinction can justify the application of entirely different moral rules to animals whose intellectual, physical, and psychological capacities are virtually identical. Thus Palmer asserts that people are obligated to feed starving horses but not starving zebras, to provide medical care to a sick dog but not a sick coyote, or to save a cat from a flood even while we watch the waters carry away equally sentient, intelligent, and complex wild creatures. This ethic is not only dualistic but also anthropocentric, even when articulated by self-proclaimed ecocentrists. It derives the value of nonhuman animals, wild or domestic, from their relationship with us and their ability to contribute to what we value.

ANIMAL ETHICS PERSPECTIVES ON DOMESTIC ANIMALS

Animal advocates pay much more attention to domesticated animals than do environmentalists but still disagree about the proper moral response. This lack of clarity comes from domestic animals' ambiguous place between wild nature and human culture. The marginality that generates ambivalence, and in some cases outright rejection, among many environmental thinkers also creates complexities for animal advocates. Most insist that animals' individual capacities, rather than their social contexts and histories, generate human moral obligations. However, this claim is far from unqualified or consistent in its application.

Rights theorists assert that domestic and wild animals share some of the same rights, most importantly the right "never to be treated as if they exist as a resource for others," as Tom Regan puts it. Animals must be treated, in Kantian terms, as ends in themselves, never simply as means to another's ends. This principle leads to a generally abolitionist position, according to which all deliberate human exploitation of both animals should end, in circuses, laboratories, zoos, farms, and other settings. The right to respectful treatment applies equally to all animals, wild and domestic, who fulfill the morally relevant conditions. Animals have rights not because of their histories or relationships to human beings but rather because of their internal capacities. As Regan summarizes, "they see and hear, believe and desire, remember and anticipate, plan and intend. Moreover, what happens to them matters to them."[33] Thus it is no more acceptable to display horses in a circus than elephants, no better to eat a sheep than a gazelle, no less wrong to dissect domestic rabbits than wild ones.

Beyond the basic right not to be used as an instrument or deliberately harmed, a number of rights attributed to nonhuman animals depend on context. Like ecological thinkers, most animal advocates believe we should leave predator-prey relations and other natural processes to unfold without interference. The injunction to let wild animals be, even when pain and premature death are involved, is grounded, as Regan explains, "in a recognition of their general competence to get on with the business of living, a competence that we find among members of both predator and prey species."[34] Such competence is not present in domesticated animals, for the most part; their dependence makes them vulnerable in a way that permits and even demands our intervention. Presumably, then, we should protect a pet rabbit from a marauding terrier but not save a wild rabbit from a hungry fox. Lacking the wild rabbit's competence, the tame one does not have much chance of evading the predator; and lacking the terrier's regular food supply, the fox is driven to procure her own meat violently.

Few if any animal rights activists or theorists propose treating domesticated animals identically to wild ones, apart from the prohibition against causing deliberate harm. Most animal advocates realize that many domesticated species, especially farm animals such as cows, pigs, and sheep, could not thrive without human care. The fact that humans have shaped the very species-character of domesticated animals creates greater responsibility.

Many activists would like to see the population of domesticated animals, especially farm animals, decline or even disappear as a result of reduced human exploitation. They would not, however, effect this decline by releasing domesticated animals into the wild. Further, activists who help feral animals such as cats work to reduce the population of such animals by trapping and neutering them, rather than simply celebrating and enabling their lives independent of human control. In the big picture, then, animal rights positions on domestic animals do not differ as sharply from that of ecocentric environmentalists as the latter often imply.

Most animal advocates accept the theoretical divide between wild and domestic, despite the occasional blurring of lines, as well as the practical differences this distinction makes in treatment of different animals. Many activists also distinguish among different types of domesticated animals. There are substantial theoretical as well as practical disagreements between farm animal advocates and people involved in dog and cat rescue, for example. For the latter, emotional bonds with companion animals are central, while the former group tends to emphasize individual capacities for suffering and sentience as grounds for protection.

CARE AND JUSTICE FOR DOMESTICATED ANIMALS

Domestic animals are a primary concern in feminist care ethics, which has emerged as a leading stream in animal ethics. Care ethics are especially appropriate in regard to domesticated animals not only because of their attention to emotions but also because they emphasize the moral obligations that emerge from relationships between individuals. Justice and rights-based ethics focus on autonomous individuals, whose relationships, histories, and contexts are largely irrelevant both to their own moral obligations and to the duties owed them by other independent agents. While an ethic of justice presumes the independence and rough equality of all moral actors, a care ethic acknowledges the inequalities in power and ability that typify relationships between humans and domestic animals. Such inequalities also characterize the relationships between parents and children, one of the original models for care ethics.

In unequal relationships, such as those between parents and children, even loving and responsible people face moral ambiguities. Such relationships pose a problem for ethics based on rights and justice, which assume exchanges between people who are equal and autonomous, and who possess the necessary capacities to be full moral agents. Many, perhaps most, interhuman relationships do not meet these conditions, and many people—including young children, mentally disabled persons, or elderly people suffering from dementia—cannot be full moral agents because they lack, temporarily or permanently, the intellectual capacities necessary for moral reflection and decision-making. Some rights theorists use the term "moral patient" for these people. While they lack many of the capacities of moral agents, moral patients still have a number of rights, including most basically the right to be treated as ends and not means.

The category of moral patient makes explicit the responsibilities of moral agents toward more vulnerable, dependent, or differently abled people. However, this concept still assumes that rationality and abstract principles such as justice exhaust our ethical commitments. It does not allow for other kinds of moral commitments or actions, such as those based on emotions, relationships, loyalties, or personal history. Care ethicists argue that rather than including all kinds of people in a framework established for a small segment of the population (fully rational, free, economically and physically independent adult males), we need different ethical models to understand and account for different ways of being moral. Perhaps, in other words, the choice is not just between moral agents in the Kantian sense and passive, incompetent moral patients who can only hope for decent treatment from their superiors. There are kinds of moral agency other than that exercised by fully rational individuals who can understand and act on abstract principles. There also exist moral relations other than those between equals.

A number of feminist thinkers propose care ethics as the best theoretical framework for thinking about human relationships with and obligations to nonhuman animals. This model is especially appropriate for thinking about domestic animals, whose unequal and dependent relations with humans, coupled with their inability to operate as fully autonomous, rational moral actors in human society, make an ethic of rights or justice problematic. An ethic based on sympathy, care, and relationality seems more applicable to our relations to nonhuman animals, especially domesticated ones. Care ethics is rooted in the private sphere of home and children, a realm with which domestic animals are also associated. Because of their ties to the private household, both farm and companion animals are usually seen as closer to women and children. While domestic animals are feminized, "wild animals—and the natural world in general—remain perceived as masculine, and therefore wild animals are seen as having higher status."[35] (This connection is not absolute, since some domesticated animals, such as hunting dogs and horses, are linked to distinctly male activities.) The practical and historical ties between women and domestic animals are important in the work of many feminist thinkers who apply care ethics to animals.

With regard to wild animals, with whom people have few direct relationships and emotional ties, care ethics are less obviously appropriate. Care ethics, which assumes close and unequal relationships between humans and nonhumans, make domestic animals the paradigm. Such an ethic, Grace Clement argues, cannot be applied easily to free-ranging wild animals. Wild animals may in fact exist in the state envisioned by ethics of justice—a society of rational, independent beings to whom our primary duties are noninterference rather than care. While domestic animals need care and support from humans, free-ranging wild animals mainly need human restraint. Further, emotional values such as sympathy may be appropriate for domestic animals whose fate is largely in the hands of humans but not for wild animals who are entangled in predator and prey relations as well as larger ecological processes.[36] In a feminist twist on Palmer's contextual ethic, Clement proposes a two-track animal ethic, in which care guides our dealings with domestic animals, and justice (understood mainly as noninterference) is our primary duty toward wild animals.

This distinction attempts to avoid the dangers of care ethics, which have a built-in subjectivity because they make moral duty dependent upon feelings and relationships. Multitrack ethics seek a way around this by distinguishing between obligations of care toward animals to whom we are connected and obligations of noninterference toward animals to whom we are not clearly tied. However, we still face the problem of deciding which interactions and relationships are morally relevant. A contextual ethic, for example, declares that I am obligated to help the baby birds who fall when I accidentally knock a nest out of a tree but that I have no such duty if a squirrel knocks down the nest. The baby birds are equally vulnerable to harm in both cases, however. This would be obvious to us in the case of human children, where considerations of context, history, and direct responsibility would not preclude a duty to help children who are at risk because of someone else's actions.

If the only ethically relevant relations are those characterized by personal interactions and mutual feelings of sympathy and love, then both distant and unsympathetic individuals fall outside our circle of moral concern. Nel Noddings argues, for example, that she may have obligations to a stray cat based on "pleasant memories of caring for cats and having them respond to me," but not to rats, because "I feel no such stirring in connection to rats."[37] Neither the animals' individual capacities nor their vulnerability to human power is relevant; human choices are all that matter: "We have made pets of cats. In doing so, we have established the possibility of appreciative and reciprocal relation. If we feel that the cat has certain rights, it is because we have conferred those rights by establishing the relation."[38] (People who keep pet rats, presumably, have obligations to other rats.) This kind of ethic limits moral responsibility to relationships that have a face-to-face component. The ethicist who insists that she has obligations only to people or animals for whom she personally cares may evade responsibility for the indirect consequences of many actions and decisions. I have no personal interactions with the polar and alpine animals who suffer as a result of climate change or, for that matter, with the impoverished adults and children who are suffering and will suffer from the same causes. If my lack of an immediate personal relationship with suffering individuals absolves me from moral duties to fight against climate change, there seems little hope of effective action on this and other large problems. It is true that we cannot save the whole world, and even, as Noddings notes, that we cannot *love* the whole world. This does not lead necessarily to the conclusion that we have no moral obligations at all toward those we do not know or love, human and other.

Palmer avoids the excesses of this position by defining human-animal relationships in broader terms. She acknowledges the history of human control and exploitation in creating situations of vulnerability for which all people may have some degree of responsibility, even though we did not personally cause a particular animal's plight. Even in this two-track ethic, however, human responsibilities toward other animals depend largely on the kinds of interactions we have with those animals. Among the most complex and ubiquitous relationships are those that people have with companion animals. An examination of these connections can clarify the issues at stake in nature ethics more broadly.

ETHICS, NATURE, AND PET-KEEPING

More than half of all contemporary Americans live with companion animals, mostly dogs and cats but also reptiles, birds, and rodents. Horses, formerly kept mainly for work or entertainment, are now commonly treated as companion animals, as are some chickens, ducks, goats, and pot-bellied pigs. Pet-keeping is not confined to modern, Western, or affluent people, but is common around the world and has been for millennia. Indigenous foragers in the Amazonian rainforest, Native American hunters, and small farmers in virtually every society keep animals as pets, as do countless urban people who otherwise have very little contact with nonhuman animals.

While almost all human cultures include pets, the definition varies widely. In some places pets are routinely given names, kept inside the home, and not eaten; in other places, these do not apply to at least some animals kept as pets. Katherine Grier provides a broad definition: a pet is an animal that has been "singled out by human beings."[39] A pet is treated as an individual and has a personal relationship with people, or at least with one person. Pets may also be working animals, like hunting dogs or mouse-catching cats; their status as pets comes from the fact that their utilitarian purpose is not the only source of their value or their only relationship with people. Many contemporary animal advocates and theorists use the term "companion animal" instead of "pet," because the latter implies passivity and subordination.

Pets are often trivialized, associated with children or women, and seen as lacking in political, moral, or intellectual significance. Because of this, they receive little attention from academics, as Erica Fudge notes: "Pets are often regarded as beneath scholarly notice to the extent that the sense of the sentimental nature of human-pet relations can make scholarship that includes pets itself seem sentimental."[40] However, pet-keeping is both an important dimension of many people's emotional and social lives and the most common and often the only way that most people interact with nonhuman animals. It raises a host of ethical questions on both environmentalist and animal welfare grounds. Pet-keeping also provides a powerful lens for thinking about the moral, political, and environmental implications of human interactions with domesticated animals.

Pets in Environmental Thought

Scholarly attention to pets has grown with the expansion of animal studies, which takes a special interest in the role of animals in human societies (and less interest in wild animals or ecology). In contrast, very few environmental thinkers or advocates pay attention to companion animals. When they do, they find them almost as problematic as factory farms. Environmentalist objections to pet-keeping have both practical and moral dimensions. In practical terms, the problem is resource consumption by companion animals, especially carnivores such as dogs and cats. In light of the ecological destruction caused by the meat industry, some environmentalists argue, it is morally questionable, at best, to feed meat to companion animals.[41] This echoes the more general complaint that wealthy Westerners should not be providing food, shelter, and medical care to nonhuman animals when so many people are starving in other countries.

This argument is easy to refute. First, many poor people in both poor and wealthy countries have companion animals that they value highly. Second, neither the environmental nor the social justice critiques of pet-keeping can be taken seriously unless the critics themselves are sending substantial resources toward the relief of Third World poverty and other social and ecological ills. Third, there is no logical need to make different kinds of care mutually exclusive. We can and do care for different people, animals, and places. I do not have to choose between love for my dog, for my child, and for my local ecosystem. Compassion, as Mary Midgley points out, "does not need to be treated hydraulically . . . as a rare and irreplaceable fluid, usable only for exceptionally impressive cases. It is a habit or power of the mind, which grows and develops with use. Such powers (as is obvious in cases like intelligence) are magic fluids which increase with pouring. Effective users do not economize on them."[42] The either-or thinking that characterizes much environmental thinking, in particular, is shaped by an economistic logic, according to which resources are always limited and there must always be winners and losers. As Midgley points out, this logic does not apply in the case of values and emotions.

This question of emotional expansiveness is separate from the real limitations on resources such as time and money. We do need to choose where to direct these resources, which sometimes requires prioritizing one value over the other. These priorities may shift depending on immediacy, but such practical decisions do not reflect a lack of care or love. Perhaps in the month that I need to buy my child new school clothes I will not be able to buy a new dog bed. If I have to take my dog on an emergency trip to the vet, I may need to cancel my participation in a local ecological restoration project. These practical questions about limited resources also apply to extensions of care beyond personal relationships. Barring unlimited personal wealth and freedom, even people who care deeply about the suffering of humans, animals, and places may have to choose where to direct time and money. An environmental disaster may prompt me to direct a donation to the Sierra Club rather than Oxfam one month, or a humanitarian emergency another time may lead me to spend time at a local homeless shelter rather than the animal rescue.

Many ecocentrists blur practical decisions about limited resources with moral and emotional priorities. Questions about resource consumption are intertwined with moral and even spiritual arguments against pet-keeping.

In the view of some environmental thinkers, companion animals, no less than "livestock," are unnatural creatures, and their interactions with humans represent a distorted relationship with nature. Paul Shepard, unsurprisingly, presents this argument most assertively. He writes that companion animals are "deformed" and have lost the fundamental difference from humans that makes them real animals: "Because of the loss of otherness in the animals we keep, there is a terrible emptiness in which they mirror our lives instead of informing them."[43] Since only free-living wild animals are natural, pets twist and impoverish our understanding of animals and nature in general. Other environmentalists echo these themes. According to James Hillman, "the pet has become an anthropomorphized little animal, a little freak. It's completely in the human world. That's not longer an animal as totem or fetish or familiarus or tribe member. It's like having a eunuch, as in the middle ages." Pet-keeping is like an unconscious religious activity that mediates the "spirit world" of animals that we have repressed in modern society.[44] The cult of domesticity, implicitly female in character, is opposed to imagined pursuits of predomestic societies, especially hunting, in which men related to nature in wilder and more virile ways.

Even when they are not as extreme as Shepard and Hillman, most environmental thinkers have an essentialist and polarized understanding of domestic animals. This reflects the larger, lingering dualisms in their views of nature and culture. The laissez-faire approach to wild animals, for example, asserts that we can clearly distinguish the animals who are directly affected by human actions and to whom people therefore have certain duties from those who are not directly affected by human actions and who thus lie outside our moral universe. If people are part of nature, as most environmentalists assert, however, then such strict divisions between nature and society, or between animals and people, are untenable both intellectually and morally.

Animal Welfare Perspectives on Pet-Keeping

Animal welfare advocates both pay more attention to companion animals and have more positive views about them than environmental thinkers, as is the case for domestic animals generally. Most animal advocates do not find pet-keeping problematic in principle but rather are concerned with proper standards of care and interaction. This position is associated, in the scholarly literature, with the "animal welfare" or "humane" movement. Activists in this category fight against individual cases of abuse and against exploitative institutions and practices, such as puppy mills or dog-fighting rings. They work for legal protection for companion animals, support spaying and neutering to reduce overpopulation, and often volunteer at municipal shelters or private rescue organizations. Many live with companion animals.

While such advocates do not believe that pet-keeping is immoral in principle, they also know that calling an animal a pet does not guarantee proper treatment. Countless dogs, cats, and other domesticated animals are not treated as companions but instead are victims of cruelty and neglect. Animal shelters across the United States overflow with abandoned cats and dogs, millions of whom are euthanized every year. Activists are overwhelmed caring for cats who have been left to forage for themselves and rescuing dogs who spend their lives at the end of a chain. This is the sobering counterpoint to claims that "most cats (or dogs) live better than people," or "you wouldn't treat a dog like that." Most do not, and even if *you* would not treat them cruelly, millions do.

Many theorists elaborate a model similar to this practical position, noting that it is possible to live with companion animals in a moral way even though in actual practice many forms are abusive. Abuse is possible not just because of human ignorance or cruelty but also because of the structural conditions of domestication. "We make the animal dependent upon us for every important facet of its life, including food, exercise, mental and emotional environment, and companionship (or lack of it)," as Andrew Linzey notes.[45] In the face of the obligations arising from this dependence, even well-intentioned pet owners can fall short. Activists take practical measures to remedy these problems, including removing animals from abusive situations, rehabilitating the victims, and providing education and support to animal guardians to prevent larger problems and keep pets with their families, rather than in a shelter or on the street.

Pet-keeping underlines the larger fact that relationships between people and nonhuman animals are always fraught with power imbalances, dependence, and vulnerability. These inequities make abuse and neglect ever-present possibilities in human-animal interactions. This is true, however, of many relationships between people, particularly in situations of structural inequality, as between adults and children or between men and women. Like marginalized humans, nonhuman animals are easily trivialized or ignored by those with more power, adding to the danger that animals' interests will be subordinated to human preferences, just as children's interests are so often subordinated to adult priorities. Most people, however, do not believe parent-child relationships are inevitably defined by cruelty and exploitation, even though these possibilities may always be present.

The fact that some marriages entail domestic abuse, or that some parents neglect their children, does not lead most people to condemn the institutions of marriage or parenthood altogether. Most animal advocates for companion animals, like most advocates for women and children, believe it is possible to critique specific instances of abuse and neglect without blanket condemnations of an entire institution. This is the attitude not only of large mainstream organizations, such as the American Society for the Prevention of Cruelty to Animals (ASPCA) or the Humane Society of the United States (HSUS), but also of most grassroots groups, including those involved in controversial issues such as care for feral cats or the rehabilitation of dogs from fighting rings. Most of these activists believe that although certain practices or institutions are inherently cruel, people need not stop interacting with domestic animals. Their position parallels the view of most environmentalists, who condemn certain practices, such as strip mining or clear-cutting, but do not believe that people should end all interactions with wild nature.

Efforts to build nondestructive relationships with animals, nature, or vulnerable humans must acknowledge that power lies at the center of such asymmetrical relationships. Even real emotional connections do not erase the reality of power. "Affection mitigates domination, making it softer and more acceptable," as Yi-Fu Tuan acknowledges, "but affection itself is possible only in relationships of inequality. It is the warm and superior feeling one has toward things that one can care for and patronize. The word *care* so exudes humaneness that we tend to forget its almost inevitable tainting by patronage and condescension in our imperfect world."[46] Pet-keeping is an instance of the inevitable mixing of power and love, perhaps not qualitatively different from similarly power-laden relationships among humans.

Against Pet-Keeping

While most animal advocates accept pet-keeping in principle, a minority believes that human interactions with domestic animals are inevitably exploitative. Pet-keeping is no better than factory farming or vivisection, and perhaps even more insidious because its exploitation is masked by affection. Like certain radical environmentalists, these animal advocates believe that humans can behave morally in relation to nonhuman nature only by avoiding contact as much as possible. Opponents of pet-keeping agree with ecocentrists like Paul Shepard that domestication in itself is a harm, because of the kind of creatures and social relations that it inevitably involves. Domestication has created a category of animals that should not exist.

In this perspective, the only way to end harm to animals is to eliminate domestic animal species or at least those who cannot live freely without human care. As Gary Francione summarizes, companion animals "exist forever in a netherworld of vulnerability, dependent on us for everything and at risk of harm from an environment that they do not really understand. We have bred them to be compliant and servile, or to have characteristics that are actually harmful to them but pleasing to us. . . . Humans have no business continuing to bring these creatures into a world in which they simply do not fit."[47] This view is shared by activists such as Lee Hall and Priscilla Feral, and the activist group People for the Ethical Treatment of Animals (PETA). They assert that people should take care of existing domestic and companion animals, but the ultimate goal is to end their populations through sterilization and contraception, so that eventually the world will include only human beings and free-ranging wild animals with whom humans have few interactions.

The argument against domestication rests on a larger critique of the property status of domestic animals. All human relationships to domestic animals, in this view, are a form of slavery, despite individual acts of kindness. It is no more possible to keep pets or raise farm animals in a moral way than it is to own slaves in a moral way. Unlike human slaves, however, most pets and farm animals cannot simply be freed to live autonomous lives, both because of the ways that domestication has reduced their ability to feed and protect themselves and because of human destruction of much appropriate habitat. Thus we must care for domesticated animals the best we can while working toward a day when such animals, and thus the inherently immoral relationships we have with them, no longer exist.

While prominent thinkers like Regan and Singer do not call explicitly for an end to pet-keeping, their abolitionist stances suggest a sharp reduction in human interactions with domesticated animals. For many abolitionists, further, personal relationships with animals are irrelevant or even detrimental to arguments about animal welfare or rights. Singer explicitly rejects personal relationships with or affection for animals as a basis for ethical claims. In fact, he explains, he has never been especially interested in animals. Neither he nor his wife "had ever been inordinately fond of dogs, cats, or horses in the way that many people are. We didn't 'love' animals. We simply wanted them treated as the independent sentient beings that they are, and not as a means to human ends."[48] Singer worries that basing moral arguments on relationships will lead inevitably to arbitrary forms of discrimination. Thus it is as wrong to use rats for experiments as beagles because what is important is not human preferences but the animals' capacity to suffer.[49]

This dismissal of emotional ties reflects the dualism between the public and private spheres. This dualism associates both rational discourse and political significance with the public sphere, while considering interpersonal relationships and domestic practices morally and politically irrelevant. Care ethics challenges both this division between public and private and the view that emotion is philosophically suspect. Instead, care ethicists take affective commitments and relationships as central to moral reflection. Such commitments can also lead to political activism, as some feminist activists have argued in the case of child-rearing. From initial focus on the well-being of a single child or family, mothers extend their care to homes, neighborhoods, other children, and "the community on which growing children depend for their projects and affections," as Sara Ruddick has argued.[50] Just as mothers may generalize the "attentive love" they feel for their own children to children in general, pet lovers may generalize their affection for their own nonhuman companions.[51] Activism is demanded, in this perspective, because our loved ones require a certain kind of society in which to thrive. In addition, our love for them leads us to look differently at others, to extend sympathy, respect, and responsibility beyond our immediate circles. It is possible that "a politicized concept of love for particular animals" can be abstracted to address the well-being of other animals and perhaps also of natural places and processes.[52]

Pet-keeping points to both ethical and political possibilities lost to much environmental and even animal ethics. Pets are the only animals most people relate to on a regular basis today, in most societies around the world, and the ways we think about and treat the animals closest to us affects the ways we think about and treat other animals and even nature in general.[53] Domestic animals are part of human history and human nature. The ways and the places that we live, the shape and size of our brains, are all the results of our intricate relationships with domestic animals. We have evolved, as Mary Midgley points out, to live in mixed communities and not in species isolation. While we should not treat animals as disposable objects for our convenience, neither should we think of them as ethical problems from which we must distance ourselves. The belief that contact, and thus moral contamination, can be avoided creates a false sense of isolation, as though it were truly possible to stop interacting with the nonhuman world. We live in nature, interact with it, and consume it continually. Rather than try to hide from these relationships, the task of ethics is to sort them out, evaluate them, and develop guidelines that can help people engage in them more responsibly.

These relationships will never make sense if we do not take seriously the agency of companion animals, a factor that seems as irrelevant for many animal ethicists as it is for most environmental thinkers. If we understand animals as complex creatures with desires, intentions, and moral capacities, then we need to think not just about the parts they play in our lives but also the parts we play in theirs. Many scholars of domestication, as noted earlier, now believe that at least some species, notably dogs and cats, participated in their own process of domestication by choosing to relate to humans. For many domesticated animals, and especially companion species, relations with humans are not just necessary evils but desirable and sought-after, at least when they are not tainted by abuse and neglect. It would be arrogant to claim to know with complete accuracy what nonhuman animals want, or what it is like to be a dog or cat. However, it is equally arrogant not to acknowledge the intentions and preferences they often express.

As I write this, three of my dogs lie around the table where I work. (The fourth is on my son's bed, keeping watch out the window for passing pedestrians, bicyclists, and other threats to our home territory.) They have free run of the house but most of the time choose to be in the room where I am, and they usually follow when I shift to a different location. I also have free run of the house, including rooms with doors that can shut out dogs, but I choose proximity as well. We like to be with each other. This is why it is cruel to isolate dogs on a chain or in a pen, depriving them of companionship, no less than it is cruel to deprive bears or tigers of room to roam. Most other domesticated animals do not stay at home as dogs and cats do. Horses, cows, sheep, and goats may roam unless constrained by fences. If they have come to expect kindness, however, they usually do not shy away from people but often approach them, and many seek out interactions with people. Companion animals can take pleasure from our mutual interactions, just as we do, and like us they are curious about other species. To ignore their curiosity, their interest, and their affection is both to deny their agency and to cut ourselves off from a world beyond our own.

The perceptual world of domesticated animals is not radically different from the world of their wild relatives and ancestors. Research in ethology does not distinguish sharply between the intellectual or social complexity of wild and domesticated animals or of captive and free-roaming individuals.[54] While different species have different capacities, domestication in and of itself does not create "stupidity" or other wholesale reductions in cognitive, social, and emotional complexity. In short, domesticated animals' historical and biological ties to humans do not take away their agency or their otherness. If we are to separate ourselves from them, we must accept a radical separation between humans and nature in general, a world in which humans and nature do not interact. Such a separation reflects and reinforces the dualisms that I have critiqued throughout this book.

This dualism is not only philosophically and morally problematic but also nonsensical. Human society is a mutual creation; domestic animals are no more foreign to it than we are. Barbara King makes this point in criticizing another writer's claim that humans must teach horses to accustom themselves to "our world." The human world, as King points out, "hasn't been separate from the horse's world for many millennia; it developed in interaction with the horse's world, through the grand sweep of animal-human interactions."[55] Our world is theirs, and vice versa. We cannot return to a blank slate and re-create ourselves without them. If we cannot transform our relationships to companion animals to eliminate, or at least minimize, abuse and exploitation, then we have little hope of reducing our exploitation of nature in general.[56]

The solution to the moral dilemma of power is not to isolate ourselves but rather to use our relationships with other animals as a lens for thinking about our interactions with nonhuman nature more broadly. In this reflection, and the personal and social transformations that should follow, "the pet's status as a creature that is somewhere between the wild animal and the human" puts companion animals front and center.[57] Domestic animals occupy a middle ground between nonhuman nature and human social worlds. They are liminal, both theoretically (in terms of how philosophy conceives of them) and practically (in terms of how environmentalists and others deal with them). Animals are never just signifiers or markers, however. They are sentient, complex beings who are competent actors in their own worlds. Domesticated animals are neither fully socialized into human society nor fully wild; perhaps they are simultaneously both.

This ambivalence is one of my main themes in this book. Because of their ambiguous status, domestic animals can either hinder efforts to build a more sustainable relationship to nonhuman nature or help clear the path toward such a relationship. The various possibilities inherent in our relations with domestic animals are linked to the ambiguities of our own self-understanding. "Once an animal is domesticated and folded into a culture," as Roger Caras points out, "there is enormous ambivalence about the role that animal is supposed to play. Perhaps the reason and the universality of that reaction stems from man's ambivalence about his own nature and role."[58] When we define domestic animals as purely social artifacts, entirely separate from their wild origins, we deny our own animal natures, just as we do when we define wild animals as entirely separate from human culture.

6

The Debate Between Environmentalism and Animal Advocacy

The relationship between environmentalism and animal advocacy is usually seen, as the only book on the topic puts it, as "The Animal Rights/Environmental Ethics Debate." The title reflects two widespread assumptions. First, there are two parties involved, which can be described as "animal rights" and "environmental ethics," each with a singular perspective. Second, there is an ongoing argument between the two fields. Although the book is over fifteen years old, no subsequent volumes have appeared to update or revise the state of the debate, and the problems and positions elaborated in this volume remain central to contemporary discussions.

The book's subtitle proclaims that it reflects the "environmental" perspective. In most of its chapters, and indeed in most of the scholarly work on the subject, this perspective entails the now familiar adherence to both holism and ecocentrism. The use of the term "animal rights" presumes that moral concern for nonhuman animals is inevitably framed within a liberal individualist model. The theoretical split between holism and individualism indicates different ways of thinking not just about ethics but about nonhuman nature overall. It reflects a division that extends beyond the theoretical disagreements between environmental ethics and animal rights to encompass broader differences between environmentalism and animal advocacy. One side conceives of nature in terms of ecological systems whose good supersedes that of any one of its parts (the "environmental perspective"). The opposing side sees nature as composed of individual organisms who have interests, rights, or goods of their own (the "animal rights" perspective).

The debate between environmental ethics and animal rights rests on deeper dualisms, beginning with the split between culture and nature. This split manifests itself in the opposition between domestic and wild animals. In addition, the debate incorporates a less familiar division, between animals and nature. This duality, in turn, depends on the presumed competition between individuals and wholes, according to which individuals and collectives have completely divergent interests and one prospers only at the expense of the other. This assumption is central to Western ethical frameworks dealing with human society and has simply been extended unquestioningly to nonhuman nature. Methodological and moral individualism is so deeply ingrained in most religious and philosophical systems of thought in the West that the majority of environmental and animal ethicists take the opposition between individuals and wholes for granted, even while criticizing dualistic thinking in general.

Because ethicists on both sides of the debate frame the issue in polarized terms, they assume that there is an irreducible conflict between various types of concern for nature. One can care for wild animals and ecological wholes, or for sentient individuals, especially domesticated ones—but not for both, because the different categories reflect mutually exclusive ways of understanding and valuing nonhuman nature. Even people advocating more radical versions of Deep Ecology or animal rights have found it difficult to shed these entrenched ways of seeing nature and the interpretations of humanness that go along with them.

Challenging the "debate" model makes possible alternative ways of seeing environmental ethics, animal ethics, and the relationship between them. These alternative perspectives point to important theoretical problems, such as the question of why we value nonhuman nature at all. Some issues are practical, and play out especially in efforts to reconcile the welfare of individual creatures (wild or domestic) and the health of larger ecosystems. When we delve into these issues, we find dominant theoretical models inadequate. Dualistic theories often do not make sense in concrete situations, as, for example, when people care for both animals and nature, even though environmental philosophy tells them this is not possible. Such failures should lead to a search for better ways of understanding and acting and, perhaps most of all, of conceiving the relationship between theory and practice.

Environmental Perspectives

Environmental philosophers from a variety of perspectives, including land ethicists, Deep Ecologists, and pragmatists, all agree that nonhuman animals have value not for individual qualities such as sentience but rather on the basis of collective characteristics such as scarcity, ecological significance, or contributions to larger goods like biodiversity or land health. The general consensus among environmental thinkers is that the "rights and interests of individuals are not a helpful basis for an environmental ethic," as Bryan Norton summarizes, because the interests of individual organisms bear only a contingent relationship to the primary value of "the healthy functioning and integrity of the ecosystem."[1] In other words, what is good for individuals is not necessarily good for the whole, which is the most important criterion for most environmental ethics.

Both the superiority of ecological holism and its fundamental incompatibility with animal ethics are affirmed in the best-known essay in *The Animal Rights/Environmental Ethics Debate*, Baird Callicott's "Animal Liberation: A Triangular Affair" (1989). The "animal liberation" movement is theoretically inadequate, he argues, both because it fails to take a holistic perspective and because it does not make full use of ecological science.[2] He calls the desire of animal rights advocates to reduce suffering and save individual animals "humane moralism," which denies the reality of ecological processes. For Callicott, this moralism only appears to challenge the anthropocentrism of dominant ethical frameworks. At root, these two apparently different approaches—a humanism concerned exclusively with human well-being, the other extending moral concern to nonhuman animals—are united by their methodological individualism. What defines humane moralism is not the expansion of moral concern beyond humans but rather a focus on individual well-being which simply continues, in different guise, the ethical and philosophical humanism that has long dominated Western philosophical ethics. Humane moralism, despite its expansion of value across species lines, is not truly innovative.

A genuine transformation of ethics, for Callicott, would not just broaden existing ethical models to include animals or other individual natural entities. Rather, it would reject the epistemological and methodological principles that underlie moral individualism and replace them with an ecologically grounded holism. Callicott sees this as the genius of the land ethic, which reverses the relative weight placed on part and whole in

traditional ethics. In fact, however, holism has precedents in anthropocentric philosophical systems, including non-Western traditions such as
Buddhism and Taoism, secular ideologies such as fascism and communism,
and some Western religions, including streams in Catholicism, Islam, and
Judaism. Even within Protestant Christianity, which is generally very individualistic, the Radical Reformation offers a collectivist alternative. It is
thus incorrect to assert that contemporary environmental philosophy is
the first ethical tradition, or even the first in the West, to reject individualism for more holistic assumptions. Environmental ethics may be the first
philosophical system to base its holism on explicitly scientific grounds, but
even that is uncertain, since the mutual influencing of moral and scientific
thinking in the West can be traced back to at least Aristotle. The land
ethic's innovation should be understood not in simple terms but rather as
a complex set of interlinked qualities, such as the combination of holism
and intrinsic value, linked by the systematic use of ecological science.

Ecological science, as adopted by holists like Callicott, frames the flaw
in humane moralism as an unwillingness to accept the fact that a healthy
environment necessarily involves harm to individuals. In this view, animal
welfare advocates are unrealistic sentimentalists who cannot accept that
pain in nature is not only inevitable but often beneficial. Thus it is not
merely sentimental but in fact morally wrong to try to eradicate or reduce
the pain of individual nonhuman entities. Individual well-being plays "a
lofty but passing role in a storied natural history," as Holmes Rolston
explains. "From the perspective of individuals there is violence, struggle,
death; but from a systems perspective, there is also harmony, interdependence, and ever-continuing life."[3] Rolston makes explicit a perspective
that pervades most ecocentric ethics: the welfare of individual animals
must often be sacrificed, sometimes painfully, for the survival of the community which alone holds intrinsic value. Individual well-being is morally relevant only when the animals involved are central to "communal
health and stability." Otherwise, animal welfare and environmentalism
are incompatible.[4]

Animal ethicists' failure to prioritize holistic goods is tied, in the eyes
of some critics, to an even more problematic refusal to accept the truths
of evolutionary science. Lisa Sideris attacks the inconsistencies of environmental ethicists and theologians who assert allegiance to evolutionary theory while denying or glossing over the suffering, competition,
and conflict that are necessary elements of evolution by natural selection. Too often, as she puts it, "interdependence" is "used interchange-
ably with such terms as *community*, *mutuality*, and even *harmony*." From a

Darwinian perspective, however, "interdependence in nature is itself the source of much conflict and struggle."[5] The key to natural selection, Sideris writes, is attrition. Evolution works because individuals who are not well-adapted to a particular environment fail to survive and reproduce and thus do not pass on traits to future generations of their species. Without the premature death of many individuals, both overpopulation and the spread of less adaptive traits would weaken the entire species' chances for success.

Like many ecocentrists, Sideris believes that nature is indeed red in tooth and claw. Nature's cruelties can be seen in predation, disease, and parasitism, all of which are essential to maintaining the health of ecosystems, species, and populations. These cruelties are difficult if not impossible to reconcile with concern for individual suffering. Such concern, at least in regard to nonhuman animals, is misplaced: "An environmental ethic should attach value to the processes of evolution, not merely their products."[6] Sideris believes that many prominent environmental ethicists and ecotheologians, as well as animal ethicists, falsely imagine "that nature functions in a way that permits the flourishing of every individual creature at once."[7] This naive optimism misreads the process of evolution by natural selection and, more generally, glosses over the need for hard choices that any ethic, and perhaps especially an environmental one, must face. Indeed, an ethic that pretends we will never have to make hard choices and thus gives us no guidelines for making them is of little use. Too often, environmental theories that claim grounding in ecological and biological realities actually seek to remake nature in the shape of cultural ideals, such as the biblical "peaceable kingdom." Such attempts, Sideris argues, are neither scientifically defensible nor practically workable.

While important, Sideris's criticism suffers from several weaknesses. First, she overstates the extent of sentimentalism among environmental philosophers, most of whom advocate an ecocentric holism that subordinates individual welfare to the greater ecological good. This approach is reflected in the positions of most environmental organizations, which consistently support the removal of nonnative species, "culling" of native animals whose numbers exceed ecological carrying capacity, sport hunting (as long as the prey animals are not endangered), and "sustainable" forms of animal agriculture. They oppose the end or limitation of any of these programs based on concern for the interests of individual animals, wild or domestic, native or exotic. Sideris's sentimental environmentalist is yet another straw man, constructed or at least exaggerated in order to bolster a provocative argument.

Equally imaginary is the agreement between animal and environmental ethicists that lies at the heart of her criticism. This conflation of two different fields reflects and reinforces an inaccurate understanding of both. Had Sideris clarified the fundamental differences between environmental and animal ethicists, she could have constructed a more precise, accurate, and persuasive critique of the subset of thinkers in either group who do misread evolutionary science in the way she describes. As it stands, she suggests an agreement about the value of individuals in contrast to wholes that does not characterize the relationship between the two fields.

Perhaps Sideris's most significant error is her failure to define humans as integral, dependent parts of larger ecological wholes and evolutionary narrative. If humans are products of natural selection, then we should be subject to the same cruelties that affect other living entities. Like most ecocentrists, Sideris brings her hard-headed commitment to evolution by natural selection to a screeching halt at the species line. Never is the pain of individual humans called valuable in ecological terms or unavoidable in light of evolution. Like other environmental thinkers, Sideris may fear both old accusations of social Darwinism and newer accusations of environmental fascism. The failure to question human exceptionalism, however, undermines claims that evolution and ecology are hard truths that lie at the heart of all serious thinking about nature.

Animal Ethics Perspectives

Most animal ethicists agree with environmental thinkers that their two fields are fundamentally incompatible and that this incompatibility rests on the opposition between individual and holistic philosophical frameworks. Animal advocates disagree, among themselves, about which kinds of animals have value, and on what basis. Most believe, however, that value lies in individuals rather than in larger wholes such as populations, species, or ecosystems.

Among various approaches to animal ethics, rights-based theories have the strongest commitment to methodological and moral individualism and the clearest rejection of holism. Tom Regan, for example, locates the difficulty of developing a rights-based environmental ethic in the problem of reconciling "the *individualistic* nature of moral rights with the more *holistic* view of nature emphasized by many of the leading environmental thinkers."[8] Paradigmatic rights holders are individuals, who are of minor importance in most environmental philosophies. For Utilitarian animal advocates, the key is not the inviolability of individual rights holders but rather the moral urgency of minimizing suffering among sentient individuals. Despite these philosophical disagreements, Utilitarian animal advocates reject ecological holism as thoroughly as do rights theorists. Peter Singer, for example, agrees with Regan that it is wrong to harm an individual animal for the health of a larger ecosystem, in explicit opposition to ecological holism. Even the leading alternative theories in animal ethics, including care ethics, accept the priority of individual suffering. Like ecofeminists, care ethicists emphasize relationships and criticize individualism. However, most feminists stop short of a thoroughgoing holism, in part because they have good reason to mistrust a position that accepts individual suffering for the good of the whole.

CONCERNS AND CRITIQUES

Ecofascism and Human Exceptionalism

The fact that environmental holism explicitly subordinates the interests of individual animals to greater ecological goods leads Tom Regan to reflect that, "It is difficult to see how the notion of the rights of the individual could find a home within a view that, emotive connotations to one side, might be fairly dubbed 'environmental fascism.'"[9] Regan's worries are echoed in an article by Michael Zimmerman entitled "Ecofascism: An Enduring Temptation," which addresses the charge of fascism made by some anti-environmentalists who oppose land-use regulations in the American West. While most environmentalists view this characterization as "the ludicrous creation of anti-environmental corporations and extractive industries," Zimmerman believes that "the threat of ecofascism cannot be dismissed out of hand."[10] He points to the fact that far-right groups in Europe and the United States have begun to incorporate environmental concerns, especially about population growth, into their political platforms. This association does not prove a philosophical link between environmentalism and fascism, and Zimmerman acknowledges that even radical environmentalists almost never advocate fascism. However, he believes that some stray dangerously near the line, including not only rightist thinkers like the German ecological advocate Walter Schoenichen but also some prominent American environmentalists, including Garrett Hardin. Zimmerman also targets Baird Callicott's early view of ecosystems as "superorganisms," which led him to argue that just as parts of a body may have to be sacrificed for the good of the whole person, so individual entities can be sacrificed for ecosystemic well-being. Zimmerman finds this model necessarily misanthropic because it treats humans instrumentally, as resources for the greater good of the ecological whole. Callicott has since rejected the superorganism model but still affirms the holism of the land ethic and a subsequent de-emphasis on individual well-being.

Zimmerman absolves Callicott's current work from ecofascism but sees a continuing risk in the fact that "dark green ideology is tempting even to highly intelligent people."[11] He cites the anti-immigration positions of some contemporary environmentalists as an example of a dangerous willingness to sacrifice human interests for environmental goods, which can ultimately lead to claims that "human freedom must be abolished to save the human species."[12] Zimmerman's fear is not that holism devalues individual nonhuman animals but that humans might be included as "plain members and citizens" of a larger ecological community that has ultimate value. He sees no circumstances in which any interest of humans should be subordinated to any nonhuman entities—individuals or wholes. He objects primarily to nonanthropocentrism, in other words, rather than to holism in general. Zimmerman's approach to environmental value rests on the same foundation as the work of most of the holists whom he criticizes—a qualitative divide between humans and other animals. As unsatisfactory as this separation is from evolutionary and ecological perspectives, it protects environmental advocates both from name-calling and from the deep philosophical, moral, and political challenges entailed in really conceiving of humans as part of nature.

The fear that environmentalists will subordinate human interests to the greater ecological good has little basis in theory or practice. While ecological holists advocate the sacrifice of individual nonhumans for larger environmental goods, they almost never apply this holistic vision to *Homo sapiens*. In theory, they ought to, since almost all environmentalists insist that people are "part of nature" and have evolved to live interdependently with other animals and plants. However, almost to a man (and occasional woman), they shy away from the ecological need to compromise the interests of individual humans, along with those of individual animals, for the greater good. Most environmental thinkers and activists criticize consumerism and call for people to tread "lightly" on the earth, but very few advocate the hard sacrifices—of well-being or even life—on which they insist for other species. The few environmentalists who even hint at such sacrifices are roundly condemned, as evidenced in Zimmerman's harsh criticism of Callicott's fairly tentative suggestions about how holism might apply beyond wild ecosystems. Ecocentrists, no less than anthropocentrists, have a strong interest in maintaining the security of the human-nonhuman border.

Many environmental thinkers leave their human exceptionalism implicit, but a few bring it into the open. Holmes Rolston is particularly unapologetic about the special status accorded to human beings in his otherwise holistic environmental philosophy. In nature, only collective goods matter. Individual suffering and individual happiness are largely irrelevant, even though healthy ecosystems are likely to provide well-adapted individuals with a generally satisfactory life.[13] In nature, the only moral significance of nonhuman suffering is the extent to which animals' lives and deaths contribute to larger ecological health. In culture, however, this holistic vision does not apply. As Rolston explains, "the fawn lives only in an ecosystem, in nature; the child lives also in culture. Environmental ethics is not social ethics, nor does it give us any duty to revise nature."[14] Rolston draws ethical conclusions from the "is" of nature but realizes that this is problematic for culture, so he draws a hard line between the two, and also between humans and animals, domestic and wild. These dualisms enable Rolston to avoid the dilemmas faced by Callicott, who asks about the possibility of extending ecological holism into human life as well. Callicott's position is politically controversial but also more intellectually consistent and morally braver.

Ecological evolutionary processes sometimes require that individuals be sacrificed for the good of the whole. Pain and suffering are necessary parts of a healthy biotic community. Few infants will survive to adulthood, few adults will live to old age, and few aging individuals can be supported by their communities past their productive lives. These claims, which ecocentrists make so assuredly for nonhuman nature, are politically and morally unpalatable when extended to humans. The only way to avoid these problems is to divide humans radically from nature and declare that ecological and evolutionary principles have no significance for humans or that their significance extends only to vague calls to "live within limits" and "respect nature." The limits within which we live do not have anything to do with the constraints on other species, however. Nor do they have much to do with the planet's actual carrying capacity.

It is not hard to see how Rolston gets himself into this Cartesian bind. No one wants to reject the use of "heroic measures" to save premature infants, for example, even though it is not hard to see the ecological trouble that would arise if we tried to save every sickly fawn. However, ultimately Rolston's position, which is shared by most ecocentric thinkers, albeit not always expressed so explicitly, lacks intellectual, political, and moral consistency. "Each is for itself, but none is by itself," he writes.[15] This powerful statement of ecological interdependence is fatally undercut by his insistence that humans are indeed by themselves as soon as the going gets tough. This inconsistency remains implicit in most environmental thought; the most common way to deal with the conflict between ecological holism and individual human interests is to ignore it. Rolston deserves credit for addressing this problem directly and gratitude for making obvious the sharp dualism between nature and culture that underlies the debate between ecological holism and animal welfare. Callicott, similarly, deserves credit for admitting that the land ethic would impose "limitations on human freedom of action."[16] The limitations placed on human action are minimal, however, and never approach the limitations that ecological holists accept for nonhuman animals.

The inconsistency of ecocentric thought raises practical and theoretical problems with no easy solutions. The first step toward an answer is simply to ask the questions and admit the inability of current approaches even to begin framing adequate answers. As a next step, both environmental and animal ethicists should explore alternative perspectives and frameworks that might challenge the polarized and stunted understandings of nature, people, and animals that underlie their views of the debate. The possibilities and limitations of such alternatives can become clearer in the context of concrete experiences in which different values and perspectives are at play.

The Conflict in Practice: Hunting

In many cases, the same policy or project supports the well-being of both individual animals and the good of larger wholes such as populations, species, or ecosystems. On concrete problems (such as climate change, animal agriculture, or endangered species habitat), animal and environmental advocates often agree and sometimes join forces. Many animal activists also support other efforts to preserve or restore ecosystemic health that do not override the rights or welfare of individual animals. Similarly, many environmentalists do not oppose protection or assistance to individual animals which does not threaten overall ecological well-being.

In some situations, however, individual and collective goods seem to be opposed or mutually exclusive. In such cases, the differing assumptions about intrinsic value and moral hierarchies lead to disagreements between animal and environmental agendas. Environmental holism suggests that individual animals, no less than individual trees, rocks, or bulldozers, should be sacrificed for larger ecological interests, while animal ethics asserts that the value of even one individual can trump the greater good. This conflict is especially clear in the case of hunting, a helpful lens for exploring the practical implications of the theoretical disagreements between environmental and animal advocates. Hunting makes it clear that the debate between animal welfare and environmentalism is not the invention of philosophers but in fact plays out in a variety of real-life situations.

Environmental Perspectives on Hunting

Hunting has long been an important theme in environmental studies and environmental philosophy. Environmental ethicists often point out that Aldo Leopold himself was a hunter, as were many other pioneering conservationists. Many hunters and anglers relate the practice directly to their interest in and love for nonhuman nature, especially wild ecosystems. Hunting and fishing both require the preservation of wild habitats and have long been connected to preservation and restoration efforts.[17] Several major environmental advocacy groups have been formed by hunters and fishers, notably Ducks Unlimited and Trout Unlimited. Despite the widespread acceptance of some forms of hunting, however, most conservationists do not consider all kinds of hunting morally or ecologically equal. They distinguish among various types of hunting and accept some while condemning others. This attitude is largely a theoretical one, since relatively few environmentalists are hunters, part of a larger recent decline in hunting generally in the United States.

The types of hunting are distinguished by the motivations and goals of the hunters as much as by the method used or the kind of animal pursued. Mere observation, without access to the intentions of the parties, cannot distinguish among these forms. In this, hunting is like animal play, and indeed many forms of nonhuman play mimic predatory behaviors. Animals at play stalk, bite, and chase, and only their intentions distinguish these from the same physical behaviors that are involved in serious fighting or hunting. Only inner subjective states, similarly, determine whether a human is hunting for "serious" reasons, such as a need for food or self-defense, or for trivial aims such as entertainment or a trophy.

The distinction between pleasure and need divides different kinds of hunting. The main types of hunting are subsistence, sport, and therapeutic, differentiated according to the motivation of the hunter rather than factors such as the weapons used, types of prey, or location. The goal of subsistence hunting is to provide food for people. Sport hunting is "aimed at maintaining religious or cultural traditions, at reenacting national or evolutionary history, at practicing certain skills, or just at securing a trophy." Within this category, as philosopher Gary Varner notes, some hunters distinguish between hunting as recreational sport and hunting as ritual. For Varner the two are fundamentally similar because both serve not ecological interests but rather fulfill less fundamental human goals. Varner's third category, therapeutic hunting, is "motivated by and designed to secure the aggregate welfare of the target species, the integrity of its ecosystem, or both."[18]

Like most complex activities, hunting often involves more than one motivation at the same time. For example, a wildlife manager involved in therapeutic hunting for ecological purposes may also enjoy it. The same is true for nonhuman predators, who can find the chase and kill pleasurable as well as useful. The lines are often fine, further, between primary and secondary motivations, which complicates the problem of moral evaluation. If hunting is acceptable for sustenance but not purely for enjoyment, then it is not clear how we should judge the practices of the many hunters who gain both pleasure and food from the practice. This issue is most relevant to environmentalists who accept some but not all sorts of hunting. Most animal advocates condemn hunting in all but a few exceptional cases and thus do not need to distinguish between primary and secondary motivations.

Aldo Leopold offers a good starting point for thinking about hunting's varied moral status in environmental philosophy. Leopold accepted "therapeutic" hunting as a necessary element of ecosystem management. He also engaged in sport hunting himself and considered it a valuable way to strengthen human connections to nature.[19] However, Leopold did not find all kinds of hunting acceptable, and in particular he deeply regretted his own participation in hunting to control predators. In the essay "Thinking Like a Mountain," Leopold describes watching a wolf die. "I thought that because fewer wolves meant more deer, that no wolves would mean hunters' paradise. But after seeing the green fire die, I sensed that neither the wolf nor the mountain agreed with such a view."[20] After this transformative experience, Leopold found hunting acceptable only when it was based on concern for the integrity and health of the ecosystem as a whole. Most environmentalists agree with Leopold that hunting is acceptable under certain conditions, but not in all cases. For example, it may generally be acceptable and even necessary to kill elk or deer but usually not to hunt predators.

Humans first hunted for food. For early hominids, trying to kill other animals was dangerous and uncertain. The domestication of *Canis lupus* was a crucial turning point, making subsistence hunting both more efficient and less risky. The assistance of dogs in finding, tracking, holding, killing, and retrieving prey may well have made possible the luxury of hunting for pleasure, and dogs remain crucial to many kinds of sport hunting today. Early humans were omnivores, able to survive without animal products, but meat provided a valuable source of protein and other nutrients. Once humans migrated to the far northern parts of the Americas and Europe, with very short growing seasons, land and sea animals provided almost all food, at least until the arrival of modern transportation and storage methods.

Today very little hunting can be called "subsistence," if that term indicates an activity necessary to a person's livelihood and basic food supply. Still, many people, including many environmentalists, accept hunting for food much more readily than purely for pleasure. As long as the prey species is not rare or endangered, hunting for food is no more (and often less) problematic, from an ecological perspective, than buying meat in a store or restaurant. Further, some environmentalists point out that hunting can be more humane than animal agriculture. Free-ranging wild animals who are killed by hunters often have better quality lives and quicker, less agonizing deaths than the domestic animals who live on factory farms. From this perspective, if one is to eat meat, hunting one's own is preferable to eating conventionally farmed domestic animals.

Most environmentalists also approve of hunting in pursuit of ecological goals. The usual goal of such killing is to reduce the numbers of an overabundant prey species, such as deer, or to eliminate invasive nonnative animals, such as feral goats or hogs. From a holistic environmentalist perspective, culling excess individuals is necessary to preserve fragile ecosystems and often to protect other, less prolific animal species. This is a way to restore a natural "balance" that humans disturbed, usually by reducing habitat or by killing predators. Because such killing is understood as necessary for the health of the larger ecological system, Varner calls it "therapeutic." Most environmentalists find both moral and scientific justification for killing a few individual animals in order to protect habitat and food for many more. Assuming the common sense of this claim, Andrew Light points to ecologically motivated hunting as a point on which animal advocates and environmentalists usually agree.[21] In making this assertion, however, Light reveals his lack of familiarity with the animal ethics literature, which in fact condemns most hunting, even in "environmentally therapeutic" form. He takes for granted an ecological holist perspective that is neither as self-evident nor as widespread as he assumes. Because animal ethics generally opposes any direct killing or harming of animals, there is a presumption against hunting except when it is necessary to prevent much greater harm.

While therapeutic hunting is controversial, the most heated and revealing discussions concern sport hunting. Environmentalists hold a wide range of opinions about hunting for pleasure alone. Some find sport hunting acceptable if the hunters follow basic ecological constraints such as not targeting rare or endangered species and obeying all relevant laws regarding the size, age, and sex of the animals hunted. As long as no larger environmental harm is done, in this perspective, causing pain or death to individual creatures is not a problem. It is probably preferable also to eat or otherwise use the animal killed, but many environmentalists do not find hunting for pleasure wrong in itself. Hunting wild animals is part of human evolutionary and cultural history, many assert, and can even be seen as a positive environmental practice, insofar as it encourages people to spend time in nature, to learn about wild animals and habitats, and to work for the preservation of these habitats.

Another type of hunting for nonbasic needs is justified on spiritual grounds. The founding text for this approach is José Ortega y Gasset's *Meditations on Hunting*, written in 1942, which describes hunting as a romantic union of predator and prey. A number of more recent environmental writers describe hunting, similarly, as a way for humans to participate in ecological processes, much as nonhuman predators do, and achieve unity with the rest of nature.[22] Hunting is one of the few ways that contemporary people experience themselves as part of natural cycles, realizing their dependence upon the bodies of other animals and upon nonhuman nature more generally. Since pain exists in nature and is sometimes beneficial, the suffering caused by human hunting is no less justified than that which results when wild animals kill to eat.

Because it accepts the reality of death in nature, hunting for some environmental thinkers indicates both scientific wisdom and ecological maturity. As Holmes Rolston puts it, "sometimes those who object to any killing in nature and in human encounters with nature have not grown up either biologically or morally." (Rolston also believes that people who kill just "for fun" have not grown up morally.)[23] Hunting may also provide a visceral knowledge that distinguishes hunters if, as Stephen Budiansky believes, "the hunter really *does* understand something that the average apartment dweller does not."[24] The notion that killing nonhuman animals is a way to care for and identify with nature represents a logical extension of the ecocentric consensus. Individual animals will suffer and die in any natural system, and in fact the system's health requires the premature deaths of many individuals. Particularly in unbalanced ecosystems, deprived of healthy populations of nonhuman predators, humans not only may but should kill prey species. This enables some ecocentrists to see hunting not as a necessary evil but as a moral high ground separating real environmentalists from deluded sentimentalists who are alienated from nature.[25]

A number of environmental thinkers expand the idea that hunting provides superior knowledge into a view of hunting as a way to experience a mystical union with nature, as Ortega y Gasset suggested. The hunter feels "perfect identification" with the "tragic drama" of creation, the "blood sacrifice" on which all of life is founded.[26] Killing animals enables humans to participate in the contradictory, painful, yet beautiful unfolding of evolutionary and ecological processes. In this view, moralists who condemn hunting do not understand nature as it really is. They fail to appreciate the aesthetic and moral value not just of wildness but of the pain and death that it necessarily includes. Rolston quotes and rejects Jeremy Bentham's assertion that the key question about animals is "Can they suffer?" For Rolston, individual suffering is beside the point. Instead, he asks, "Is nature at the level of sentient life a passion play? Ought humans to transform this nature into something else? Or refuse to join in, having learned something better? One answer is that hunting, a seeming sport, has sacramental value because it unfolds the contradictions of the universe."[27] A sacrament is, in the traditional Roman Catholic definition, an "outward and visible sign of an inward and invisible grace." Presumably hunting is the visible expression of the grace—a divine gift—inherent in evolutionary processes such as predation. We need not simply accept the painful reality of predation, in this view, but can contribute to it and celebrate it.

Advocates of hunting as a spiritual exercise often point to Native American practices as a model of ecologically and morally sound interactions with nature. In such cultures, hunting is part of a mutually respectful relationship between humans and wild animals, including ritual requests for permission before the hunt and expressions of gratitude after the kill.[28] Some writers cite animal behaviors, such as the fact that many large herbivores pause to look back at hunters before running, as evidence that animals "offer" themselves to hunters. This suggests, in ritualistic interpretations of hunting, that animals are willing participants in their own deaths because they want to contribute to larger ecological (and spiritual) processes. This reading receives particularly strong criticism from animal ethicists, who object to efforts not only to accept hunting but to present it as evidence of moral and spiritual superiority.

Animal Ethics Perspectives on Hunting

In contrast to the environmentalist tendency to make ethical distinctions among different kinds of hunting, almost all animal ethicists find hunting both unacceptable and unnecessary in most contemporary settings. The work of Tom Regan reflects the usual animal rights position on hunting. Regan condemns all kinds of hunting, except for necessary self-defense from dangerous animals, such as a rabid fox who attacks children. Apart from such rare cases, he sees hunting as an unjustified violation of an animal's basic rights to life and freedom from unnecessary suffering. Even if sport hunting provides "communion with nature," such communion can also be found in ways that do not lead to the deaths of animals. Subsistence hunting is unnecessary because humans can and should be vegetarians. Regan also rejects claims that death by hunting or trapping involves less suffering than the death these animals would endure otherwise. He notes that many hunters only wound, leaving the animals to die long and painful deaths, and trapping is always painful. Thus "the defense of hunting and trapping on the grounds that they kill 'more humanely' is specious."[29]

Some animal ethicists might expand the category of necessary killing a little further than Regan, but most condemn hunting for anything other than urgent needs, such as protection or food. Hunting for sport is dismissed easily; most animal advocates believe that taking pleasure in the fear, pain, and death of another sentient being indicates serious ethical and perhaps psychological problems. This is true whether the hunted animal is a member of an abundant species or a rare one. The key moral question is not about the larger population, species, or ecosystem but about the capacities and experiences of the individual animal. A nonhuman animal who is one of many suffers no less than one who is the last of her kind, and in fact some animal ethicists prefer the death of a rare but cognitively simple invertebrate to that of a common but complex bird or mammal. Most sport hunters pursue "higher" animals, whose very intelligence and adaptability is what makes the hunt pleasurable. Pursuing an oyster provides no sport in comparison to the challenges of tracking down a deer, bear, or caribou.

Many animal ethicists reserve special scorn for those who claim to hunt for spiritual or ritual reasons. Feminist thinkers, in particular, dismiss assertions that hunting demonstrates love for animals or facilitates spiritual union with them. Marti Kheel offers a systematic critique of the contradiction between hunters' expressions of love for nature and their willingness to kill animals. She sees assertions of nature's intrinsic value and professions of ecological concern as whitewashing or perhaps, to use Callicott's phrase, sugarcoating. Expressions of care ring hollow in the face of lethal practices. As Kheel puts it, "Caring for other living beings cannot be conducted in the privacy of one's interior psychic state. It must take into account a genuine recognition of the response of the one we are caring for. . . . It is our actions, more than our state of mind, that are crucial in the realm of ethical conduct."[30] A feeling of union with nature, in other words, does not make it acceptable to destroy natural entities. As Kheel puts it, saying a prayer before killing an animal is no more acceptable than saying a prayer before raping a woman. This provides a counterpoint to Rolston's notion that hunting "has sacramental value because it unfolds the contradictions of the universe."[31] (So does death in childbirth, one is tempted to add, but that does not make it holy.)

In addition to feelings of mystical unity with nature, some environmental supporters of hunting repeat the common Native American belief that prey animals "offer" themselves willingly by stopping to gaze at human hunters. The scientific explanation for such actions is that the hunted animal is evaluating the number, location, and probable speed of potential pursuers. Turning to look makes good sense since there is no point in wasting energy and risking injury by running if a predator is too far away to pose a serious threat. Prey animals use many other practices to examine predators. Some antelopes, for example, jump straight up in the air—called "stotting"—probably both to get a better look at the predator and to demonstrate their own speed and agility, thus perhaps deterring the hunter. For similar reasons, prey animals sometimes approach predators and even engage them in fights (which they often win). Such behaviors are frequently very effective with nonhuman predators, and it makes good sense to apply them to human hunters as well. If we do not believe that antelopes offer themselves to lions, or caribou to wolves, it seems self-serving to assert that they do offer themselves to humans.

A successful hunt ends with the death of the prey animal. This makes the claim that hunting is an example of mutual respect, interaction, and animal agency problematic. We do not call interactions that are supposed to lead to the death of a human participant mutually respectful. It is illuminating, in this regard, to note the subgenre of horror films and stories in which humans are hunted by other humans. A classic example is Richard Connell's 1924 story (made into a film in 1932), "The Most Dangerous Game," in which a "big game" hunter is stalked on an isolated island by a human adversary. This theme has made its way into a wide range of media, including classic dystopian novels like *The Lord of the Flies* and films such as *Platoon* (1986), as well as many television shows, comic books, and video games.[32] Fictional narratives in which humans are prey underline the particularly nightmarish quality of being tracked and hunted. The experience cannot be less terrifying for nonhuman creatures, especially cognitively complex mammals.

Abolitionists also criticize efforts to justify hunting on the grounds of "tradition." Regan insists that even the practices of indigenous communities with long histories of relying on hunting today have no more justification than do other forms of exploitation. The claim that all animals who are subjects-of-a-life should not be deliberately harmed trumps all arguments in favor of any kind of deliberate, unnecessary suffering. Appeals to tradition as a justification in and of itself "are themselves symptomatic of an impoverished view of the value animals have in their own right and thus can play no legitimate role in defending a practice that harms them."[33] People have often defended the exploitation or harming of some groups of people on similar grounds, Regan points out, but most people today recognize that "tradition" cannot justify practices such as slavery, rape, or child labor. He finds animal exploitation no different.

Many animal advocates agree with defenders of subsistence hunting on the evils of industrial farming and the superiority of life in the wild to life in a feedlot. They also acknowledge the contradiction, and perhaps even hypocrisy, of opposing hunting while eating the flesh of farmed animals. Vegetarian and vegan animal advocates point out that since it is not necessary for humans to eat meat at all, we need not debate the moral status of different types of meat. Although human beings evolved as omnivores, they argue, we can live just as well without meat, and probably better, given the well-documented negative consequences of consuming many animal products. Even some animal advocates who do eat meat find hunting distasteful because of the association of killing with pleasure or sport. Central to these discussions are the distinctions between different categories of domesticated animals and their advocates. Many companion animal activists are not vegetarian or vegan, while some farm animal advocates reject pet-keeping.

Since humans evolved as omnivorous predators, it is in one sense natural for us to hunt. However, this does not make hunting either biologically necessary or morally right. Environmental philosopher Gary Varner points out that contemporary humans have ceased doing many things that are "natural" in the sense that they were common and often necessary during earlier evolutionary periods. For example, he notes, most people no longer routinely defecate in the woods. "Acknowledging that hunting is in one sense natural for humans," he concludes, "implies nothing compelling about the morality of hunting."[34] Many animal ethicists share his skepticism about moving from "our ancestors did this" to "therefore we are justified in doing this." This contrasts with the position of many ecocentric thinkers, who draw explicitly moral conclusions from descriptions of natural processes.

Many environmentalists and some animal advocates accept therapeutic or ecological hunting as an unfortunate necessity. However, a number of animal activists criticize the instrumental view of animals underlying ecological arguments for culling certain individuals or populations. In response to the claim that the killing of some animals may be necessary for the good of the larger population or habitat, Peter Singer charges that such arguments rarely include genuine concern for the interests of individual animals. "The use of the term 'harvest'—often found in the publications of the hunters' organizations—gives the lie to the claim that this slaughter is motivated by concern for the animals," according to Singer. "The term indicates that the hunter thinks of deer or seals as if they were corn or coal, objects of value only in so far as they serve human interests." This attitude overlooks the fact that "deer and other hunted animals are capable of feeling pleasure and pain. They are therefore not means to our ends, but beings with interests of their own."[35] According to Singer and many other animal advocates, the only morally acceptable way to control wild animal populations is through nonlethal methods such as contraception, which many wildlife managers reject because they do not consider the suffering and death of nonhuman animals significant enough to justify more difficult or costly methods.

ANIMALS OUT OF PLACE

A special case of ecological hunting occurs when officials in charge of parks or other natural areas determine that a certain kind of animal is threatening native habitats and must be reduced, removed, or eliminated. Such threats frequently result from human actions. For example, the killing of natural predators can lead to "excess" populations of other species, most notably in the case of white-tailed deer, who face few or no predators in many parts of the United States due to the extirpation of large carnivores such as wolves and cougars. Another source of apparent overpopulation is reduction of habitat, often through urban sprawl and agricultural activities, which causes wild animals to range into areas where they threaten other native animals and plants or human settlements. This has occurred, for example, with coyotes and bears in many parts of the United States, and with elephants in some parts of Africa.

In addition to native wild animals who exceed the carrying capacity of a particular habitat, domestic animals frequently damage native species and ecosystems. Environmental advocates point to the erosion and habitat damage caused by cattle allowed to graze in wilderness areas in the West. Even more destructive, in the eyes of many environmentalists, are feral animals—members of domesticated species who are not "owned" by humans and live without direct human assistance. The conflicts between feral animals and native species are among the most frequently cited case studies in environmental ethics courses and texts.[36] The most common example of this in the United States occurs when feral cats kill large numbers of songbirds and rodents, often including endangered species. In other cases, introduced or escaped domestic herbivores, such as pigs and goats in Hawaii and rabbits in Australia, encroach on native plants. Mustangs, the feral descendants of domesticated horses, are for many a symbol of the American West, but they compete with ranched cattle for fragile grazing land and thus have been targeted for removal and other population-control plans.

Other problems emerge when nonnative wild animals inhabit a new place. Introductions of wild animals to novel habitats are usually the result of human actions. Many hitch rides on planes, trucks, or ships carrying produce or other products across state or national borders. A number of destructive species have entered the United States in this way, including fire ants in the Southeast and Zebra mussels in the Great Lakes.[37] Sometimes people release exotic animals deliberately, often because they no longer want to care for an unusual pet. The growing population of Burmese pythons in south Florida is a result of this practice. A number of nonnative species have been deliberately released, often to provide fishing or hunting opportunities. Introduced nonnative fish species, including carp and some types of trout, have become serious threats to wild native populations in rivers and lakes around the United States. Island ecosystems such as Australia, New Zealand, and Hawaii are especially vulnerable to the threats posed by exotic species because there are often no native predators or diseases to limit the newcomers' population growth. Free from indigenous threats, these nonnative species not only speed the extinction of numerous plant species but also contribute to erosion and other ecological problems. They often cause much greater damage than native species and can be more difficult to control. Many exotic plants, introduced both deliberately and accidentally, also threaten native species. Lethal removal of these invaders is not usually controversial, however.

Some wild animals establish populations outside their original ranges by migration. Armadillos, for example, are now common in the southeastern United States, far from their original homes in the Southwest. Another well-known migrant is the Virginia opossum, which is native to the Atlantic seaboard but has spread throughout North America. Some animals migrate or expand their ranges because humans have killed or greatly reduced the numbers of competing species. Thus coyotes now live throughout the southeastern United States in areas originally occupied by red wolves.

Regardless of place of origin or the method of introduction, out-of-place animals can cause stress and sometimes permanent damage to the physical landscape and native plant and animal species. They can create problems for human communities as well, usually involving the destruction of plants in home gardens or on farms or the killing of farm and companion animals. (Coyotes are a nuisance for watermelon farmers in Florida; the omnivorous canids apparently enjoy watermelon so much that they can devastate entire fields of them.) Much more rarely, wild animals pose physical threats to human safety, as has been the case with mountain lions in some suburbs in southern California. In all these cases, conflicts emerge between the interests of individual animals, on the one hand, and larger social or ecological goods, on the other.

The varied responses of environmental and animal advocates to these conflicts underline the diverse issues and perspective at stake. Holistic environmentalists usually advocate killing some or all of the excess or misplaced animals. Because the pain or death of individual creatures is not morally significant, in their view, it is right to eliminate problem animals in order to preserve the stability and health of larger natural and social communities. Lethal control should be done as efficiently and humanely as possible, without excessive suffering, but there is little question that it should be lethal. Many environmentalists acknowledge that human actions such as destruction of habitat and elimination of predators have caused current imbalances. While condemning such practices, they contend that in the face of existing problems, humans must strive to restore ecological balance to the extent possible, even if that requires killing particular animals. Environmentalists occasionally support nonlethal solutions. Most notably, wildlife managers have provided deer with contraceptives, laced in food or shot in darts, especially in the northeastern United States. This method has worked fairly well where there is greater opposition to hunting or where hunting is prohibited or considered too dangerous.[38] It is not practical, however, in many situations, due to the high cost and the difficulty of treating large numbers of animals.

Many animal advocates reject all lethal methods of control. While acknowledging the ecological threats posed by animals who are out of place, they point out that the animals themselves are hardly villains. They are simply trying to survive in circumstances not of their own choosing. In most cases, they are in these problematic situations because of human actions. This is especially obvious for domestic or nonnative animals who have been left to live on their own, but even the overpopulation of native species such as deer or coyotes usually has anthropogenic causes such as urban sprawl or the elimination of predators. Animal ethicists argue that individual animals are blameless and should not be killed simply for living in fragile ecosystems that humans have disturbed or for trying to cope in the face of relentless human demands for space and resources.

The conflict between animal and environmental advocates is especially clear-cut in the case of feral animals. Members of domestic species who range freely in the wild are especially problematic for ecological holists, who usually consider domesticated animals both inferior to wild ones and implicated in the larger human assault on wilderness. Even environmentalists who might hesitate to advocate lethal control of native species such as deer usually support the killing of destructive feral species. Animal advocates, on the other hand, find special appeal in precisely the feature that puts off many environmentalists—the connection of feral animals to domesticated farm and companion animals. They acknowledge, at the same time, that feral animals can pose serious threats not just to non-sentient parts of nature but also to other animals and should not simply be allowed to multiply unchecked. They thus seek nonlethal solutions, usually through contraception, relocation, or a combination of both.

The most widespread model, used especially with feral cats, is "trap, neuter, and release" (TNR), in which volunteers set out humane traps to catch cats, have them sterilized and vaccinated, and rerelease them in the same area where they were caught. (Volunteers often try to find adoptive homes for kittens, who can be acclimated to life as house pets, although feral adults rarely adapt.) TNR is supported by major animal welfare organizations including the American Society for the Prevention of Cruelty to Animals (ASPCA) and the Humane Society of the United States (HSUS). It has been implemented by many local governments as well as private organizations. Advocates say that TNR prevents the growth of feral cat colonies while avoiding mass killings of animals. Since most adult feral cats do not make good pets, TNR seems to provide the most acceptable alternative to killing the cats, which receives much less local support and which, according to some critics, can be more expensive than trapping and returning the cats.[39]

On the other hand, usually only a small proportion of feral cats are captured in TNR programs. Thus even the most successful efforts permit the continuation of large colonies that cause significant ecological damage. Both the Audubon Society and the American Bird Conservancy, for example, oppose TNR programs because feral and other free-roaming cats kill millions of songbirds in the United States every year, including many whose populations are already in decline. The Bird Conservancy prefers solutions that would trap and neuter cats and then "relocate them to enclosed cat sanctuaries or shelters, or, where possible, adopt them out to safe and comfortable homes."[40] TNR advocates point out that few of the cats are adoptable, and the number of feral cats far outstrips the capacities of sanctuaries able to provide lifetime care for them. Several recent scientific studies of feral cats in California support the Bird Conservancy's claims. Research in the San Francisco Bay Area documented a significant negative impact on the numbers of native rodents and birds due to predation by feral cats, despite active TNR programs in the study area.[41] Another study, conducted on Catalina Island, found both that neutered cats continued to roam widely in search of prey and that TNR programs did not significantly reduce the cat populations. That study recommends that feral cats should be trapped and either adopted or euthanized.[42]

While feral cats generate the most frequent conflicts, some larger species have been trapped and relocated, as in the case of feral goats who threaten native plants in Hawaii. A different approach has been used with mustangs in the American West. Large numbers of the feral horses are captured and held in pens managed by the Bureau of Land Management (BLM), which then tries to sell them at auction. Many mustangs, especially when captured young, adapt well to domesticated life, although a large number are held indefinitely in the BLM facilities. In the United States there are many more horses than available homes, especially since the economic downturn in 2008. The equine overpopulation problem is not as well known or as severe as that of dogs and cats but still poses an obstacle to placing mustangs with adopters. Like feral cats, feral horses are not very appealing companions compared to the many well-socialized and well-trained individuals also in need of homes. Nonlethal removal programs, while imperfect from both the environmental and animal rights perspectives, attempt to balance concerns for long-term ecological health with protection of individual animals' basic interests. Animal advocates point out that, in practice, many of the mustangs suffer both physically and psychologically from confinement, which is frequently long-term. (Some go to a much crueler fate—slaughterhouses in Mexico or Canada.)

Most arguments in favor of killing animals who create problems rest upon a conviction that the good of the larger ecosystem is more important than the well-being or survival of individual animals. Some observers, however, also argue for lethal control on the basis of animal welfare. They point out that animals whose numbers have exceeded their habitat's carrying capacity frequently die of starvation or disease. Hunting, in such circumstances, proves more humane than slow death by other causes. In some cases, then, the "therapeutic hunting of obligatory management species" is justified not only from an ecological perspective but also, as Gary Varner argues, "from a true animal rights perspective," since overpopulation will cause the suffering and death of many individual animals.[43]

People who oppose lethal methods of population control point out that animals become problems only as a result of human actions, such as the abandonment of pets, the introduction of nonnative species, or predator removal leading to population explosions among wild herbivores such as deer. Our own mistakes do not justify causing pain and premature death to other creatures. The animals in question are frequently intelligent and highly social mammals, who suffer both physically and psychologically as a result of eradication campaigns.[44] In such cases, it is no more ethical to override the interests of individual nonhuman animals for the good of a system than it would be to ignore the interests of individual humans in a similar situation.

These stark choices suggest that the debate between environmental and animal ethics may in fact be as intractable as advocates on both sides generally assume. A number of thinkers, however, have looked for common ground, and their efforts are worth examining in light of both the theoretical and the practical problems we have encountered so far. In the next chapter I discuss a number of the efforts at reconciliation, which point to both the difficulties and the possibilities of constructing an ethic that can do justice to all aspects of nonhuman nature, including both individual subjects and the ecosystems in which they are embedded.

7

Between Animals and Nature

Finding Common Ground

ANIMALS OR NATURE?

In both theory and practice, the conflict between concern for animals and concern for the environment as a whole seems to be unavoidable and perhaps permanent. The theoretical dimensions of this split rest in dominant ways of thinking about nature and culture, animals and humans, wildness and domesticity, and individuals and wholes. All these pairs resist efforts at reconciliation because the elements are defined as mutually exclusive rather than constitutive. As long as we think about nature, animals, and humans in terms of these conceptual oppositions, integration of the different values at stake will remain impossible. We will continue to have animal ethics, environmental ethics, and an insoluble debate between them. To move beyond this theoretical and practical dead end, we need an ethic that accounts for and does justice to all of nature, including individual nonhuman subjects and entire ecosystems, as well as the many natural places and entities in between.

Such an ethic is far from simple. It is elusive partly because attempts at reconciliation have sought to encompass one "side" or the other within preconceived and abstract categories. Rather than tweaking existing models, we might find better grounds for a more encompassing ethic in the experiences of people who care for nature in its various guises and scales. Many people feel and act in ways that do not mirror the theoretical debates about natural value. They care about nature in general and about nonhuman animals in particular. They give money to both the Humane Society and the Sierra Club; they love their pets and they love wilderness; they are horrified by massive oil spills and by the suffering of a single abused animal. The love for nonhuman life that E. O. Wilson calls biophilia seems expansive enough, most of the time, to encompass concerns of many kinds, at many scales. Few people believe that they have to choose, once and for all, between loving nature in general and animals in particular, any more than they must choose between people and animals.

Popular attitudes about animals and nature are often inconsistent: people who oppose sport hunting eat meat; people who worry about climate change drive gas guzzlers; people who love their pets buy dogs bred in puppy mills. Such inconsistencies are not limited to attitudes about nonhuman nature but permeate many areas of our lives. People who desire good public schools also want lower taxes, people who support gender equality do not let their sons paint their nails, and so on. These contradictions commonly divide our expressed values and our actual practices. The split between animal welfare and ecological concern, however, is different. It reflects not simply a failure to follow principles in concrete situations but a more foundational problem. Following ecocentric values in all our actions would make it impossible to respect individual animals' intrinsic value, and vice versa.

Conflicts exist between many different value systems: being a free-market libertarian makes it impossible to be a socialist, and upholding patriarchal values makes it impossible to be a feminist. However, the clash between animal welfare and environmentalism is not like these other contrasts because the two value systems seem aligned in many ways. Many people combine concern for nature and for animals, which is not true for libertarianism and socialism or patriarchy and feminism. This combination thrives because animals are part of nature. They reflect, embody, and make real the more-than-human world to which we are so powerfully and so ambivalently connected. This is why the dilemma requires not just practical guidance—ways to live up to our felt values—but a deeper theoretical reconciliation. If animals are a vital, defining part of nature, we need to develop an ethic that can make sense of that fact and also of the ambiguities and contradictions inherent in our relations with nature.

RECONCILIATION, PART 1: SHALLOW VERSIONS

Perhaps the most common strategy for reconciliation is to acknowledge the differences between animal and environmental ethics but seek common ground in between. I describe such approaches as shallow, not because they lack gravitas but because they do not seek agreement on foundational principles. I discuss three versions here, which I call the separate but equal (or separate spheres) approach; moral pluralism; and pragmatism. The models have many shared features, and each exists in different variations. Despite the fact that the divisions are not always clear, sorting them out into these categories helps us understand the issues at stake and the strengths and weaknesses of each approach.

Separate but Equal

Many environmental and animal philosophers propose two separate value systems, one for wild nature and another for the individual animals for whom we have some sort of historical, social, or personal responsibility. This parallels two-pronged approaches in social ethics advocated by feminists who believe, as Virginia Held puts it, "we need different moral approaches for different domains of society."[1] While justice may be the most appropriate principle to apply in the public sphere, in this view, ethics based on care are better suited to the home. Similarly, many environmental and animal ethicists argue that we should follow different guidelines in the disparate domains of wilderness and human society. The distinction between spheres leads to different standards for treating animals in nature and animals out of nature.

The definition of these spheres depends on a clear separation between domestic and wild animals, which makes possible the claim that domesticated animals are no longer part of nature. They have diverged so much from their wild relatives, in both character and circumstances, that the same ethic cannot apply to both. The resulting two-track ethic uses a holistic environmental ethic for free-ranging wild animals, who are beyond human influence and responsibility. Domestic animals, on the other hand, are human creations and dependent members of human societies, which gives humans special responsibilities to them. For a number of environmental ethicists, including many ecocentrists, the elaboration of two distinct ethical models seems a satisfactory and even necessary way to address the categorical differences between domesticated and wild animals. Baird Callicott, for example, argues that duties to domestic animals "differ in a general and profound way from our duties toward the wild animal members of the biotic community."[2] He acknowledges that "animal rights is not a preposterous notion if restricted to domestic animals," although to extend rights to wild animals would be in effect to domesticate them.[3]

The separate spheres model also appeals to many animal ethicists, including Singer and Regan, who apply a laissez-faire approach to wild animals while insisting that we have direct duties to domestic and captive animals. Some feminist philosophers also believe that domestic and wild animals should be subject to two different ethics, paralleling care ethicists' distinction between home and civil society. Grace Clement summarizes this approach: "our relations to domestic animals should be based on an ethic of care, while our relations to wild animals should be based on the ethic of justice. That is, perhaps in relation to domestic animals, our primary obligation is to meet their needs and to protect them, while in relation to wild animals our primary obligation is to leave them alone, or to stop interfering with them."[4]

Many different thinkers prefer the separate but equal approach because it takes seriously the claims of both environmentalism and animal welfare while avoiding the daunting task of integrating disparate notions of value. Without trying to reconcile two competing approaches, it acknowledges that each is appropriate in its own place. The separate spheres model has several disadvantages, however. First, it assumes that domestication and wildness are completely separate. This belief rests on and perpetuates a dualism between nature and culture that both environmentalists and animal advocates describe as inaccurate and destructive. These divisions are inaccurate because humans are animals and because people are formed by continual interactions between nature and culture. They are destructive because ideas of human separation from nature almost always entail claims of human superiority, what Karen Warren calls the "logic of domination" that justifies the subordination of the "lower" terms.[5] Separate spheres models also view individuals and groups as fundamentally opposed to each other, enmeshed in a necessary competition that will end in the destruction of one or the other.

The separation of spheres model divides not only individuals and wholes or nature and culture but also wild and domestic animals. This split rests on a number of problematic assumptions: we can clearly define and distinguish both wildness and domesticity; humans do not interact with wild animals; wild and domestic animals do not interact with each other; and wild and domestic animals are radically dissimilar in character, capacities, and ways of life. These assumptions make it possible to distinguish animal ethics and environmental ethics: one deals with domestic animals, who are part of human society, and the other deals with wild animals, who are part of ecosystems. From this perspective, human societies do not include wild animals, and ecosystems do not include humans. However, this neat division cannot be sustained in light of evidence from ecology, ethology, and evolutionary science as well as from social scientific and historical studies of human cultures and human-animal interactions. Ecosystems and societies are created and maintained by multiple interactions that continually cross lines between wild and domestic, human and animal, and social and natural.

Moral Pluralism

Another effort at shallow reconciliation expands the separate spheres model by acknowledging not just two but many systems of value. This model, usually called moral pluralism, is distinguished from monist approaches in which all values can ultimately be traced to a single, originating source. While the separate spheres model applies two different moral approaches for two different domains, pluralism affirms multiple approaches for the same domain (or the same person or object). We care about important things for many reasons. We may value simple things for a single reason: I value a paper clip because it holds papers together. However, we usually have multiple reasons for valuing more significant or complex parts of our lives. I appreciate a particular vase because it is useful, because it is beautiful, and because it was a gift from a beloved friend. I value my friend because of her moral probity, her sense of humor, and her generous habit of giving me a ride to work every morning. I value my job because it is interesting, because it contributes to the common good, and because it pays the mortgage. At times, a specific reason for loving a friend or appreciating a job may take precedence, but this does not exclude other values.

Further, the fact that one entity possesses primary value does not mean that others do not also have substantial value. Just as many people "can both intrinsically value persons and works of art," as Dale Jamieson observes, so "animal liberationists can value nature intrinsically and intensely, even though they believe that nonsentient nature is of derivative value." Further, Jamieson believes, "because what is of derivative value can be valued intensely and intrinsically, animal liberationists can join environmental ethicists in fighting for the preservation of wild rivers and wilderness areas. Indeed rightly understood, they can even agree with environmental ethicists that these natural features are valuable for their own sakes."[6]

Jamieson points to one of the major attractions of moral pluralism: its ability to create coalitions of people who differ on foundational concerns but reach similar conclusions about policies and practices. In this sense, pragmatism is a version of moral pluralism, although pragmatism is distinguished by its explicit rejection of foundational principles, in contrast to pluralists' attempt to combine them.

In relation to animal and environmental ethics, moral pluralists believe that we need different approaches for different scales and aspects of the nonhuman world. Nature, like human society, is too large and complex to fit within a single theory of value. In relation to animals and nature, pluralists do not try to encompass individuals in a holistic ethic or wholes within an individualistic ethic. Instead, they value both for different reasons. Pluralism is not only possible but required, as Marti Kheel puts it, because "moral worth can exist *both* in the individual parts of nature *and* in the whole of which they are a part."[7] However, pluralists still must develop models for thinking about different values and differently valued entities in concrete situations, as well as theoretical dilemmas, in which choices must be made to prioritize one or the other. Usually such choices are made according to an implicit hierarchy of values, in which the primary good (individuals or wholes, for example) takes precedence. In such models, the acknowledgment of multiple goods does not translate into equal consideration.

Pluralism makes important contributions to the animal rights–environmental ethics debate because it points to a more expansive way of valuing nonhuman nature. Pluralism counters the argument, implicit in both individualist and holist models, that we should minimize concern by applying it to the smallest number of beings possible. This approach falsely assumes, as Mary Midgley puts it, that moral concern and compassion exist in fixed quantities. To the contrary, she notes, such qualities grow with use, and "effective users do not economize on them."[8] Love and care are not involved in a zero sum game. Just as no one expects parents to reduce care for their first child by half upon the birth of the second, we need not expect people to care less for ecosystems because they love individual animals. We think that individuals and ecosystems compete with each other only because we are trained to do so. This sort of lifeboat thinking, which sees moral decisions as choices between mutually exclusive opposites, is a social construct. It is not the only or the best way to make most ethical decisions. Pluralism is valuable, despite certain theoretical and practical difficulties, because at the very least it undercuts narrow ways of thinking about the value of nonhuman nature.

Even though love is not limited, resources such as time, energy, money, and space are sometimes in short supply, and we need guidelines for how to distribute them. Simply saying we value them all does not resolve the problem in concrete cases. For such situations, we need further guidance. Another shallow approach, philosophical pragmatism, seeks such guidance in problem-solving and consensus-building. The fact that people with divergent philosophical positions agree on many issues, pragmatists argue, indicates that philosophical issues such as intrinsic value or holism are less significant than practical consensus. Pragmatists believe that "the goal of seeking a unified, monistic theory of environmental ethics" has led environmental philosophers to focus on internal intellectual disagreements and to fail in the urgent task of contributing to environmental policy and activism.[9] Metaphysical foundations are largely irrelevant to these tasks. Pragmatists seek to overcome the divide between animal welfare and environmental concern in order to solve concrete problems in ways that can benefit both animals and ecosystems.[10]

In terms of the relations between animals and ecological wholes, many pragmatists develop a de facto holism. They focus on protecting ecosystems, species, and habitats not because these are the only sources of intrinsic value but rather because preserving these natural wholes seems the best way to preserve a wide range of nonhuman goods. As Bryan Norton puts it, "because of the complexity of the interrelationships in nature, and because there are so many different values exemplified in nature, the only way to be able to protect *all* of these diverse and pluralistic values is to protect the integrity of community processes."[11] In this view, special arguments or provisions in favor of individual animals are not necessary, a claim accepted by many philosophical holists and disputed by many animal rights advocates.

The pragmatist rejection of philosophical foundations makes it possible to sidestep the choice between holism and individualism and focus instead on philosophical work that is "more relevant to environmental advocates on the ground."[12] Both animal and environmental activists, according to Andrew Light, should ask, "What argument is actually going to work? That is, which argument can offer appeals for stronger and better policies and laws to promote the welfare of animals and ecosystems, a goal on which these two communities converge, which will be intuitively appealing for those who do not count themselves as either environmentalists or animal advocates?" Such an approach makes it evident that "the divide between environmental ethicists and animal liberationists is not nearly as wide as has been suggested."[13] Further, adds Dale Jamieson, environmental and animal advocates might find that they share not only common goals but also "many of the same enemies: those who dump poisons into the air and water, drive whales to extinction, or clear rainforests to create pastures for cattle, to name just a few."[14]

The value of a pragmatist approach is evident in many concrete situations. One is the common opposition of animal and environmental advocates to industrial agriculture, and especially concentrated animal-feeding operations (CAFOs). Both environmentalists and animal advocates oppose industrial farming of animals, albeit for very different reasons. Environmentalists point to the air and water pollution caused by high concentrations of animals such as pigs, chickens, or cattle in CAFOs. Animal advocates emphasize the suffering of these animals, who have little room to move and are treated in purely instrumental ways from conception to slaughter. (Many social justice activists also oppose CAFOs because of their detrimental effects on local economies and community relations, and health advocates oppose them because they make possible cheap meat, often full of steroids and antibiotics.) Both environmental and animal activists use opposition to factory farms not only to build coalitions with other groups but also to appeal to broader audiences. This issue thus provides an excellent illustration of how a pragmatic approach can unite a variety of moral and political concerns.

Other policies supported by both animal and environmental advocates share similarly diverse theoretical foundations, uniting not only individualistic and holistic perspectives but also ecocentric and anthropocentric values. Concern for human well-being, not ecological integrity, underlies many environmental laws, and movements that highlight human welfare often wield greater practical influence than those focused explicitly on nature's intrinsic value. On the other hand, ecocentric values do have some public resonance, and a number of laws and policies explicitly recognize natural value apart from human use. The 1973 Endangered Species Act (ESA) is an outstanding example of the codification of intrinsic value into law. It asserts that nonhuman species should be protected even if they have no known or potential value for humans. This perspective has been ridiculed and legally challenged, but the ESA still stands both as one of the most significant pieces of environmental legislation in history and as evidence that ecocentric values can receive wide-scale public support.

The ESA also reflects the paradoxical role of nonhuman animals in modern environmentalism. On the one hand, animals generate support and concern powerful enough to inspire unprecedented legal protection. On the other, the focus is not on individual animals themselves but on abstractions such as species and on collective harms such as extinction. To some extent the ESA fulfills goals of both animal advocates and ecocentrists because it acknowledges that threatened species require protection both as individuals who should not be hunted or trapped and also as members of larger ecosystems that require preservation or restoration. Environmental holists, pluralists, and pragmatists all cite the ESA as a major victory, as do animal advocates opposed to the killing of individual creatures. Sometimes the ESA has supported major efforts to protect a few individuals, as in the case of condors, red wolves, and other rare animals, who have been bred in captivity and released into wilderness areas at significant cost. In other cases, it justifies the destruction of individual animals, feral or exotic, who threaten the survival of native species.

The ESA's primary unit of value is neither individuals nor wholes but the middle-level category of species. The success of the ESA suggests that attention to middle categories such as species can benefit efforts to reconcile concerns for animals and ecological wholes. The middle ground is not necessarily a compromise between two poles, but a territory that both includes and blurs boundaries. It encompasses not just individuals and collectives but also, and above all, the relationships and dynamic processes that connect them. On this middle terrain, an alternative theoretical framework is necessary.

Even though the ESA shows that there is not always a conflict between individual and collective welfare, it does not please all sectors all the time. There is a partial truth in the common framing of the environmental ethics—animal rights debate: it is not always possible for both individual animals and ecological wholes to thrive equally; in some cases, one does in fact threaten the well-being of the other. Such lifeboat scenarios are much less common than ethics textbooks suggest, although it is true that not all issues are amenable to pluralist approaches. Few institutions are as generally bad for nature, animals, and people as factory farms, and few policies have the broad appeal of the Endangered Species Act. A number of practices and policies are clearly good for one sector and not for another. Lethal control of feral hogs or white-tailed deer, for example, is good for native ecosystems and plants but not for the complex, sentient animals who are killed in the process. Similarly, trap—neuter—release programs respect the interests of feral cats in living relatively free and healthy lives, but they can come at a significant ecological cost. In harder cases such as these, the marriage of animal and environmental concerns falls apart when the impossibility of doing equal justice to both becomes obvious. This dilemma prompts a renewed search for an ethic that can reconcile different kinds and scales of nonhuman value at more foundational levels.

RECONCILIATION, PART 2: DEEPER VERSIONS

The failings of shallow reconciliations, especially evident in difficult situations such as ecological restoration, suggest we need to look deeper for an ethic that can encompass animals and nature together. A number of philosophers have made this attempt, usually on the basis of an existing ethic which they modify to encompass other concerns. I look here at several different approaches. The first builds an environmental ethic on the basis of concern for individual natural entities, while another tries to include respect for individual animals within an overarching communitarianism or holism. A third alternative begins with a theological foundation, in which God subsumes both individual entities and ecological wholes.

Starting with Individuals

Some philosophers believe that concern for individual animals can ground a coherent environmental ethic. Since animals are the most important elements of nature, Gary Steiner argues, attitudes toward nature and animals are intimately connected. Therefore, "a fundamental change in our moral estimation of animals would require a corresponding change in our relation to nature as a whole."[15] This claim is elaborated more fully in Paul Taylor's ethic of "respect for life," which begins not with ecological wholes but with life itself. Life is a property only of individual organisms, so value lies in individual natural entities, which Taylor calls "teleological centers of life." Taylor's primary target is not holism or individualism but anthropocentrism, the automatic privileging of humanness over all other qualities. In this sense, his ethic resembles the anti-speciesist approaches of Peter Singer and Tom Regan. He also echoes these animal ethicists in framing his ethic as fundamentally concerned with the good of individuals. Because individual natural entities have their own inherent worth, they deserve respect, which in turn "determines our moral relations with the Earth's wild communities of life."[16]

Taylor is among the few environmental philosophers who do not distinguish sharply between the moral value of domestic and wild animals, and he may be the only one who addresses plants as centers of value. Even domestic animals, he writes, "are entities that have a good of their own. They can be benefited or harmed. In this matter they are exactly like wild animals and plants in natural ecosystems." Neither capacities nor relationships to humans make a difference in our moral obligations toward them. Specifically, he adds, the dependence of domesticated animals does not lessen their value or the consideration they deserve.[17] Even under conditions of domestication or captivity, animals remain teleological centers of value.

Taylor extends moral considerability much more broadly than either ecocentrists or animal rights advocates, while sharing common values with both. Like most animal advocates, he locates value in the "unique, irreplaceable individual."[18] Although Taylor's methodological individualism resembles that of animal ethics, he identifies as an environmental philosopher, and his primary concern is with wild animals and ecosystems. He believes that this concern does not require a methodological holism because individualism and anthropocentrism are not necessarily connected. He thereby turns Callicott's claim about the land ethic upside down: what is innovative about environmental ethics is not holism but rather the perception of intrinsic value in nonhuman entities. This claim has the potential to undermine the dualistic opposition between animals and nature that defines much ecocentric thought.

The dependence of nonhuman animals on overall ecological health can expand concern for individual animals ethics into a comprehensive environmental ethic. Thus environmental concern requires not a holistic perspective but merely concern for individuals, multiplied. Since habitat destruction, climate change, and pollution all harm individual creatures, animal advocates should oppose these ecological problems as well. Taylor makes this explicit: it is wrong to destroy the habitat of many plants and animals because such large-scale destruction means that many moral subjects, "each having the same inherent worth, will also be wronged, namely all the members of the population that are killed or injured." However, the ecological community as such has no moral standing. He opposes the destruction of ecosystems and the extinction of species, "not because the group as *such* has a greater claim-to-be-respected than the individual, but because harming the group necessarily involves harming many individuals."[19]

This individualistic ethic links care for animals, especially but not exclusively wild ones, into care for the ecological processes and communities on which they depend. This is a sort of bottom-up approach, in which one can arrive at concern for wholes without explicit theoretical attention to wholes. As Dale Jamieson puts it, "one can go quite far towards protecting the environment solely on the basis of concern for animals." No significant obstacles need prevent either alliances between animal and environmental advocates or the conversion of the former into the latter. Jamieson concludes, with refreshing though perhaps excessive optimism, that "where Callicott saw a 'triangular affair' and Mark Sagoff saw 'divorce,' I see the potential for Hollywood romance" between animal rights and environmentalism.[20]

Starting with Wholes

Jamieson's enthusiasm for a bottom-up approach finds a mirror image in the conviction of some environmental thinkers who believe that ecocentric holism provides sufficient grounds for protecting individuals and should therefore be embraced by animal rights advocates. The most influential approach of this sort was developed by Baird Callicott, in an effort to resolve the conflict he helped ignite with his 1980 article "Animal Liberation: A Triangular Affair," which declared animal rights and environmental ethics fundamentally incompatible. The article generated numerous responses, both positive and negative. In 1989 he replied with an essay titled "Animal Liberation and Environmental Ethics: Back Together Again," in which he regrets the "acrimonious estrangement" between advocates of animal welfare and environmental ethicists that his earlier work encouraged. Because the two camps have overlapping concerns, he notes, "it would be far wiser to make common cause against a common enemy— the destructive forces at work ravaging the nonhuman world—than to continue squabbling among ourselves."[21]

Callicott echoes the optimism of pragmatists and moral pluralists: given that we seek similar goals, our philosophical differences should not prevent us from finding common ground on many concrete issues. Consistent with his pursuit of a monist theory of value, however, he rejects purely pragmatist grounds for this collaboration. We cannot shy away from the substantive theoretical differences that divide animal rights and ecocentrism, because those differences will lead, ultimately, to practical divisions. Thus we still need "a moral theory that embraces both programs *and* that provides a framework for the adjudication of the very real conflicts between human welfare, animal welfare, and ecological integrity."[22] (Callicott adds human welfare to the equation here but does not elaborate how this fits into his overall ethic.)

While Callicott acknowledges that animal and environmental ethics can be complementary rather than contradictory, he finds proposals for parallel ethical codes "philosophically unsatisfying." They are also practically inadequate, he adds, because "when competing moral claims cannot be articulated in the same terms, they cannot be decisively compared and resolved. Ethical eclecticism leads, it would seem inevitably, to moral incommensurability in hard cases." All the shallow approaches to reconciling animal rights and ecocentrism, including the separate spheres model, moral pluralism, and pragmatism, fail because they do not provide the necessary theoretical commensurability. We require, Callicott believes, "something more than a mere coalition of convenience," which although satisfactory to pragmatists cannot ground the lasting alliance required to achieve both animal welfare and environmental goals.[23] We still need, in short, a deep reconciliation based on foundational principles.

This integration begins with the holistic framework provided by the land ethic. Callicott's challenge is to find a way, within ecocentrism, to acknowledge the claims of individual natural entities in a more than cursory manner. He finds the grounds for such a reconciliation in Mary Midgley's concept of the mixed community. "Midgley's marvelous insight," he writes, "is that, however exclusive of other human beings the perceived boundaries of historical human societies may have been, they all, nevertheless, have included some animals." Like Leopold's biotic community, the mixed community suggests that "we are members of nested communities each of which has a different structure and therefore different moral requirements."[24] Callicott joins these two versions of a more-than-human moral community to create "the basis of a unified animal-environmental ethical theory."[25]

Callicott's theory combines environmental and animal welfare concerns by asserting that wild and domestic animals are qualitatively different centers of value: "Domestic animals are members of the mixed community and ought to enjoy, therefore, all the rights and privileges, whatever they may turn out to be, attendant upon that membership. Wild animals are, by definition, not members of the mixed community and therefore should not lie on the same spectrum of graded moral standing as family members, neighbors, fellow citizens, fellow human beings, pets, and other domestic animals." Wild animals, however, have value as members of the biotic community, to which humans also belong.[26] Wild animals' membership in this biotic community gives them certain "moral entitlements," chiefly the now-familiar right to be left alone. They do not have the right to life, however, because leaving nature alone means allowing predation and other sometimes violent ecological processes to unfold.

This sounds very much like a separate spheres argument, grounded on the notion that different groups require different attitudes and actions from their members. People have obligations to members of their immediate families that they do not have to nonrelated people and duties to pets that they do not have toward wild animals. These personal commitments, however, do not preclude morally significant connections to unknown people and to wild animals, with whom we also share membership in larger communities. Callicott describes these communities as "nested," in the form of concentric circles, although for Midgley they are more like "petals" which overlap but need not supersede each other in most cases. While holistic environmental duties are important, in the biosocial model they are not "preemptive," because "we are still subject to all the other more particular and individually oriented duties to the members of our various more circumscribed and intimate communities."[27] This does not identify clear grounds for decisions in tough cases, the problem Callicott rightly identifies in the separate spheres model and other pluralist approaches.

Callicott seeks such coherence by using the land ethic as an overarching communitarian model: "The integrity, stability, and beauty of the biotic community depend upon *all* members, in their appropriate numbers, functioning in their co-evolved ways." This sets limits on the entitlements and rights of all members, human and other, domestic and wild, who should be permitted to function in their various "co-evolved" ways as long as they do not threaten the overall health of the land community. Callicott makes this explicit when he explains that his combined theory is offered "on terms favorable to ecocentric environmental ethics," inverting Tom Regan's attempt to combine environmental and animal rights concerns on terms favorable to animals. This suggests a clearer hierarchy than the simple idea that we belong to various communities, all of which exert claims upon us. When these claims come into conflict, the "common theoretical structure" of the land ethic offers "a means, in principle, to assign priorities and relative weights and thus to resolve such conflicts in a systematic way."[28] However, Callicott does not spell out the precise way in which this assigning works out, hinting that the task of theoretical reconciliation is more difficult than it appears.

Starting with God

Another way to connect people, nature, and animals is by placing them all in the context of a larger theological meaning. Many secular environmentalists hold Christianity responsible for, or at least complicit in, Western culture's generally negative attitude toward nonhuman nature. However, the tradition also contains alternative streams, sometimes deeply buried, that challenge accustomed ways of relating to nature. Particularly valuable is the Christian critique of individualism and especially of the oppositional relationship between individuals and wholes that is common in secular philosophies. Especially in its non-Evangelical forms, Christianity asserts that human freedom and creativity are most fully realized within, not apart from, community. This is expressed with particular clarity in Roman Catholic social thought, which consistently affirms that "God did not create man for life in isolation, but for the formation of social unity," in the words of *Gaudium et Spes* (1965), the final document of the Second Vatican Council.[29] Anabaptist theology, radically distinct from the Catholic tradition in many respects, similarly rejects any definition of the human person "as a self-centered reacting organism."[30]

Among contemporary Christian ecotheologians, Jay McDaniel brings together concern for animals and for nature most explicitly. McDaniel uses the concept of God's larger good to unite diverse values and moral claims in an explicitly holistic framework. This approach, he explains, "is not human-centered, animal-centered, plant-centered, or systems-centered, at the expense of these other centers; rather it is divinely centered, in a way that understands the divine life as including all life, individually and communally, within an interconnected, diverse whole."[31] The overarching whole that gives value is not, as in the land ethic, a natural system or community but rather God. This model creates a radically different kind of hierarchy, in which the most meaningful boundary is not between humans and animals or nature and culture but rather between the creator and the creation.

This echoes the theocentric environmental ethic developed by Protestant theologian James Gustafson, in which God's creation is good in and of itself even though individuals within it sometimes suffer. As Gustafson explains, "If there is a sense of divinity, it has to include not only dependence upon nature for beauty and for sustenance, but also forces beyond human control which destroy each other and us. If God saw that the diversity God created was good, it was not *necessarily* good for humans and for all aspects of nature."[32] From this perspective, anthropocentric and ecocentric models do not exhaust the possibilities, as Gustafson asserts: "The good that God values must be more inclusive than one's normal perceptions of what is good for me, what is good for my community, and even what is good for the human species."[33] Gustafson's theocentric approach conceives of humans, animals, and nature as parts of a larger community, created and sustained by God, always subordinate to divine purposes and meaning. The community envisioned here is neither purely a human creation—"nurture"—nor merely a biological fact—"nature." Rather, God creates and provides meaning to all forms of human and nonhuman life and the larger ecological processes that support them.

Theocentric thinkers have a significant advantage over secular philosophers. This larger context makes sense of the diverse claims made by individuals and wholes, wild and domestic, human and nonhuman. All these claims are valid because all emerge from God's good creation, but none is ultimately decisive because their foundation lies outside nature and human society. This avoids the problems of pragmatism and pluralism, which provide no foundation at all. The problem is that the theocentric solution is limited to people with the relevant theological convictions. In responses, Callicott proposes that we "purge" Christian ethics of their "literal elements," but this may reduce rather than increase the power of moral demands. Without literal belief that God created the world and said that it was good, there is no compelling reason to abide by the ethical guidelines that follow.[34]

IS ANTHROPOCENTRISM THE PROBLEM?

Most of the efforts at deep reconciliation—holistic, individualistic, and religious—share a common conviction that the human-centered value systems are the root problem. In particular, they criticize, and try to replace, the notion that humans are separate from the rest of nature. This separation is usually justified on the basis of uniquely human qualities, which make us superior to all other species and entitle us to use other animals and natural resources for our own purposes. If this analysis is correct and anthropocentrism is the problem, then building more sustainable and humane societies will require revised understandings of our own place in relation to nature and other animals. To this end, much scholarly energy has gone into descriptions both of the destructive consequences of existing attitudes and of the positive new attitudes that should emerge.

Many environmental thinkers believe that better attitudes must begin with acknowledgment of membership in larger natural wholes, exemplified by Leopold's call for a shift in the human role "from conqueror of the land-community to plain member and citizen of it."[35] This ecological citizenship should be understood, further, as part of an overarching vision of the meaning and shape of human life. Environmental problems are more about philosophy and theology than about economics or science. "What we do about ecology," as historian Lynn White put it, "depends on our ideas of the man-nature relationship. More science and more technology are not going to get us out of the present ecologic crisis until we find a new religion, or rethink our old one."[36] This new religion, as articulated by environmental philosophers of various persuasions, emphasizes humans' dependence upon nature, the value of nature apart from its utility for people, and our duty to consume fewer resources and respect natural places and entities.

These environmental worldviews rarely confront the fact that we are animals—not vegetables, minerals, mountains, or rivers, and not, as Mary Midgley points out, just rather *like* animals. This self-evident truth, however, raises difficult questions about our own character and behavior. Acting "like an animal" means many things—aggressive, violent, crude, primitive, or uncivilized, for instance—but few of the qualities associated with animalness are positive. Because being animal is conceived in this way, we value in humanness what separates us from "the animals." We emphasize our differences and deny both the many similarities between humans and other creatures and the uniqueness of every nonhuman species. Mary Midgley's magisterial *Beast and Man* remains the best discussion of this problem, beginning with her assertion that defining human features must be understood not as unprecedented gifts of fate but rather as "continuous with our animal nature," evolved like and alongside many qualities we share with other species.[37]

The question about what finally distinguishes humans from animals is, as Midgley notes, wrong from start to finish. First, we should ask "what distinguishes humans *among* the animals, unless we think we're machines or angels." Second, the question is wrong because "it asks for a single, simple, final distinction, and for one that confers praise." However, no single mark distinguishes humans from other animals. Rather, Midgley continues, "We resemble different ones in different ways. It is also essential to remember how immensely they differ from one another. In certain central respects, all social mammals, including us, are far more like each other than any is like a snake or a codfish, or even a bee." This conclusion is affirmed, at least genetically, by DNA analyses showing that *Homo sapiens* differs less from chimpanzees than chimpanzees do from gorillas. For many people, such information seems to diminish the meaning and value of humanness. Animals are driven by blind instinct, while "man makes himself." This is, Midgley points out, wrong on both points. Other animals are much more complex than we have generally allowed, and humans are more like these animals than we have wanted to admit. Human dignity is not harmed by acknowledging that we, like other animals, "have a nature" and are not pure creatures of culture or spirit.[38] Being animal is neither an insult nor a tragedy, unless we make it so.

The first difficulty with acknowledging that we are animals is that it means that we are neither as special nor as separate from the rest of nature as we have thought. The next problem follows from this conclusion: if we are not so different, we ought not to treat other animals as we do. Human exploitation of other species, even those most closely related to us, has been justified by the conviction that we are radically Other. Something momentous separates all of us from all of them and makes it acceptable to wear, capture, and vivisect them according not just to our needs but to our desires and whims. Without this qualitative difference, almost every aspect of our individual lives and our larger societies becomes morally questionable. It is much more comfortable to leave our feelings of connection to nature ambiguous and abstract.

We avoid examining the details of our connections to nature not only to sidestep moral dilemmas but also because of unavoidable epistemological limitations. It is not possible to know nature in general any more than it is to know humanity in general. Nature is not an undifferentiated mass but countless nonhuman individuals, places, communities, processes, and interactions, all in constant flux. Because we experience and think about nature in partial and heterogeneous ways, we cannot value or feel connected to all its diverse parts equally. Inevitably, we care about or admire certain nonhuman entities and places more than others.

Some environmental thinkers, such as stewardship advocates, make the hierarchies explicit. Even those who proclaim species equality, however, usually take some hierarchies and exclusions for granted, which permits them to declare domestic animals "travesties," for example, or to seek lethal control of nonnative species. Animal advocates do the same thing, as even anti-speciesists such as Singer and Regan grant greater status and protection to animals who possess morally relevant traits. Ecocentric, biocentric, and anti-speciesist thinkers all assert that nonhuman nature has value apart from humans, but few question our right to decide what counts in nature and as nature.

Even if we could develop an ethic of nature that does not put humans at the center, it would still be anthropogenic—human-created. We are always within the process of interpreting and evaluating our world, and therefore our vision and knowledge are always particular, embodied, limited, and, in Donna Haraway's term, "non-innocent." Humans cannot simply take nature on its own terms; we must take it "as it comes" to particular people embedded in specific contexts. These limitations persist even when we seek the universalism implied in nonanthropocentrism. Despite all our efforts, we can never obtain full and complete knowledge of nature. The "view of infinite vision," of nature or anything else, "is an illusion, a god-trick," as Haraway puts it.[39] Just as we cannot achieve a view from nowhere by removing individual subjectivity from our interpretations of the world, neither can we escape our species perspective.

While we cannot jump our skins, we can acknowledge that consciousness, knowledge, and agency do not stop at the limits of those skins. There is something that it is like to be a bat, as the philosopher Thomas Nagel concluded, but we can never know what it is like, because humans cannot experience batness.[40] Alexandra Horowitz criticizes Nagel for treating interspecies difference as something wholly unlike an intraspecies difference. The problem of understanding bat consciousness seems to him qualitatively different from the problem of understanding the consciousness of another human being. Horowitz notes that we do not hesitate to talk about what it is "like" to be another person, even though we can never know completely what it is like. We can come closer with more information and greater empathy. The same is true of our efforts to understand other animals.[41] The fact that we cannot achieve total comprehension, either of another person or of a member of another species, should not prevent us from trying to understand their perspectives, subjectivity, and experiences as fully as possible.

Nagel's epistemological dead end need not lead to a moral dead end. Rather, it leaves us with the challenge of valuing something, in this case the subjectivity of other creatures, that remains always outside our grasp. The anthropologist Clifford Geertz put this problem neatly in relationship to studying other human cultures: although it may be impossible to achieve an ethnography of witchcraft as done by a witch, he wrote, it is not necessary to settle for an ethnography of witchcraft as done by a geometer.[42] Returning to Nagel's problem, we might say that although we cannot achieve a psychology of bats as done by a bat, we can certainly do better than a psychology of bats as done by René Descartes.

Descartes is the flag-bearer for a worldview that denies not only reason and subjectivity but even sentience to all nonhuman animals. One of his "proofs" was that animals lacked language, which distinguished *Homo sapiens* from both animals and machines. Even stupid or insane people can use language to convey their thoughts, Descartes believed, based on what must have been an extremely limited experience of other humans. His conviction that all humans and no nonhumans have language supported his claim "not merely that animals have less reason than men, but that they have none at all, for we see that very little is needed in order to talk."[43] Animals make sounds, he acknowledged, but we should not confuse these with human speech. The sounds made by animals are no different than those made by clocks or other machines, and no more expressive of consciousness, reason, or even physical pain.[44]

In the centuries since Descartes wrote, many philosophers and psychologists echoed his conviction that consciousness requires language. Today, however, this claim is widely discredited. Research in ethology has demonstrated that many animals, including not only nonhuman primates but many other mammals and birds, use language in deliberate and creative ways: they put words together to talk about new situations, create new words, use human language with other members of their own species who have not been taught that language, and they understand and use general conceptions. Dogs, for example, can understand the category of novelty and thus when faced with an unknown word, find and retrieve the single unfamiliar item amidst dozens of known ones.

Cognitive psychology has also shed light on the processes of thought in humans without language, including some autistic people. These experiences can help explain animal intelligence and consciousness, animal scientist (and autistic person) Temple Grandin has suggested.[45] Scholars studying early childhood development have explored these issues, demonstrating that even prelinguistic babies "think, observe, and reason. They consider evidence, draw conclusions, do experiments, solve problems, and search for the truth."[46] If prelinguistic or nonlinguistic humans are conscious subjects, on the one hand, and nonhuman animals can learn human language, on the other hand, then Descartes's arguments are doubly implausible. Consciousness does not depend upon language ability, although language ability may depend upon consciousness. Certainly language makes consciousness easier to recognize and thus is particularly valuable for identifying conscious intentions, desires, and perspectives. Understanding the other in the absence of language is harder but, as caretakers of infants can attest, far from impossible.

With or without language, we come to know others' subjectivity in and through the practices that build relationships. The next chapter explores the philosophical resources and concrete encounters that can help us develop an ethic that values both subjectivity and relationship, as well as the social and natural communities in which both are embedded.

8

Being Animal

All mysteries which mislead theory into mysticism find their rational solution in human practice and in the comprehension of this practice.[1]

ANIMALS, NATURE, AND MARX

To develop an alternative nature ethic, we need to challenge the usual ways of thinking not just about animals and the environment but also about ethics. Mainstream moral theory assumes that wrong ideas cause destructive practices and, therefore, that changed ideas will lead directly to changed practices. This framework permeates environmental ethics, reflecting the endemic idealism of Western social thought, in which ideas always precede action. According to this "linear model of action," new knowledge leads to different attitudes, and those attitudes, in turn, cause shifts in behavior.[2] In reality, however, the connections between values and practices are more complicated and subtle than direct cause and effect. Ideas always interact with social conditions, over time and across different places and cultures, and their practical consequences are rarely what the original thinkers intended.[3] This means that we cannot attack destructive practices and relationships, in social or natural communities, merely at the level of mental criticism. Instead, the challenge must begin on the ground, in and through confrontations with the social relations that gave birth to the problematic ideas.

This emphasis on concrete experience and practice characterizes the radical revision of theology and ethics developed by a number of Latin American thinkers in the 1970s. They began with the "hermeneutic circle," a theological method grounded on "the continuing change in our interpretation of the Bible, which is dictated by continuing changes in our present-day reality, both individual and societal," as Juan Luis Segundo summarizes.[4] In this interpretive circle, practical experiences shape people's readings of the Bible, and these readings in turn affect the way they act. The point at which theology begins and to which it always returns is a concrete commitment to the liberation of oppressed people. The ultimate criterion of success, further, is not theoretical sophistication but rather the capacity to alleviate human suffering and be liberative.[5]

Liberation theologians have not applied this methodology directly to nonhuman nature, but there are parallels in Anthony Weston's work in environmental philosophy. Weston argues that it is possible to develop the philosophical language necessary for a non-anthropocentric ethic only by "reconstituting the sorts of relationships and environments that have been destroyed. We need to deanthropocentrize the world rather than, first and foremost, to develop and systematize non-anthropocentrism — for world and thought co-evolve. We can only create an appropriate non-anthropocentrism as we begin to build a progressively less anthropocentric world."[6] Like radical Catholics in Latin America, Weston argues that new ways of thinking about philosophy, theology, and ethics must begin with committed practice.

In the task of building a coherent and expansive practice-based nature ethic, among the most helpful resources is the work of Karl Marx, who insisted that all ideas begin and return to actual human subjects and lives, because "for man the root is man himself." Every other aspect of our world, including ideologies, institutions, cultures, and economies, is created by human activity. It is dangerously easy, however, to forget what came first. This risk is especially acute under capitalism, which inverts the proper order of things, diminishing and demeaning living, active subjects while elevating their products. This reversal is reflected in and also reinforced by the idealist philosophy that places abstractions over real individuals and their practical experiences. Marx thus turned Hegel on his head, as he explained in *The German Ideology*:

> In direct contrast to German philosophy which descends from heaven to earth, here we ascend from earth to heaven. That is to say, we do not set out from what men say, imagine, conceive, nor from men as narrated, thought of, imagined, conceived, in order to arrive at men in the flesh. We set out from real, active men, and on the basis of their real life-process we demonstrate the development of the ideological reflexes and echoes of this life-process.[7]

Marx not only begins with "men in the flesh" as the source of meaning and value but always keeps them front and center as the end of political action. Because of his focus on structural change, especially in his later writings, Marx did not spend much time on ethics. Nor did he pay attention to animals, or at least not positive attention. Like most Western thinkers, Marx discussed animals mainly as a negative foil, defined by their lack of what makes people truly and fully human. Also like most other philosophers, his human exceptionalism rests on his distinctive view of human nature. Marx identifies several uniquely human qualities, the most important of which is the capacity to work freely, creatively, self-consciously, and collectively. As Marx explains, "man makes his life-activity itself the object of his will and of his consciousness. He has conscious life-activity. It is not a determination with which he directly merges. Conscious life-activity directly distinguishes man from animal life-activity." This is because "the animal is immediately identical with its life-activity. It does not distinguish itself from it. It is *its life-activity*."[8] Free, conscious activity can be distorted or aborted in human life, especially as a result of alienated labor, but it appears not even to be a possibility for other species.

Most of Marx's references to animals contrast their failings in this respect. For example, he writes in the first volume of *Capital* that "what distinguishes the worst architect from the best of bees is this, that the architect raises his structure in imagination before he erects it in reality."[9] Marx was not aware, of course, of the complexities of apian behavior, and especially the ability of bees to plan, adapt to changing circumstances, coordinate their work, and communicate in extremely complex ways.[10] It remains an open question whether bees create their hives in imagination before they build the material forms. Marx, however, has no doubts about what bees—or any animals—do and do not do, especially in their imaginations. Like many other great thinkers, he takes animals' dullness for granted. Nonetheless, Marx's thought points to other possible ways of thinking about animals, nature, and the relations between them. In particular, his insistence that theory must be rooted in practice and his key categories of *relationship*, *alienation*, and *practice* challenge not only the dominant idealism of animal and environmental ethics but also the boundaries and categories that have hampered both fields.

Relationships

Liberal philosophers often describe Marxism as a holistic system of thought that subordinates individuals to the greater good. This interpretation of socialism provides common ground with ecocentric environmentalism, which rejects the focus on individual well-being common to theories of animal rights and welfare.[11] The apparent holism of socialism creates conflicts with animal rights advocates, who believe that holistic approaches encourage the subordination of individual interests for the greater good. Marx's ethic, however, is best read not as holistic but as relational. He starts his analysis of social life with the living practices of and interactions among the individuals comprising it. Both entire societies and smaller groups such as classes are not abstractions or preexisting wholes but rather, as E. P. Thompson puts it, "something which in fact happens . . . in human relationships."[12] Not only collectives but also individuals are shaped by relationships, as Marx explains in his sixth Thesis on Feuerbach: "The human essence is no abstraction inherent in each single individual. In its reality it is the ensemble of social relations."[13] Both individuals and groups are always constituted by social interactions and socially embedded practices. There is no prior essence, for individuals or societies, but only endless practical encounters.

From a Marxian perspective, relationships also lie at the heart of our troubled connections with nonhuman nature and animals. Nature, according to Marx, is "man's *inorganic body*—nature, that is in so far as it is not itself the human body. Man *lives* on nature—means that nature is his *body*, with which he must remain in continuous interchange if he is not to die. That man's physical and spiritual life is linked to nature means simply that nature is linked to itself, for man is a part of nature."[14] Humans' relationships to nature are as constitutive and foundational as are relationships between people.

Alienation

If relationships are Marx's central positive category for understanding humanity's "essence" and social life, his equally important negative category is alienation. Alienation is the thread that unites his early philosophical reflections with his later work on political economy. Marx defines alienation, most basically, as the breakdown of relationships. This breakdown is both an inversion—reversing the proper order of things—and a separation of things that should be united.[15]

Marx first identified the dynamic of alienation in his criticism of religion, which begins with Feuerbach's insight: "*man makes religion; religion does not make man.*" Religion portrays real human individuals as abstractions, while an imaginary being, God, appears supremely real. This inversion is possible because of deep contradictions in human experience. Religion is "the fantastic realization of the human being inasmuch as the human being possesses no true reality. The struggle against religion is, therefore, indirectly a struggle against that world whose spiritual aroma is religion."[16] From religion, Marx developed his general theory of alienation. The process that begins with religion extends to society itself, which is reified as the "State." In the State, contradictions appear between the interests of individuals and of society as a whole, which is now understood as an abstraction standing over and against the subjects who constitute it.[17] Similarly, the products of human work and imagination appear alive and powerful, and in the face of their fictive subjectivity, human beings become objects. This reversal prompts the poignant cry of the proletariat: "I am nothing and I should be everything!"[18] Communism promises to achieve "the *genuine* resolution of the conflict between man and nature and between man and man—the true resolution of the strife between existence and essence, between objectification and self-confirmation, between freedom and necessity, between the individual and the species."[19] Communism is the radical transformation of economic and political structures that will repair the relationships that are constitutive for human beings and, although Marx does not explore this, perhaps for other creatures as well.

Four kinds of relationships suffer particularly in capitalism, leading to four types of alienation—from the labor process, labor products, other people, and our own species-being (*Gattungswesen*). Marx's concept of nature as our "inorganic body" suggests a further type of alienation, that of humans from nature itself. Marx hints at this in his most extended discussion of alienation, in *The Economic and Philosophic Manuscripts of 1844*, where he writes "in estranging from man (1) nature and (2) himself, estranged labor estranges the *species* from man."[20] Species-being is tied up with our relations to nature, and alienation from nature separates us from important dimensions of humanness.

Marx does not explore the possibility that alienation might be experienced by nonhuman subjects. Like other Marxian categories, alienation is usually defined in terms that rule out nonhuman animals and that make an explicit contrast between human and animal existence. Animal existence represents a pathological and alienated version of human life, radically divided from fulfilled (non-alienated) human experience by virtue of what it lacks. By using the contrast between humans and other animals to explain alienation, Marx suggests that the concept is by definition inapplicable to animals. Several contemporary thinkers, however, have pointed to the possibility of using alienation to explain certain features of nonhuman life as well. Barbara Noske argues that all four types of Marxian alienation can be experienced by nonhuman animals and can illuminate the plight of animals under oppressive human regimes. Alienation is especially relevant to animals who labor in exploitative institutions such as factory farms, research laboratories, and circuses. Like humans, these animals are estranged from their products, their productive activity, and their fellow animals. Even battery hens and veal calves have natural behaviors that can be suppressed. Animals can also experience alienation from surrounding nature, as a result of being forced to live in sterile and artificial environments.

Marx's model also suggests that animals can be alienated from their species-being. Species-being has usually been taken as an exclusively human category, but it can be helpful for thinking about nonhuman animals if we define humanness not as the opposite of animal life but rather as "everything that makes humans human, that is: both the continuity and the discontinuity between humans and animals."[21] Under this revised notion of species-being, humans are animals living amidst other animals, with similarities and relationships as well as unique traits. Each species is distinctive in its own characteristic way, and each has a *Gattungswesen*, a characteristic life-activity, of its own. For humans, species-being includes connections to other animals and nature in general. This totality of relationships, including relations with nature and animals as well as with other people, breaks down in capitalist processes of production.[22]

The most severe forms of alienation are experienced by the proletariat, a class so degraded that it represents a "dissolution of all classes," such that the wrong done to it is wrong in general. From every vantage point, this group occupies the bottom rung. Its exploitation is so universalized that it can redeem itself only by redeeming society in general. No moderate reforms, no tinkering with the existing system, can liberate the classless class. Only a comprehensive revolution in ideas, practices, and social structures can effect the necessary improvement. This revolution is made simultaneously necessary and possible by the fact that the proletariat both demands the negation of private property and at the same time already is this negation.[23]

Nonhuman animals are the proletariat of environmental thought: the perpetual poor relation in both environmental and social ethics, they demand and embody the negation of human exceptionalism. Their demand, like that of the proletariat, comes from the fact that only this negation can liberate them. Proletarians embody the negation of private property because they exist without it. Nonhuman animals embody the negation of human exceptionalism in similarly concrete form, by living their own exceptional lives. Each species is exceptional by its own lights. The mouse eats the farmer's seeds and the hawk hunts the mouse. Mouse and hawk both give the lie to human self-importance by pursuing their own goods as though they matter. They reveal, paradoxically, the fact that human goods are not all that matter. Even though our hierarchies are not the only ones, they are the dominant and most destructive ones. The fetishism of our own specialness, no less than the fetishism of capital, has caused immeasurable suffering and death.

Practice, Labor, and Play

The link between alienation and labor in regard to nonhuman animals comes through Marx's concept of natural being. In contrast to species-being, which he sees as only human, Marx describes natural being as a "suffering, limited, and conditioned" existence that humans share with other animals.[24] As natural beings, people are identical to their activities, meaning that they do not distinguish themselves in their imaginations from what they are doing and are controlled by natural forces. For Marx, natural powers serve as the basis for species powers and retain the possibility of becoming species powers, if and when they are exercised in distinctively human ways.[25] The relationship between natural and species powers is thus a continuum rather than simple opposition. If natural and species powers are not mutually exclusive, and if natural powers are shared by humans and other animals, then nonhuman animals might possess species powers, by Marx's own definitions. He already admits that both natural and species powers can involve activities that are not unique to humans. The difference lies not in the activity itself as much as in the meaning attached to it. The defining human activity is labor, which is both a species and a natural power. What distinguishes labor as a natural power from labor as a distinctively human species-activity is creativity and self-consciousness. If nonhuman animals engage in creative, free, self-conscious activity, the species line begins to blur.

In labor, "we make ourselves collectively and individually in a constant interaction with all that has not yet been humanized," as Donna Haraway notes.[26] Such labor is a relationship. Free human praxis entails continual interaction between persons, between individuals and groups, and of creativity and power within an individual. One of the most important characteristics of free labor is that it includes its own intrinsic rewards, by expressing creativity and connecting people to each other, as well as meeting people's needs. Absent intrinsic rewards, capitalism offers external incentives (in the form of wages) and coercion, which further alienate the worker from the process of labor. Under capitalism, work is "not voluntary, but coerced; it is *forced labour*. It is therefore not the satisfaction of a need; it is merely a *means* to satisfy needs external to it." In this situation, "Life itself appears only as a means to life."[27] Labor becomes merely an instrument for earning wages, when it should be the deepest source of meaning and satisfaction. Work should also be thoroughly social, a contribution to a larger community, an appropriation of both natural and social resources, and a mediator of human relations to other people and to nature, instead of a force dividing people from each other. Labor, in sum, constitutes the fundamental human condition. As such, it ought to be an expression of human identity, power, sociability, and creativity.

Marx and subsequent Marxists have defined labor as uniquely human. Marx writes in the *Economic and Philosophical Manuscripts* that with the alienation of labor, "man (the worker) no longer feels himself to be freely active in any but his animal functions—eating, drinking, procreating, or at most in his dwelling and in dressing-up, etc.; and in his human functions he no longer feels himself to be anything but an animal. What is animal becomes human and what is human becomes animal."[28] When work is merely a means to satisfy physical needs, it lacks the features that make it both distinctively human and nonpathological; it becomes animal-like and alienated. Marx believed that animals undertake activities to meet their needs purely in mechanistic, unthinking, non-intentional, and inflexible ways; when humans are forced into this condition, it is unnatural, the result of exploitative and alienating social conditions.

However, labor may be open to a less species-bound definition, if we substitute for the dualism between human and animal the contrast between healthy and alienated forms of life. The latter distinction enables us to ask whether any nonhuman activities fulfill the conditions for distinctively human labor—free, creative, social, and intrinsically satisfying. Research on animal behavior shows that Marx, along with most other Western thinkers, seriously underestimated the complexity and flexibility of much nonhuman activity. We now have abundant, rigorously documented evidence that all sorts of nonhuman animals perform complex behaviors in which they not only appropriate resources to meet their needs but also make and use tools to adapt to changing material circumstances and shifting social contexts, communicate their desires and intentions, and establish partnerships and coalitions to accomplish their goals. All animals, wild and domestic, have species-specific ways of meeting their needs, and all require particular social and environmental conditions to be able to do so with freedom and creativity. Under other conditions, they may still meet their physical needs but not express the mental, social, and emotional powers entailed in a fuller understanding of labor.

Some of the most fascinating research documents animal play, which sheds light on the distinctive features of work as well. Ethologists define play as intrinsically rewarding (autotelic) behavior that, unlike work, is not "functional."[29] Marx's definition of labor involves elements of both work and play, since it is both a functional way to meet needs and an intrinsically rewarding way to express creativity and connect to other people. Many things that animals do also blur the boundaries between work and play. Animals frequently perform the behavior involved in work in "non-work" situations—they explore, wrestle, chase, hide, dig, and manipulate their habitats even when they are not meeting any practical needs. Predators, for example, play by stalking imaginary prey or teasing prey animals whom they have no intention of actually catching. To distinguish between play and work in such instances, mere descriptions of an animal's behavior are inadequate, since the same physical behavior can have different meanings in different contexts. Are the head-butting rams fighting or playing? Is the cat stalking a bird or a leaf? A similar ambiguity characterizes much human activity. Are the children rolling together on the ground fighting or playing? Is the woman measuring ingredients in the kitchen practicing her hobby or engaged in domestic drudgery? Without knowing about intentions, mood, and relationships, we cannot categorize a particular activity as play, work, or aggression.[30] Similarly, merely observing a laborer's actions does not tell us, in Marxian terms, whether the worker is alienated or not, or in what ways.

Like humans, other animals do not labor only on their own behalf. For thousands of years, humans have established partnerships with working dogs and horses to hunt, to guard and herd sheep and cows, and to engage in military conflicts. More recently, dogs have been trained to guide blind people, to warn of impending medical crises, to provide therapy for people with emotional or physical disabilities, and to sniff out not only drugs and bombs but also melanomas, invasive species, the scat of endangered animals, and even peanuts (for children with severe allergies).[31] These animals do not work blindly, pathologically, or under compulsion. They cannot perform their jobs without thoughtful engagement and a large degree of freedom. A service dog, for example, must practice "intelligent disobedience," when human knowledge fails regarding, for example, whether a road is safe to cross or a seizure is over. The dog must first gather information that may be unavailable even to nondisabled humans. While most people can see a car coming, none can predict the onset of a seizure. Then the dog uses that information, her prior training and experience, and her own intelligence to make the right decision. The dog's rewards are intrinsic—the protection of the partner and the continuation of the partnership and the work.

Similar processes are at work when humans and animals play together, as Haraway describes in relation to agility trials, in which the dog's chief reward is the run itself.[32] The same is true for the terrier in pursuit of a rat, the collie gathering sheep, and the retriever finding fallen ducks. It may also be true for the quarter horse cutting cattle or the thoroughbred running full-out. Like human work, these activities can be exploitative; they can use the animals' energy, skill, and courage in purely instrumental ways. A dog or horse, like a human, may come to hate an activity that was once pleasurable. (Is the woman in the kitchen enjoying her hobby or shackled to her stove?) The specific abilities of domestic animals are products of a particular evolutionary history and genetic makeup, but so are the human capacities for language, music, art, and sport. People do not talk, sing, paint, or play ball only on demand, any more than dogs retrieve or herd, or horses run, only to satisfy the whim of another. As Yi-Fu Tuan notes, "work presumes necessity, play freedom."[33]

Animals, like people, excel at particular kinds of play because they are intrinsically satisfying and even necessary expressions of their species-being. This is why trainers often say that a given dog or horse is the type who "needs a job" in order to be happy and healthy. Even when the work is as serious as saving a life, it can bring deep joy. Animals, no less than people, must be able to express their species powers in order to live full, unalienated lives. A border collie's species powers differ not only from those of a human being but also from those of a terrier. However, there is just as much difference between a satisfying and unsatisfying life for a border collie or a terrier, or a horse, dolphin, or bat, as there is for a human being. It is as incoherent to say that a suffering dolphin is living "like a human" as it is to say that an alienated person is living like an animal.

Alienation is a loss of what really matters, for a dolphin, a dog, or a human being. It involves the breakdown of the relationships that make a practice, or a life, valuable. The connections between alienation, value, and relationship unfold in Marx's discussion of the commodity. Every commodity, for Marx, has two types of value—exchange-value and use-value. Exchange-value is linked to price, while use-value is based on a commodity's capacity to fulfill the purpose for which it was intended.[34] Both kinds of value are factors of relationships, but the relations that determine exchange are abstract, functions of the "market," while human practices endow an object with use-value.

In capitalism, as under most other regimes, animals are treated as commodities. They are property, and their usefulness to human beings determines their value. In capitalism, this value is exhausted by the categories of use and exchange. Their worth, in other words, comes from their practical utility to others (as workers, food, etc.) or from their reification into property that can be bought or sold. Exchange-value is a kind of alienation, made possible because the properties and powers of real living individuals are transferred to an abstraction created by humans—in this case, money. Money is an abstraction, rooted like all abstractions in real human activities. "The extent of the power of money is the extent of my power," Marx explains. "Money's properties are my properties and essential powers—the properties and powers of its possessor. Thus, what I *am* and *am capable* of is by no means determined by my individuality. I am ugly, but I can buy for myself the most *beautiful* of women. Therefore I am not *ugly*, for the effect of *ugliness*—its deterrent power—is nullified by money." This power, however, is always derivative. The real source of all power is human creativity and practice; money derives its apparent "divine power" by alienating human abilities.[35]

The money economy recognizes only exchange- and use-value, which cannot make sense of the relationships between humans and companion animals. They categorize active subjects, human and other, as commodities or tools. Use- and exchange-value do not encompass the sort of property that Haraway describes: "the living, breathing, rights-endowed, doggish bit of property sleeping on my bed."[36] Since "Marx always understood that use- and exchange-value were names for relationships," we need another category to describe the relationships between humans and companion animals. Haraway proposes "encounter value," which cannot be exchanged or used, but only experienced in and through relationship.[37] In encounter-value, relationships and practices have value in and of themselves, not for their usefulness to another. If we "assume *man* to be *man* and his relationship to the world to be a human one," Marx wrote, "then you can exchange love only for love, trust for trust, etc. . . . If you love without evoking love in return—that is, if your loving as in loving does not produce reciprocal love; if through a *living expression* of yourself as a loving person you do not make yourself a *loved person*, then your love is impotent—a misfortune."[38] One great gift of companion animals is that exchange- and use-value mean nothing to them. They make possible the good fortune—often more difficult between humans—of exchanging love only for love, trust only for trust.

Such encounters across species lines possess revolutionary potential. "Loving an animal," as Stephen Webb writes, "does violate species barriers, and it does provide an alternative expression to human relationships. It disturbs the speciesist assumption that only humans are worth loving."[39] It also disturbs the taken-for-granted beliefs that only humans can love and be loved, that we can live without loving anything outside our own species, that we cannot have and do not need other kinds of relationships. Relationships with companion animals also suggest an expanded conception of value, grounded on relationship itself. We understand value differently, as Haraway notes, in light of "the insight that to be a situated human being is to be shaped by and with animal familiars."[40] The animals that make us human are not, or not only, the distant wild creatures on which ecocentrists fix. Rather, we are made human in intimate, everyday relations with familiar animals. Our shared, mundane practices of work and play enable us to recognize and then to educate and expand our natural desire for a mixed community, for cross-species bonds, for better relationships with all aspects of nonhuman nature.

COMPANION ANIMALS AND NATURE ETHICS

Although Marx was not an ethicist, nor an animal or environmental advocate, his thought points toward an ethic that connects and accounts for both individual subjects and expansive processes and communities in nature. This link is made possible by the practices that create relationships and mediate between scales. Beginning with practices enables us to avoid forced choices between mutually exclusive, preestablished polarities, such as the familiar opposition between an ecological holism that subordinates individuals and an individualism that sees all forms of community as threatening and foreign. Attention to practice also makes evident the socially constructed nature of many definitions and boundaries, including the lines between wild and domestic, nature and culture, and human and animal—precisely the problematic dualisms that bedevil most attempts to value animals and nature together. We challenge these dualisms in and through our constant interactions with nature. We breathe, we eat and drink, we walk upon the earth, we wear clothes and live in houses built from natural materials. Nature is indeed our "inorganic body," and also, in Saint Augustine's evocative phrase, "the earth we carry."[41] Both images point to the connections of body and earth—not in dualistic opposition to heaven and soul, but as an affirmation of human life as natural, embodied, and relational.

Our relationships with nonhuman animals differ from encounters with landscapes, places, rivers, or trees.[42] Although experiences with nonsentient nature can be profound, they do not involve mutual engagement with other agents. Such encounters are possible only with individual subjects, not with "nature in general." This does not mean that only interpersonal relationships, and thus only individual creatures, have value. However, our relationships with individual animals are a distinctive and important form of engagement with nature. This includes domesticated animals, which most environmental thinkers do not "count" as nature. Further, our most common and intimate encounters with the more-than-human world are with companion animals, who receive virtually no attention from environmental philosophers. Even animal advocates usually think about domesticated animals only in relation to their exploitation and suffering at the hands of humans. There is no reflection on the "naturalness" of domesticated animals, on farms, feedlots, homes or shelters, on their relations to wild landscapes and creatures, or on what our encounters with them mean for our larger relationship to nature.

A number of environmental ethicists explicitly question not only the naturalness but also the moral significance of relationships with domesticated animals. For many ecocentric thinkers, human interactions with animals should engender awe and respect but not affection or close bonds, which is why wild animals are the paradigmatic and perhaps only kind of animals whom we should consider. To claim that humans can interact meaningfully with nonhuman animals diminishes the animals' wildness and otherness, the qualities that make them valuable and that define humans in opposition. "'Bonding' to animals," for Paul Shepard, "is a willful, Disneyish dream."[43] This denial of the possibility of relationship rests not only on a dualistic understanding of domestic and wild but also on an equally sharp dualism between humans and nature, undermining the ecocentrist claim to embed people in the environment.

Less frequently, some animal advocates also reject relationships with animals, as described in chapter 4. They maintain a principled commitment to justice and the elimination of harm but have no intimate engagement with real animals. Peter Singer asserts that his commitment to animal liberation rests not on affection for animals but merely a desire that they be "treated as the independent sentient beings that they are, and not as a means to human ends."[44] While Singer rejects Shepard's holism and his emphasis on wilderness, he agrees that humans' attitude toward animals should be one of respect rather than intimacy. This conviction is shared by a few other animal rights theorists and activists, who reject pet-keeping and other relationships with domestic animals as inherently exploitative.

Most animal advocates, however, and even many environmentalists, experience close, affectionate relationships with companion animals. Not many, however, explicitly connect these relationships with their larger attitudes toward nonhuman nature. Their love for particular animals seems entirely separate from their attitudes toward "the environment." Against this separation, Kathy Rudy asserts that "the greatest resource we have in the struggle for animal advocacy is the deep connections many of us form with other animals." The denigration of emotional ties to animals has negative practical consequences, including the prevention of strong links between commitments to animal and environmental advocacy and concrete practices of animal rescue and care. Rudy believes that "if everyone who ever cared about a specific dog or cat or bird could be persuaded to re-create and reexperience that love toward lots of different kinds of animals, the earth would experience an unprecedented change."[45]

Rudy's insight is important: emotional attachments, to humans and other creatures, have moral significance because they illuminate what we value and why, they motivate us to act, and they help us build communities with other people who share our commitments. To denigrate emotion and relationship, as many environmental and animal (and other) ethicists do, denies us access to the ways most people think about moral value. Rudy's ethic, however, remains undeveloped, in part because she does not connect it to more systematic reflections on the role of emotion and relationships in ethical theory. She thus fails to address a number of important advantages as well as weaknesses of a care-based ethic.

The removal of emotion from ethics is rooted in a healthy suspicion for the partiality and subjectivity of interpersonal bonds and priorities. Further, as feminists point out, not all relationships—among people or between people and animals—are equally admirable or healthy. The simple fact that a relationship exists does not guarantee emotional, psychological, or moral quality. Intimate relationships can include violence and exploitation as often as care and nurture. Human interactions with nature and animals contain inevitable imbalances of power. As Yi-Fu Tuan notes, such inequities are almost impossible to avoid in any sort of relationship, with other people, with nonhuman animals, or with natural landscapes. Power, he adds, "is subject to abuse."[46] This abuse is sometimes blatant, as in cases of slavery, domestic violence, vivisection, factory farming, or clear-cutting. Sometimes, however, abuse is mixed with genuine love. In such cases, as Tuan explains, "affection mitigates domination, making it softer and more acceptable, but affection itself is possible only in relationships of inequality. It is the warm and superior feeling one has toward things that one can care for and patronize." Further, "the word *care* so exudes humaneness that we tend to forget its almost inevitable tainting by patronage and condescension in our imperfect world."[47]

It is difficult, perhaps impossible, to maintain perfectly egalitarian relationships with human others; it is even harder with nonhuman animals. The moral dilemmas involved in any relationship, with people or with parts of the more-than-human world, should not be taken lightly. It is not necessary, however, to give up on emotion, relationships, and community as a result. We are social beings, and we need the society of other species as well as other people. As even Tuan notes, power is not inevitably abused.[48] To avoid abuse, or at least minimize the destructive effects of structural inequities in our relationships with nonhuman animals, we need to identify where value lies and the kinds of relationships we value. Socialist emphases on institutions, material forces, and historical context provide an important corrective and complement to the apolitical and parochial tendencies of some care ethics and also of some animal advocacy.

Political engagement and effectiveness pose distinctive challenges for both environmental and animal ethics. Relationships with and care for nature are often seen as emotional or aesthetic preferences rather than political issues. Animal advocacy, in particular, has been disconnected from larger political discussions and ideologies, in part because it often defines issues in terms of individuals: the animals, their abusers, and those who help them are all seen in isolation. To counteract this individualism, an emphasis on practices can underline the connections between animals and larger communities, both natural and social, and thus make it possible to think critically about the ways that animal advocacy is related to other political and moral agendas. There is a danger, however, if the focus on relationships leads to parochialism, as is the case in Nel Noddings's early work on care ethics, which made personal relationships not only a starting point but the entire scope of moral obligation.[49] As an explicitly political alternative, Sara Ruddick uses mothering to begin thinking about problems such as war, violence, and structural injustice. Ruddick argues that it is possible to construct a political ethic based on an expansive notion of "maternal protectiveness," in which mothers extend their care to their homes, neighborhoods, and beyond.[50] This political ethic expands care in a critical and systematic way, by identifying the structures that link diverse experiences, feelings, and relationships.

A politicized nature ethic can start with companion animals, the elements of nature with whom humans are privileged to establish intimate relationships. "Spending time with companion animals: dogs and cats, for example, or dwarf hamsters and snakes," can nurture an ethic of care for nature and wild animals, according to theologian Jay McDaniel. Empathy and care for larger aspects of nature, he suggests, begin "with the knowledge of the life of an animal 'other' with whom we are in daily relationship."[51] Domesticated animals are not enemies of nature but rather aspects of it with unique connections to human society. Rather than dismiss or simply exploit that closeness, we can use it as a doorway to more positive interactions with nonhuman nature as a whole. We begin at home, but cannot stop there. A better nature ethic has to help us think about and relate to a wide variety of nonhuman others, including both the cat who sleeps on our bed and the feral colony at the edge of town; the owls who nest in our neighborhood and the chickens that our neighbors eat; the mouse chewing wires in the attic and the squirrel living in a city park; the threatened baby seals pictured on fund-raising letters and the equally threatened gopher tortoises whose homes are bulldozed in a new suburb. A nature ethic must also take account of the ecological communities and processes in which all these creatures, as well as all humans, are embedded.

Companion animals open new ways of thinking about nature because their very existence challenges the boundaries that undergird dominant theories about humans, animals, and the environment. In contrast to common ecocentric views of domesticated animals as the opposite of nature, we can see companion animals as "a sign of the inextricable intermingling of the human and the animal world."[52] They show that taken-for-granted theoretical dualisms—between humans and animals, nature and culture, home and wilderness, and love and utility—collapse in actual practice. Pets are boundary breakers—animals out of place, living in our homes, given individual names, treated as members of families. By their very nature, as Erica Fudge explains, pets "challenge some of the key boundaries by and in which we live and thus they cannot provide ontological security, but instead undermine it."[53]

Among the certainties undermined by pet-keeping are rules for treating nonhuman animals. The contrast between our treatment of pets and our treatment of most other animals, domestic and wild, can make "the constructed character of all animal categories more visible," as Katherine

Grier puts it.[54] The expectation that people will act with kindness and affection to companion animals, which Grier calls "the domestic ethic of kindness," calls into question our interactions with other kinds of animals. This points back to the question raised by animal rights advocates: why do people love animals called pets and eat animals called meat? In relation to environmental philosophy, we might also ask, for example, why we value animals called wild and kill animals called exotic or feral. These terms have nothing to do with the animals' own subjective experiences, capacities, or desires and everything to do with the context in which they relate to humans. Human-centered institutions and experiences define not just the meaning but also the life expectations of virtually all animals, domestic and wild alike. Rather than setting companion animals in an entirely different category, Grier proposes, we might view pet-keeping as "one part of the larger narrative of our relations with other sentient beings generally."[55]

THE FAMILIAR WOLF, REDUX

Critical thinking about companion animals can help us understand, and perhaps begin to reshape, our relations with other animals and other elements of the more-than-human world. Dogs offer a unique window into this world. As the animals who have been longest and most fully domesticated, they have served as spirit mediums in a number of cultures, including Egypt and pre-Buddhist China, where "dogs embodied familiarity and proximity between the human and animal world. They lived on the threshold of the realms of the living and the dead, and their mediating role between the domestic world and the world outside is well attested."[56] Similarly, in Australia, "The dingo inhabits two worlds simultaneously—the natural and the supernatural, the culturally constructed cosmos and the untamed wilderness."[57] No animal crosses the border between nature and culture as easily, as often, or as variably as the domestic dog, *Canis lupus familiaris*.

Dogs are not only the animal who lives most intimately with humans but also the only large predator who has been domesticated. They live peaceably in our homes in part because artificial selection has dulled or refocused the prey drive, to varying extents in different breeds and individuals. Thus hounds track and corner their prey but do not kill; collies nip and harass sheep but must never take a serious bite; retrievers bring back dead birds (or tennis balls) using mouths "softened" by artificial selection. In greyhounds, terriers, and a few other types of dogs, selective breeding has not dampened the prey drive but heightened it. Responsible greyhound rescuers do not adopt out their dogs to homes with cats or other small pets, because all it takes is the promise of a chase for an otherwise tranquil couch potato to remember that she is one of the fastest land predators around.

Terriers are dogs developed to find and kill rodents and other small animals deemed "vermin." The term *terrier* comes from *terre*, earth, reflecting their habit of taking the hunt underground when necessary. While many hounds, retrievers, and other hunting dogs specialize in a particular type of prey and sometimes show no interest in other animals, terriers often have a catholic taste for most small animals. They are not sporting dogs, bred to accompany humans on recreational outings, but working dogs. The hound has only to show the human hunter the prey's location, and the retriever or spaniel simply brings back the animal the hunter has shot, but the terrier works independently, locating, chasing, and killing unwelcome creatures without human supervision or assistance. It is important to remember that all animals are individuals and that prey drive varies widely even within a breed type. Some golden retrievers chase and kill cats, while some Jack Russell terriers live alongside them. While the peaceable terrier shows that all dogs are individuals, the hunting golden retriever reminds us that even dogs stereotyped as gentle family companions are still the descendants of wolves. Both reveal the paradoxes involved in domesticating a large, powerful predator.

Based on their long and intensive interaction with our species, dogs have a unique ability to read human meanings, intentional and not. Recent scientific studies have confirmed that dogs, apparently alone among nonhuman species, follow the human gaze, gaining as much information from us as from the physical world around them. They interpret not just human language but signals too subtle for other people to read—signs of an impending epileptic seizure, a blood sugar crisis, a dangerous tumor. They know us better than ourselves, in some respects. Dogs remind us—if we listen—that the animals we take into our lives and homes are independent subjects with preferences and desires that sometimes coincide with ours, and with the ability to influence us just as we influence them.

Although the balance of power is never equal in cross-species relationships, they need not be instrumental or abusive. Relations with companion animals, those whose agency we are most likely to acknowledge, raise the question, as Kathy Rudy puts it, of "When and under what circumstances do we get our relationships with animals 'right,' and how can those examples serve as a model for treatment of other animals?"[58] In other words, the fact that we have some respectful, loving encounters with animals points to possibilities for other interactions with nonhuman nature. This parallels Bill Jordan's argument that ecological restoration shows the possibility of a positive relationship to wild landscapes, a break from the "unrelieved negativity about the future of natural landscapes" that is common to much environmental thought.[59] At the same time, as Jordan emphasizes, in even our most intense interactions—the reconstitution of a damaged ecosystem, the intensive collaboration entailed in training—nonhuman nature remains outside our complete grasp. Dogs lead us to the edge of wild nature but never fully across the threshold, not unlike Pablo Neruda's dog, mentioned in the epigraph to this book, waiting in a heaven that his human partner will never enter.[60]

Our intimacy does not make dogs into humans, or even into perfect companions who always respond as we would wish. Dogs are capable of acting in ways that remind us of their wildness, most obviously in cases of aggression or predation but also in less dramatic encounters. They show us not only that they are not simply four-legged human beings but also that they are individuals who, like each person, negotiate differently the social and ecological networks in which they are embedded.

As individuals and as species-beings, dogs raise crucial philosophical questions: "Can the closeness of dogs enable us to see their very otherness? Can their similarity shed light on difference? Can dogs be both our 'best friends' and an intrusion of something persistently other, demanding respect and attention on their own terms? Are they more than what we need from them?"[61] What, in other words, do dogs tell us about the world beyond our species? After all these years, they remain boundary creatures, not so much between the living and the dead, for most contemporary Westerners, but between human society and wilderness. Too often we forget one side or the other.

Dangerous Dogs and Pit Bull Ecologies

Certain versions of *Canis lupus familiaris*, especially very small, very fluffy, or very neotenous dogs, do seem to be human artifacts, so radically do they differ from their wolf ancestors. However, other types of dogs, including those often called "dangerous," retain clear connections to their wild and predatory heritage. Diane Antonio makes this point in passing, when she notes that her interest in wolves "began, not with an encounter with an individual wolf, although I have observed a wolf pack in captivity, but as a result of my acquaintance with an admirably wolf-like canine, an American pit bull terrier."[62] What Antonio finds admirably wolf-like about pit bulls[63] is the promise of wildness lurking just below the surface. This wildness is present in every dog, "the wolf in the parlor," as a recent popular book pronounces.[64] Pit bulls and other dogs considered "dangerous" are special, however, if only in the meanings we give them.

Of my four dogs, two are pit bulls and one a pit bull–type mix. One of these, Tozi, has the most impeccable domestic manners of perhaps any dog I have met. We first met her at the Alachua County (Florida) Humane Society, where I had taken my youngest son, Rafael, then three years old, to play with the cats. At the time, we had two elderly and infirm dogs, had lost a third old dog not long before, and were not actively seeking to adopt another dog. We saw Tozi when a volunteer brought her to the play yard just as we were leaving the building. Breaking all the rules for approaching a strange dog, Rafael ran over and took a toy from her mouth. She wagged her tail and licked his face. A few days later, we brought her home. That same day, our friend Nick brought his two-year-old son Reuben to visit, not knowing we had a new dog. Upon entering the house, Reuben barreled into Tozi, knocking her over. She wagged her tail and licked his face.

Tozi's unfailing good manners extended to her interactions with our old, sick, and often cranky dogs. She never raced fifteen-year-old Inti to the tennis balls we threw for him, but instead waited as he hobbled painstakingly toward his treasure. She never took toys or treats from him or our other old dog, Balo, even though she was much stronger and faster. She cuddled next to Inti on his bed all winter, and when both dogs died (two weeks apart, almost exactly a year after we had adopted Tozi), she lay in the doorway and did not eat her dinner.

Tozi continues to be a paragon of canine etiquette. She has passed both the Canine Good Citizen and American Temperament Testing Society tests of obedience and temperament, baseline standards for therapy and service dogs. She visits schools, libraries, and various public events to teach children about dog safety and to be a "reading dog." She is particularly fond of children, from whom she accepts high-pitched screams as well as overly enthusiastic pats and bearhugs. Her protective instincts also focus on children; she twice chest-butted a beagle who was jumping on Rafael at a local dog park. Her fondness for children and tolerance for roughhousing echoes the history of pit bull–type dogs, who were called "nanny dogs" in the nineteenth and early twentieth centuries.

Against both those who demonize pit bulls and those who believe that "it is all in how they were raised," it is important to note that Tozi's unfailing courtesy is not the result of careful early nurturing by responsible human guardians. Her previous owner left her and her four puppies at our county shelter. Despite her instincts for domesticity, she did not appear to have lived inside a house before we adopted her. In addition, she is missing a few teeth, just below a long scar on her muzzle, likely caused, according to our veterinarian, by a human blow or kick.

Tozi is completely gentle with humans and firm but polite with other dogs, as befits her confident leadership style. As discussed in chapter 1, she is also a coldly efficient killer of smaller animals. She does not chase squirrels for fun; she knows she cannot catch them amidst all the trees in our yard and leaves them to our other pit bull, Boomer, whose prey drive is more about play than deadly serious business. Boomer lives for the chase, and will take it vertical if needed; he has climbed trees in search of raccoons. Once he catches his unhappy prey, however, he remembers that he is a well-trained domestic pet and responds promptly, if not enthusiastically, to a command of "leave it." He has twice caught and "left" opossums, who stop playing dead and hurry off as soon as he leaves the scene. Tozi does not leave her victims alive, and despite her willing obedience in almost all other matters, it is useless to suggest that she "leave" her prey. She will, however, let toddlers remove cookies from her mouth without a protest and usually gives them a kiss afterwards.

Tozi is, as Lévi-Strauss might say, good to think with. She embodies, in sleek brindle form, the paradoxes of nature and culture, danger and domesticity, wilderness and home. The puzzles are resolved by Tozi herself. She knows who is prey and who is family. She knows when to ask politely for dinner (by nuzzling my hand, licking my elbow, dancing a bit on her white-toed feet), and she knows when she can outrun dinner. She is not driven by blind instinct; she negotiates her territory, her relationships, and her desires with intelligence, creativity, and bulldog persistence.

This ability to discriminate lies at the heart of the human fascination with dangerous dogs. Their appeal comes precisely from their paradoxical nature. They are dangerous; they can kill a man; yet their power can be harnessed by certain people for their own purposes, which may be self-protection, self-esteem, or even another kind of predation. The essence of the human-dog bond, as Karen Delise proposes, lies in the fact that

> dogs will exhibit or inhibit natural canine behaviors in service or defense of those with whom they have formed attachments. In fact, the dog is the only animal in the world which can be expected to attack another being in defense of the humans with whom they have formed

a bond. This behavior is one of the cornerstones on which thousands of years of dog ownership and maintenance has been based. And implied in this relationship is the expectation and acceptance of canine aggression in certain circumstances.

Delise quotes Plato, who declared in *The Republic* that "the disposition of noble dogs is to be gentle with people they know and the opposite with those they don't know."[65] (In the case of terriers like Tozi, their disposition is to be gentle with humans and merciless with vermin.) It is when this capacity to discriminate goes awry, or is misused, that problems arise for humans and dogs alike. Often their human guardians encourage or force them to direct their protective instincts against the wrong people. On occasion the dogs themselves fail to discriminate properly between threatening and innocent humans. Human responsibility for the damage that dogs do is obvious in the former cases, but people are usually at fault when dogs attack indiscriminately as well. Dogs who attack humans, as Delise documents, have almost always been abused, neglected, and socially isolated. They have not learned to trust people and to relate to them properly as companion animals. (Remarkably, even most dogs who are abused or neglected continue to treat humans with generosity and affection.)

Dogs' dangerousness is a factor of their relationships to us, not just in the present but over our long history together. Dogs are dangerous, to begin with, because ten, twenty, or a hundred thousand years ago our ancestors made friends with large predators. The pets who sleep in our beds still share virtually all their DNA with wolves. We have taken wild nature in one of its most powerful, predatory forms into our homes and created the most intimate of companions. This remarkable relationship carries equally extraordinary responsibilities. When we fail in these, we have dogs that we, or other people, fear. All dogs, but especially ones we label as "dangerous," reveal our ultimate inability to control wild nature or to escape from it. Our attempts to separate nature and culture, to oppose animals and humans, to exclude wilderness from the home, all fail in the presence of our favorite canid, who is simultaneously *lupus* and *familiaris*.

Every day, Tozi reminds me that nature lives not just in culture but inside our homes. She is living proof that individual animals, like individual humans, are shaped by context, including evolutionary history, personal biography, and social communities. At the same time, like all sentient creatures, she remains a unique individual whose subjectivity is never fully explained or exhausted by these contexts. In her complexity, she points to the best way to deal with nature, or animals, or people. This way begins with recognizing that, to paraphrase Thomas Nagel, there is something that it is like to be a pit bull. There is certainly something that it is like to be Tozi. We need to know this, and also to know that we will never fully grasp all that it means to be a pit bull in general or Tozi in particular. Our comprehension, like our power, is both limited and real. This power creates responsibilities and often inequalities, exploitation, and suffering. This suffering is made worse when we give up our efforts to understand or, worse, believe that there is nothing to understand.

Whoever knocked Tozi's teeth out presumably did not pause to consider her subjectivity in general or her particular thoughts or feelings at that moment; perhaps he did not believe she was capable of feeling or thinking anything. This person (statistically likely to be a man, although I do not really know) apparently did not reflect on the fact that her teeth could easily break his wrist or his ankle. Nor, I imagine, did he think about the most remarkable fact of all: she chose not to hurt him. She decided not to break her part of the domestic bargain, even when faced with human betrayal. Tozi reminds us that other animals, even the tamest ones, have not only physical power but also intellectual powers of discrimination and decision. Both are part of their wildness. That Tozi consistently chooses to use her strength not against a violent adult, nor even against the screaming toddler pulling her tail, but rather against a harmless lizard or mole in the backyard is the mystery of her subjectivity.

These facts, so crucial to dealing with the real and imaginary problems of dangerous dogs, also help us deal with other parts of the nonhuman world. Animals are others but not *the Other*. They are different from us, but not so different that we can never understand them: "The problem is that their difference is both distant and intimate."[66] The ethical response to this paradox is to seek neither separation nor identity but rather connection and relationship. This is infinitely easier with a pit bull than a wolf. Humble gratitude is the appropriate response.

MARX'S PIT BULL

In order to obtain full benefit from the potential of Marx's thought for nature and animals, we need to turn Marx on his head, as Marx himself did with Hegel. Such a change in perspective is made easier with the help of new conversation partners. I propose Tozi and her kind as Marx's new ally and goad. Darwin had his bulldog, Thomas Henry Huxley, a loyal and tenacious defender of the theory of evolution by natural selection. Friedrich Engels was sometimes called "Marx's Bulldog," for the same reason. What if Marx had, however, a companion who was not only stalwart and faithful, in a bulldoggy way, but who also had that terrier "something" that Vicki Hearne describes: "a sprightliness in the stance, some suggestion of the possibilities of tap dancing and vaudeville, some impish gleam in the eye"?[67] Terriers allow us to take nothing for granted, perhaps especially what we thought we knew about ourselves and about them. Anthropocentric prejudice is easy prey for a dog who does not hesitate to tackle a six-foot fence or a full-grown raccoon.

The impish terrier uncovers the tools to challenge human exceptionalism buried under Marx's modernist inheritance. First and most important is his conviction, against not only the Enlightenment but most of Western philosophy before and since, that theory takes root in practice and must always circle back to it. Marx insisted that thought should begin not with ideal categories but with real life, for "the first premise of all human history is, of course, the existence of living human individuals."[68] If we start with abstractions, we not only misread reality but make it impossible to challenge and ultimately change that reality. This was Marx's criticism of the young Hegelians, the preeminent idealists of his time, who mistakenly believed that by fighting ideas only with ideas, phrases with phrases, they were actually combating the real existing world.[69] Marx saw that only by rooting our theory in life itself can we correctly perceive ideas as expressions of real life, not determinants of it.

From this perspective, the chief problem with the animal rights–environmental ethics debate is that both sides seek resolution in theory, clinging to preestablished categories even when they fail to make sense of reality, insisting that categories such as *wild* and *domestic* are both separate and unproblematic even when faced with what Marx might call their sensuous intertwining. This intermingling is evident not only in interactions among animals but in the very bodies and lives of the many creatures who fall in between the categories upon which both animal and environmental ethics rely. Claire Palmer addresses this problem, at least in part, with her concept of a "contact zone" occupied by feral and opportunistic wild species, to whom we have limited responsibilities.[70] For Palmer, this in-between category makes it possible to maintain an ethic divided between wild and domestic. These liminal animals, however, are not the exceptions who prove the rule but rather the living subjects who reveal the fragility of the whole structure built upon the far from solid categories of wild and domestic, individual and whole.

Such in-between creatures rest, impatiently, at the heart of our troubled, complicated, and rich relationships with the more-than-human world. The dilemmas they present can only be resolved, as Marx reminds us, in concrete practice, as we move back and forth across the boundaries not only between ourselves and other animals but also between nature and culture. Companion species not only keep us company on this continual back and forth but in fact make it possible. They help us put our human imaginings in perspective, not by means of a disinterested, divine valuer but in and through their very interested, earthy embodiment of intimacy and otherness. By showing us—by *being*—wildness and family together, they point the way to possible reconciliations of the theoretical mysteries that trouble us. They remind us that our theory is useless if it cannot respond constructively to aspects of life that do not fit into established categories. Idealism presumes that abstract categories come first and then questions the reality that does not fit. A practice-based ethic, on the other hand, pushes us to question abstractions themselves and not to assume as a fact that which needs to be explained.[71] Instead of forcing reality into abstractions that are not rooted in actual experience, we must develop theories that make sense of real experiences, people, animals, and relationships. As Erica Fudge notes, when animals do not match our preconceptions, "it shows how frail our structures of thought are. Maybe animals are like us: maybe we're like them. Perhaps it is our categories themselves that give us our separation?"[72] This is precisely Marx's point: ideas that appear more true than actual experiences, people, and creatures are "an inverted world consciousness," the result of an "inverted world."[73] We can use Marx's own method and start with living nonhuman individuals as well.

Marx's insights provide powerful tools for understanding how categories of thought shape and are shaped by relationships and practices. The fact that he found it impossible, or at least unnecessary, to apply this critical thinking beyond the boundaries of his own species does not mean that we are similarly limited. "Of all philosophers," as Donna Haraway writes, "Marx understood relational sensuousness, and he thought deeply about the metabolism between human beings and the rest of the world enacted in living labor. As I read him, however, he was finally unable to escape from the humanist teleology of that labor—the making of man himself." Marx might have succeeded in escaping, Haraway suggests, had he brought companion species and the intimate intermingling of human and animal that they represent into his story. Had he done so, he might have reworked the categories of the natural and the social that presently hamper our understanding of humans, animals, and almost everything else.[74] This task may have been easier with a bull-headed terrier at his back.

Marx probably would not have looked to *Canis lupus familiaris* for help. However, dogs can be our partners in exploring the philosophical and moral questions surrounding animals, nature, and people. Like every creature, Tozi unites many supposedly antithetical qualities—in her case, tameness and wildness, independence and obedience, predation and domesticity, love and aggression, property and friendship. These are theoretical mysteries that can be resolved only in concrete practice. Tozi embodies these paradoxes because nature and nurture have made her so, and because they are not so paradoxical as we thought. Refusing to stay on her side of the fence, she leads us, again and again, across the boundary between human and more-than-human worlds.

NOTES

I. INTRODUCTION: ANIMALS AND NATURE

1. Stephen R. L. Clark, *The Nature of the Beast: Are Animals Moral?*, 112.

2. The "more-than-human" world is David Abram's phrase; see *The Spell of the Sensuous: Perception and Language in a More-Than-Human World*.

3. Wikipedia reports that the world record was set in 1862 by a terrier named Jacko, who killed sixty rats in less than three minutes, an average of 2.7 seconds per rat; see http://en.wikipedia.org/wiki/Rat-baiting.

4. Marti Kheel is one of the few scholars who use the term "nature ethics" to describe a theory that reflects on the value of both animals and ecosystems; see *Nature Ethics: An Ecofeminist Perspective*.

5. Donna J. Haraway, *When Species Meet*, 3.

6. Karl Marx, *The German Ideology, Part 1*, in Robert Tucker, ed., *The Marx-Engels Reader*, 154.

7. Karl Marx, "Theses on Feuerbach," in Tucker, ed., *The Marx-Engels Reader*, 145.

8. John Bellamy Foster, *Marx's Ecology: Materialism and Nature*, 1.

9. Important exceptions include the work of Ted Benton, especially *Natural Relations: Ecology, Animal Rights and Social Justice*, and, less systematically, Barbara Noske in *Beyond Boundaries: Humans and Animals*.

10. Mary Midgley, *Beast and Man: The Roots of Human Nature*, xxxiv.

11. Among the best critiques are Antonio Damasio, *Descartes' Error: Emotion, Reason, and the Human Brain*; Carolyn Merchant, *The Death of Nature: Women, Ecology, and*

the Scientific Revolution; and the work of Mary Midgley, especially *Beast and Man* and *Animals and Why They Matter*.

12. Claude Lévi-Strauss, *The Savage Mind* (Chicago: University of Chicago Press, 1968).

13. See Jennifer Howard, "Presses, Journals, and Meetings Buzz with Animal Studies," *Chronicle of Higher Education* (October 18, 2009); see http://chronicle.com/article/Presses-Journals-and/48805/.

14. Gail F. Melson, *Why the Wild Things Are: Animals in the Lives of Children*.

15. Aaron Katcher, "Animals in Therapeutic Education: Guides into the Liminal State," in Peter H. Kahn, Jr., and Stephen R. Kellert, eds., *Children and Nature: Psychological, Sociocultural, and Evolutionary Investigations*, 187, 188.

16. Hal Herzog, *Some We Love, Some We Hate, Some We Eat: Why It's So Hard to Think Straight About Animals* (New York: HarperCollins, 2010).

17. One of the founders of cognitive ethology is Donald Griffin, author of *Animal Thinking*, among other books. See also Marc Bekoff and Dale Jamieson, eds., *Readings in Animal Cognition*, as well as Bekoff's other writings.

18. This self-identification includes a wide variety of definitions of what "love" means. Feeling affection for either animals or nature does not guarantee particular kinds of practices. For example, some nature lovers drive ATVs through wilderness areas or hunt wild animals; some animal lovers eat meat or keep their cats or dogs outside all the time. To other nature or animal lovers, such practices express something very unlike love as they define it.

19. Bryan G. Norton, "Why I Am Not a Nonanthropocentrist: Callicott and the Failure of Monistic Inherentism." *Environmental Ethics* 17.4 (Winter 1995): 343. See also Andrew Light, "Methodological Pragmatism, Animal Welfare, and Hunting," in Erin McKenna and Andrew Light, eds., *Animal Pragmatism: Rethinking Human-Nonhuman Relationships*, 119.

20. Katherine C. Grier, *Pets in America: A History*, 23.

2. ANIMALS IN ENVIRONMENTAL PERSPECTIVE

1. Gary P. Nabhan and Stephen Trimble, *The Geography of Childhood: Why Children Need Wild Places*.

2. See Anna L. Peterson, *Being Human: Ethics, Environment, and Our Place in the World*, esp. ch. 2, for a fuller discussion of human exceptionalism in Western tradition.

3. Merchant, *The Death of God*.

4. Eugene C. Hargrove, *Foundations of Environmental Ethics*, 203.

5. Aldo Leopold, "The Land Ethic," in *A Sand County Almanac; with Essays on Conservation from Round River*, 239 (all citations for this work are from the 1970 reprint edition).

6. Leopold, "The Land Ethic," 239, 240.

7. Ibid., 238, 245, 262.

8. Ibid., 240.

9. J. Baird Callicott, "The Conceptual Foundations of the Land Ethic," in *In Defense of the Land Ethic*, 84.

10. Callicott, "The Conceptual Foundations," 87.

11. Good discussions of the various models in contention can be found in Donald Worster's history of ecology, *Nature's Economy: A History of Ecological Ideas*, 2d ed. (1994).

12. Callicott, "The Conceptual Foundations," 88–89.

13. J. Baird Callicott, "Animal Liberation: A Triangular Affair" (1980), in Eugene C. Hargrove, ed., *The Animal Rights/Environmental Ethics Debate: The Environmental Perspective*, 55.

14. Eric Katz, *Nature as Subject: Human Obligation and Natural Community*, 26–27.

15. Holmes Rolston III, *Environmental Ethics: Duties to and Values in the Natural World*, 191.

16. Rolston, *Environmental Ethics*, 176. Rolston presumably knows that lions live in the savannah, not jungles.

17. Ibid., 232.

18. See, for example, "'Birdbrain' No Longer Means 'Stupid,' Asserts Scientific Consortium," by Duke Medicine News and Communications (January 31, 2005); see www.dukehealth.org/health_library/news/8401.

19. Leslie Paul Thiele, "Evolutionary Narratives and Ecological Ethics," *Political Theory* 27.1 (1999): 6–38.

20. Paul W. Taylor, *Respect for Nature: A Theory of Environmental Ethics*, 51.

21. J. Baird Callicott, *Earth's Insights: A Multicultural Survey of Ecological Ethics from the Mediterranean Basin to the Australian Outback*, 189.

22. Thomas Berry, *The Dream of the Earth*, 87.

23. Christopher Manes (writing as "Miss Ann Thropy"), "Population and AIDS," *Earth First!* 7.5 (1987); see also Manes, "Technology and Mortality," *Earth First!* 7.1 (1986).

24. Arne Naess, "The Shallow and the Deep, Long-Range Ecology Movement," *Inquiry* 16 (973): 95–100; see www.ecology.ethz.ch/education/Readings_stuff/Naess_1973.pdf.

25. J. Baird Callicott, "The Metaphysical Implications of Ecology," in J. Baird Callicott and Roger Ames, eds., *Nature in Asian Traditions of Thought*, 60.

26. Arne Naess, *Ecology, Community and Lifestyle*, trans. and ed. David Rothenberg, 28.

27. Naess, *Ecology*, 167, 168, 169–70.

28. Val Plumwood, "Nature, Self, and Gender: Feminism, Environmental Philosophy, and the Critique of Rationalism," *Hypatia* 6.1 (Spring 1991): 15, 14.

29. Naomi Klein, "After the Oil Spill," *The Nation* (January 31, 2011): 11–18.

30. Callicott, "Animal Liberation: A Triangular Affair," 43.

31. Avner de-Shalit, *Why Posterity Matters: Environmental Policies and Future Generations*, 12.

32. Frank Fischer and Maarten A. Hajer, "Introduction: Beyond Global Discourse: The Rediscovery of Culture in Environmental Politics," in F. Fischer and M. Hajer, eds., *Living with Nature: Environmental Politics as Cultural Discourse*, 2.

33. Callicott, *Earth's Insights*, 212.

34. Bryan G. Norton, "Environmental Ethics and Nonhuman Rights," in Hargrove, ed., *The Animal Rights/Environmental Ethics Debate*, 86, 90.

35. Norton, "Why I Am Not a Nonanthropocentrist,"53.

36. Don E. Marietta, Jr., *For People and the Planet: Holism and Humanism in Environmental Ethics*, 16.

37. Marietta, *For People and the Planet*, 7.

38. Ben Minteer, "Beyond Considerability: A Deweyan View of the Animal Rights-Environmental Ethics Debate," in McKenna and Light, eds., *Animal Pragmatism*, 114; and Light, "Methodological Pragmatism," 129.

39. Willett Kempton, James S. Boster, and Jennifer A. Hartley, *Environmental Values in American Culture*, 95–96.

40. Kempton, Boster, and Hartley, *Environmental Values in American Culture*, 112.

41. Callicott, "Animal Liberation and Environmental Ethics: Back Together Again" (1989), in Hargrove, ed., *The Animal Rights/Environmental Ethics Debate*, 251.

42. See, for example, Ben A. Minteer, *The Landscape of Reform: Civic Pragmatism and Environmental Thought in America*.

43. Taylor, *Respect for Nature*, 55,13.

44. Ibid., 100.

45. Ibid., 286, 118.

46. Merchant, *The Death of Nature*, 69.

47. Karen Warren, "The Power and Promise of Ecological Feminism," *Environmental Ethics* 12.2 (1990): 128.

48. See, for example, Mary Daly, *Gyn/Ecology: The Meta-ethics of Radical Feminism* and Susan Griffin, *Woman and Nature: The Roaring Inside Her*.

49. Val Plumwood, *Feminism and the Mastery of Nature*, 35.

50. Ibid., 154.

51. Plumwood, "Nature, Self, and Gender," 20–21.

52. Max Oelschlaeger, *Caring for Creation: An Ecumenical Approach to the Environmental Crisis*, 13.

53. Kempton, Boster, and Hartley, *Environmental Values in American Culture*, 92.

54. Callicott, *Earth's Insights*, 234.

55. Sierra Club statement on religious partnerships, available at www.sierraclub.org/ej/partnerships/faith/.

56. James Gustafson, *A Sense of the Divine: The Natural Environment from a Theocentric Perspective*, 44.

57. Gustafson, *A Sense of the Divine*, 48 and 133.

58. E. Roberts, "Gaian Buddhism," in Allan Hunt Badiner, ed., *Dharma Gaia: A Harvest of Essays in Buddhism and Ecology*, 153.

59. See the essays in *Dharma Gaia* and another edited volume, *Buddhism and Ecology: The Interconnection of Dharma and Deeds*, eds. Mary Evelyn Tucker and Duncan Ryuken Williams, and the work of Rita Gross, Joanna Macy, Gary Snyder, among others.

60. See, for example, J. Baird Callicott and Michael P. Nelson, *American Indian Environmental Ethics: An Ojibwa Case Study*.

61. Richard Nelson, *Make Prayers to the Raven: A Koyukon View of the Northern Forest*, 242.

62. Nelson, *Make Prayers to the Raven*, 246.

3. ANIMAL ETHICS

1. Jeremy Bentham, *Introduction to the Principles of Morals and Legislation*, 2d ed. (1823), ch. 17, footnote; see www.econlib.org/library/Bentham/bnthPML18.html.

2. Jeremy Bentham, *Anarchical Fallacies*, art. ii, in *The Works of Jeremy Bentham* 2: 501.

3. Peter Singer, *Animal Liberation*, 5, quoting Bentham, *Introduction to the Principles of Morals and Legislation*. All references to Singer's volume are to the 1990 edition.

4. Singer, *Animal Liberation*, 7.

5. Ibid., 5.

6. Ibid., 20.

7. Ibid.

8. Immanuel Kant, *Foundations of the Metaphysics of Morals*, trans. L. W. Beck, 437.

9. Tom Regan, *The Case for Animal Rights*, xvi. All references to this work are to the 2004 edition.

10. Regan, *The Case for Animal Rights*, xvii.

11. Ibid., xviii, 356, 388.

12. Gary L. Francione, *Animals, Property, and the Law*, 5, 4.

13. Regan, *The Case for Animal Rights*, xxix.

14. Gary Steiner, *Animals and the Moral Community*, 101.

15. John Stuart Mill, "Utilitarianism," in *On Liberty and Other Essays*, ed. John Gray, 140.

16. Singer, *Animal Liberation*, 20.

17. Ibid., 21.

18. Callicott, *Earth's Insights*, 21.

19. Andrew Linzey, *Christianity and the Rights of Animals*, 82.

20. Linzey, *Christianity and the Rights of Animals*, 95.

21. Ibid., 97.

22. Stephen H. Webb, *On God and Dogs: A Christian Theology of Compassion for Animals*, 40.

23. Midgley, *Animals and Why They Matter*, 61.

24. Webb, *On God and Dogs*, 41.

25. Christopher Key Chapple, "Animals and Environment in the Buddhist Birth Stories," in Tucker and Williams, eds., *Buddhism and Ecology*, 131–48.

26. Singer, *Animal Liberation*, 5.

27. Farm Sanctuary describes its mission on its website, www.farmsanctuary.org. It uses the "If you love . . . " slogan in a number of materials and products promoting vegetarian and vegan eating, e.g., see www.vegforlife.org/IMAGES/ads/for_animals.pdf.

28. Bay Area Vegetarians, see www.bayareaveg.org/flyers/bav_animals.pdf.

29. On the "Butcher's Cat" campaign, see www.butcherscat.com/. See also the Vegetarian Society's main website for postcards and posters featuring the "butcher's cat," at www.vegsoc.org/page.aspx?pid=575.

30. Singer, *Animal Liberation*, 7.

31. For PETA's position statement, see www.peta.org/about/default.aspx.

32. Clare Palmer, *Animal Ethics in Context*, 5.

33. Regan, *The Case for Animal Rights*, 363.

34. Palmer, *Animal Ethics*, 6.

35. Singer, *Animal Liberation*, iii.

36. Kheel, *Nature Ethics*, 1.

37. Carol Gilligan, *In a Different Voice: Psychological Theory and Women's Development*, 28, 30, 32, 33.

38. Carol Gilligan, "Moral Orientation and Moral Development," in Eve Feder Kittay and Diana T. Meyers, eds., *Women and Moral Theory*, 23.

39. Gilligan, "Moral Orientation and Moral Development," 23.

40. Nel Noddings, *Caring: A Feminine Approach to Ethics and Moral Education*, 83.

41. Noddings, *Caring*, 86.

42. Nel Noddings, *Starting at Home: Caring and Social Policy*, 48.

43. Noddings, *Caring*, 3.

44. Lori Gruen, "Dismantling Oppression: An Analysis of the Connection Between Women and Animals," in Greta Gaard, ed., *Ecofeminism: Women, Animals, Nature*, 79.

45. Kheel, *Nature Ethics*, 226.

46. Carol J. Adams and Josephine Donovan, "Introduction," in C. Adams and J. Donovan, eds., *Animals and Women: Feminist Theoretical Explorations*, 7.

47. Susanne Kappeler, "Speciesism, Racism, Nationalism . . . or the Power of Scientific Subjectivity," in Adams and Donovan, eds., *Animals and Women*, 324, 344.

48. See, for example, Carol J. Adams, "Woman-Battering and Harm to Animals," in Adams and Donovan, eds., *Animals and Women*, and James Garbarino, "Protecting Children and Animals from Abuse: A Trans-Species Concept of Caring" (1998), in Josephine Donovan and Carol J. Adams, eds., *The Feminist Care Tradition in Animal Ethics*.

49. Adams and Donovan, "Introduction," in *Animals and Women*, 5.

50. J. J. Eldridge and J. P. Gluck, "Gender Differences in Attitudes Toward Animal Research," *Ethics and Behavior* 6.3 (1996): 239–56.

51. See, for example, Carol J. Adams, "Caring About Suffering: A Feminist Exploration" (1995), and Josephine Donovan, "Attention to Suffering: Sympathy as a Basis for Ethical Treatment of Animals" (1994), both in Donovan and Adams, eds., *The Feminist Care Tradition in Animal Ethics*.

52. Callicott, *Earth's Insights*, 207.

53. Rolston, *Environmental Ethics*, 239.

54. Webb, *On God and Dogs*, 51, 53.

55. Lisa H. Sideris. *Environmental Ethics, Ecological Theology, and Natural Selection*.

56. Jonathan Balcombe, *Second Nature: The Inner Lives of Animals*, 171.

57. Balcombe, *Second Nature*, 172.

58. Midgley, *Animals and Why They Matter*, 20.

59. Ibid., 29–30.

4. WILD ANIMALS

1. Callicott, "Animal Liberation: A Triangular Affair," 52.

2. Worster, *Nature's Economy*.

3. Charles Darwin, *The Origin of Species by Means of Natural Selection, or the Preservation of Favoured Races in the Struggle for Life*, 443.

4. Jonathan Weiner, *The Beak of the Finch: A Story of Evolution in Our Time*.

5. Darwin, *The Origin of Species*, 443.

6. Palmer, *Animal Ethics in Context*, 116.

7. Isabella Hatkoff, Craig Hatkoff, and Paula Kahumbu, *Owen and Mzee: The True Story of a Remarkable Friendship*.

8. Among the many stories about Tarra and Bella, see www.thebark.com/content/dogs-are-elephant%E2%80%99s-best-friends?page=2 and www.cbsnews.com/stories/2009/01/02/assignment_america/main4696340.shtml. On Maximus, see http://badrap-blog.blogspot.com/2010/04/elephant-saves-stray-houston-pit-bull.html. Maximus even has his own Facebook page: www.facebook.com/#!/pages/Maximus/104871389634.

9. Leopold, "The Land Ethic," 239.

10. Ibid., 253.

11. Ibid., 262.

12. Aldo Leopold, "Wilderness," in *A Sand County Almanac*, 276, 277.

13. Leopold, "Wilderness," 277.

14. Worster, *Nature's Economy*, 274, 287–88.

15. Rolston, *Environmental Ethics*, 58, 59.

16. Callicott, Review of Tom Regan, *The Case for Animal Rights*, in *In Defense of the Land Ethic*, 47.

17. Callicott, "Animal Liberation: A Triangular Affair," 47.

18. Ibid., 53.

19. Mark Sagoff, "Animal Liberation and Environmental Ethics: Bad Marriage, Quick Divorce," *Osgoode Hall Law Journal* 22.2 (1984): 297–307; reprinted in Michael E. Zimmerman, J. Baird Callicott, George Sessions, Karen J. Warren, and John Clark eds., *Environmental Philosophy: From Animal Rights to Radical Ecology* (1993 ed.), 92.

20. One of the few authors to advocate positive duties to wild animals is Joan Dunayer, whose book *Speciesism* (2004) criticizes Singer, Regan, and other prominent animal ethicists for failing to be consistent in their interpretation and application of species-equality. This book and Dunayer's earlier *Animal Equality: Language and Liberation* (2001) are not widely cited, and some of her positions—such as extending rights to insects—are rejected by even abolitionists within the animal rights movement; see www.animalrights.net/2002/joan-dunayer-on-steven-wise-and-peter-singer/. A more mainstream thinker, Martha Nussbaum, appears to call for some human intervention in wild nature when she advocates a "gradual supplanting of the natural by the just." Martha Nussbaum, *Frontiers of Justice: Disability, Nationality, Species Membership*, 399.

21. Regan, *The Case for Animal Rights*, xxxvii (ellipses in original).

22. Midgley, *Animals and Why They Matter*, 97.

23. Palmer, *Animal Ethics in Context*, 26.

24. Ibid., 6.

25. Ibid., 36.

26. Taylor, *Respect for Nature*, 100.

27. Ibid., 295.

28. Palmer, *Animal Ethics in Context*, 115.

29. Bill McKibben, *The End of Nature* (New York: Random House, 1989).

30. Joan Tronto, "Women and Caring: What Can Feminists Learn About Morality from Caring?" in Virginia Held, ed., *Justice and Care: Essential Readings in Feminist Ethics*, 110–11.

31. Tronto, "Women and Caring," 111.

32. Jane Goodall, *In The Shadow of Man* (1971 ed.), 239–40.

33. See, for example, B. Kenward, A. Weir, C. Rutz, and A. Kacelnic, "Tool Manufacture by Naive Juvenile Crows," *Nature* 433 (2005), available at http://users.ox.ac.uk/~kgroup/publications/pdf/weir_thesis.pdf#page=145; and B. Heinrich and T. Bugnyar, "Problem Solving in Ravens: String-Pulling to Reach Food," *Ethology* 111.10 (October 2005): 962–76, available at http://onlinelibrary.wiley.com/doi/10.1111/j.1439-0310.2005.01133.x/full.

34. Frans de Waal, *Good Natured: The Origins of Right and Wrong in Humans and Other Animals*, 210.

35. Eugene Linden, *Apes, Men, and Language* (New York: Penguin; rev. ed., 1981), 99.

36. Dorothy L. Cheney and Robert M. Seyfarth, *How Monkeys See the World: Inside the Mind of Another Species*, 102 ff.

37. Sherlyn Meinz, "Prairie Dogs: They Talk & Kiss!"; see www.alienlove.com/modules.php?name=News&file=print&sid=122. Con Slobodchikoff has

published widely on the basis of his groundbreaking research on prairie dog language; see, for example, "Cognition and Communication in Prairie Dogs," in Marc Bekoff, Colin Allen, and Gordon Burghardt, eds., *The Cognitive Animal: Empirical and Theoretical Perspectives on Animal Cognition*, 257–64.

38. Jane Goodall, quoted in Meinz, "Prairie Dogs: They Talk & Kiss!"

39. Balcombe, *Second Nature*, 28–29.

40. Robert L. Trivers, "Parental Investment and Sexual Selection," in B. Campbell, ed., *Sexual Selection and the Descent of Man, 1871–1971* (Chicago: Aldine, 1972); reprinted in Lynne D. Houck and Lee C. Drickamer, eds., *Foundations of Animal Behavior: Classic Papers with Commentaries*, 795–838.

41. William Hamilton, "The Genetical Evolution of Social Behaviour," parts 1 and 2, *Journal of Theoretical Biology* 7 (1964): 1–52; reprinted in Houck and Drickamer, eds., *Foundations of Animal Behavior*, 764.

42. Hamilton, "The Genetical Evolution of Social Behaviour," 765.

43. Ibid., 765.

44. Ibid., 778.

45. Ibid., 779.

46. De Waal, *Good Natured*, 24. See also Robert Trivers, "The Evolution of Reciprocal Altruism," *Quarterly Review of Biology* 46 (1971): 35–37.

47. See Charles Goodnight, "Evolution in Metacommunities," *Philosophical Transactions of the Royal Society B* 366.1569 (May 12, 2011): 1401–1409; abstract available at http://rstb.royalsocietypublishing.org/content/366/1569/1401.short.

48. Midgley, *Beast and Man*, 136.

49. Gordon M. Burghardt, *The Genesis of Animal Play: Testing the Limits*, 6.

50. Burghardt, *The Genesis of Animal Play*, 70–77.

51. Konrad Z. Lorenz, *The Foundations of Ethology*, trans. by Konrad Z. Lorenz and Robert Warren Kickert, 333–35.

52. Burghardt, *The Genesis of Animal Play*, 382–383.

53. Ibid., 7.

54. Ibid., 399.

55. Marc Bekoff, *Animal Passions and Beastly Virtues: Reflections on Redecorating Nature*, with a Foreword by Jane Goodall, 141.

56. Bekoff, *Animal Passions*, 142.

57. Ibid., 47; and Colin Allen and Marc Bekoff, "Intentionality, Social Play, and Definition," in Bekoff and Jamieson, eds., *Readings in Animal Cognition*, 229–30.

58. Jonathan Balcombe, *Pleasurable Kingdom: Animals and the Nature of Feeling Good*, 83.

59. Burghardt, *The Genesis of Animal Play*, 382–83.

60. Ricard Louv, *Last Child in the Woods: Saving Our Children from Nature-Deficit Disorder* (Chapel Hill, NC: Algonquin Books, 2005), 133.

61. "America's Great Outdoors," executive summary, p. 1; see http://americasgreatoutdoors.gov/files/2011/02/AGO-Executive-Summary-Text-Only-2-7-11.pdf.

62. "Obama: Outdoors More Precious Than Ever," *Environment News Service*, February 16, 2011; see www.ens-newswire.com/ens/feb2011/2011–02–16–092.html.

63. Anthony Weston, *Back to Earth: Tomorrow's Environmentalism*, 122; Wendell Berry, "Getting Along with Nature," in *Home Economics*, 13, 14.

5. Domesticated Animals

1. Stephen Budiansky, *The Covenant of the Wild: Why Animals Chose Domestication*, 50.

2. Budiansky, *The Covenant of the Wild*, 24.

3. See Edward O. Price, "Domestication and Behavior," in Marc Bekoff, ed., *The Encyclopedia of Animal Behavior*, 512.

4. Jennifer Viegas, "World's First Dog Lived 31,700 Years Ago, Ate Big," *Discovery News* (October 17, 2008); see www.msnbc.msn.com/id/27240370/.

5. Mietje Germonpréa, Martina Lázni ková-Galetováb, and Mikhail V. Sablinc, "Palaeolithic Dog Skulls at the Gravettian Predmostí Site, the Czech Republic," *Journal of Archaeological Science* 38.9 (2011): 2123–40; see www.sciencedirect.com/science/article/pii/S0305440311003499.

6. Ned Rozell, "Alaska Science Forum: Old Dogs, Alaska, and the New World" (December 29, 2010); see http://capitalcityweekly.com/stories/122910/out_763002290.shtml.

7. Temple Grandin, with Catherine Johnson. *Animals in Translation: Using the Mysteries of Autism to Decode Animal Behavior*, 305.

8. Marion Schwartz, *A History of Dogs in the Early Americas*, 2.

9. Budiansky, *The Covenant of the Wild*, 27.

10. David Brown, "Why Do Cats Hang Around Us? (Hint: They Can't Open Cans): Genetic Research Suggests Felines 'Domesticated Themselves,'" *Washington Post*, June 29, 2007; see www.washingtonpost.com/wp-dyn/content/article/2007/06/28/AR2007062802343.html.

11. Budiansky, *The Covenant of the Wild*, 15, 64.

12. Ibid., 64–65.

13. Bennett G. Galef, Jr., "The Making of a Science," in Houck and Drickamer, eds., *Foundations of Animal Behavior: Classic Papers with Commentaries*, 9.

14. There is some evidence that dogs, at least, do perform basic addition and subtraction; see Stanley Coren, "Do Dogs Know Mathematics?" *Psychology Today*; see www.psychologytoday.com/blog/canine-corner/201103/do-dogs-know-mathematics.

15. Roger Caras, *A Perfect Harmony: The Intertwining Lives of Animals and Humans Throughout History*, 247, 41.

16. Grandin, with Johnson. *Animals in Translation*, 305.

17. In some form or another, the proverb is at least 500 years old: "For want of a nail the shoe was lost. / For want of a shoe the horse was lost. / For want of a horse the rider was lost. / For want of a rider the battle was lost. / For want of a battle the

kingdom was lost. / And all for the want of a horseshoe nail." The story preaches that ignoring details can have disastrous consequences; the fact that it involves a horseshoe reflects the crucial role of horses to military and political endeavors.

18. Schwartz, *A History of Dogs*, 3, 4.

19. Caras, *A Perfect Harmony*, 19.

20. See, for example, Paul Shepard, *Coming Home to the Pleistocene*.

21. Paul Shepard, *The Others: How Animals Made Us Human*, 267.

22. Shepard, *The Others*, 267, 244.

23. Callicott, "Animal Liberation: A Triangular Affair," 53.

24. Hargrove, *Foundations of Environmental Ethics*, 196.

25. Rolston, *Environmental Ethics*, 83.

26. Shepard. *The Others*, 250. See also Rolston, *Environmental Ethics*, 79.

27. Callicott, "Animal Liberation: A Triangular Affair," 48.

28. Grier, *Pets in America*, 284.

29. Ibid.

30. Rolston, *Environmental Ethics*, 80.

31. Balcombe, *Second Nature*, 178.

32. Callicott, review of Tom Regan, *The Case for Animal Rights*, in *In Defense of the Land Ethic*, 46.

33. Regan, *The Case for Animal Rights*, xvi.

34. Ibid., xxxvii.

35. Carol J. Adams and Josephine Donovan, "Introduction," in Adams and Donovan, eds., *Animals and Women*, 6.

36. Grace Clement, "The Ethics of Care and the Problem of Wild Animals," in Donovan and Adams, eds., *The Feminist Care Tradition in Animal Ethics*, 304–305.

37. Noddings, *Caring*, 156.

38. Ibid., 157.

39. Grier, *Pets in America*, 10, 11.

40. Erica Fudge, *Pets*, 14.

41. It is possible to keep dogs healthy on a vegetarian diet, but cats are "obligate carnivores" who cannot obtain all the nutrients they need without animal products. It goes without saying that the issue of resource consumption by companion animals should be raised only by environmentalists who are themselves vegetarian, or better yet vegan, although it also goes without saying that such moral consistency does not in fact exist.

42. Midgley, *Animals and Why They Matter*, 31.

43. Shepard, *The Others*, 287.

44. James Hillman, "Let the Creatures Be," *Parabola* 8.2 (1983): 53, quoted by Kimberley Patton, "'Caught with Ourselves in the Net of Life and Time': Traditional Views of Animals in Religion," in Paul Waldau and Kimberley Patton, eds., *A Communion of Subjects: Animals in Religion, Science, and Ethics*, 36.

45. Interestingly, Linzey is ambivalent about spaying and neutering companion animals, which virtually all animal advocates consider essential to reduce the

overpopulation of dogs and cats in particular. He acknowledges the necessity of neutering but believes that the animals lose something in the process. Linzey, *Christianity and the Rights of Animals*, 136–37.

46. Yi-Fu Tuan, *Dominance and Affection: The Making of Pets*, 5.

47. Gary Francione, "Pets: The Inherent Problems with Domestication" (n.d.); see www.opposing views.com/arguments.pets-the-inherent-problems-with- domestication), quoted in Palmer, *Animal Ethics in Context*, 126. For similar arguments, see also Lee Hall, *On Their Own Terms: Bringing Animal-Rights Philosophy Down to Earth*.

48. Singer, *Animal Liberation*, ii.

49. Ibid., iii.

50. Sara Ruddick, *Maternal Thinking: Toward a Politics of Peace*, 79–80.

51. Sara Ruddick, "Maternal Thinking," *Feminist Studies* 6.2 (Summer 1980): 359, 361.

52. Kathy Rudy, *Loving Animals: Toward a New Animal Advocacy*. Minneapolis: University of Minnesota Press, 2011), 68.

53. Caras, *A Perfect Harmony*, 160. See also Webb, *On God and Dogs*, 3, 4; and Grier, *Pets in America*, 23.

54. See, for example, the selections in Bekoff and Jamieson, eds., *Readings in Animal Cognition*, and in Houck and Drickamer, eds., *Foundations of Animal Behavior*.

55. Barbara J. King, *Being with Animals: Why We are Obsessed with the Furry, Scaly, Feathered Creatures Who Populate Our World* (New York: Doubleday, 2010), 44. The review that King cites is Michael Korda, "Thundering Hooves," *Washington Post Book World*, July 13, 2008, 9.

56. Tuan, *Dominance and Affection*.

57. Fudge, *Pets*, 8.

58. Caras, *A Perfect Harmony*, 160.

6. The Debate Between Environmentalism and
Animal Advocacy

1. Norton, "Environmental Ethics and Nonhuman Rights," 86, 85.

2. Callicott, "Animal Liberation: A Triangular Affair," 46.

3. Rolston, *Environmental Ethics*, 225.

4. Katz, *Nature as Subject*, 16–27, 16.

5. Sideris. *Environmental Ethics, Ecological Theology, and Natural Selection*, 265.

6. Sideris, *Environmental Ethics*, 149 .

7. Ibid., 82.

8. Regan, *The Case for Animal Rights*, 361.

9. Ibid., 361–62.

10. Michael Zimmerman, "Ecofascism: An Enduring Temptation," in Michael Zimmerman et al., eds., *Environmental Philosophy: From Animal Rights to Radical Ecology*, 1.

Cited from version available online at www.colorado.edu/philosophy/paper_zimmerman_ecofascism.pdf.

11. Zimmerman, "Ecofascism" (online version), 18.

12. Ibid., 24.

13. Rolston, *Environmental Ethics*, 57.

14. Ibid.

15. Ibid., 219.

16. Callicott, *Earth's Insights*, 1.

17. This is especially true for angling. See Samuel Snyder, "The Rodman Standoff: A Dam Critique of Bioregionalist Politics of Place," paper presented at the First International Conference on Religion and Nature, Gainesville, Florida, April 7, 2006.

18. Gary Varner, *In Nature's Interests? Interests, Animal Rights, and Environmental Ethics*, 100–101.

19. Aldo Leopold, "Game and Wild Life Conservation" (1932), in Susan J. Armstrong and Richard G. Botzler, eds., *The Animal Ethics Reader*, 451–53.

20. Aldo Leopold, "Thinking Like a Mountain," in *A Sand County Almanac*, 138.

21. Light, "Methodological Pragmatism."

22. Jan Dizard, *Going Wild: Hunting, Animals Rights, and the Contested Meaning of Nature*, and Richard Nelson, *Heart and Blood: Living with Deer in America*. See also Mary Zeiss Strange, *Woman the Hunter*; James Swan, ed., *The Sacred Art of Hunting: Myths, Legends, and the Modern Mythos*; and David Petersen, ed., *A Hunter's Heart: Honest Essays on Blood Sport*, among many other examples.

23. Rolston, *Environmental Ethics*, 91.

24. Budiansky. *The Covenant of the Wild*, 161.

25. Shepard, *The Others*, 6.

26. Rolston, *Environmental Ethics*, 92.

27. Ibid., 93.

28. One example of this perspective is Howard Harrod, *The Animals Came Dancing: Native American Sacred Ecology and Animal Kinship*.

29. Regan, *The Case for Animal Rights*, 354–55.

30. Marti Kheel, "License to Kill: An Ecofeminist Critique of Hunters' Discourse," in Adams and Donovan, eds., *Animals and Women*, 111.

31. Rolston, *Environmental Ethics*, 93.

32. The topic merits its own Wikipedia page: http://en.wikipedia.org/wiki/Human_hunting.

33. Regan, *The Case for Animal Rights*, 354.

34. Varner, *In Nature's Interests?*, 119, 120.

35. Singer, *Animal Liberation*, 234.

36. For example, *Case Studies in Environmental Ethics*, by Patrick G. Derr and Edward M. McNamara, includes sections on feral cats in Australia and feral pigs in Hawaii, along with a number of other cases in which domesticated or feral animals threaten native wild ecosystems and species.

37. For more on ferals, see Roger King, "Feral Animals and the Restoration of Nature," *Between the Species* 9 (August 2009): 1–27, available at http://digitalcommons.calpoly.edu/bts/vol13/iss9/1; and Jo-Ann Shelton, "Killing Animals That Don't Fit In: Moral Dimensions of Habitat Restoration," *Between the Species* 4 (2004): 1–21, available at http://digitalcommons.calpoly.edu/bts/vol13/iss4/3.

38. See http://audubonmagazine.org/webstories/deer_birth_control.html.

39. Ed Boks, "Analysis of Feral Cat Solutions"; see www.edboks.com/uploads/Analysis_of_Feral_Cat_Solutions.pdf.

40. See www.abcbirds.org/newsandreports/releases/090601.html.

41. Cole C. Hawkins, William E. Grant, and Michael T. Longnecker, "Effect of House Cats Being Fed in Parks on California Birds and Rodents," *Proceedings of the 4th International Urban Wildlife Symposium* (2004), 168; see http://cals.arizona.edu/pubs/adjunct/snr0704/snr07042l.pdf.

42. Darcee Guttilla and Paul Stapp, "Effects of Sterilization on Movements of Feral Cats at a Wildland–Urban Interface," *Journal of Mammalogy* 91.2 (April 2010): 482–89; see www2.allenpress.com/pdf/mamm-91-02-482-489.pdf.

43. Varner, *In Nature's Interests?*, 111.

44. The most poignant example of this has occurred when matriarch elephants have been killed in parts of Africa where habitat has been reduced so sharply that elephant populations are encroaching on human farms and settlements. Elephants depend heavily on the older females to lead the group.

7. BETWEEN ANIMALS AND NATURE: FINDING
COMMON GROUND

1. Virginia Held, "Feminist Moral Inquiry and the Feminist Future," in Held, ed., *Justice and Care*, 165.

2. Callicott, "Animal Liberation and Environmental Ethics," 257.

3. Callicott, review of Regan, *The Case for Animal Rights*, in *In Defense of the Land Ethic*, 46, 47.

4. Clement, "The Ethics of Care and the Problem of Wild Animals," *Between the Species* 3 (2003); available at http://cla.calpoly.edu/bts/issue_03/03clement.htm.

5. Warren, "The Power and Promise of Ecological Feminism," 128.

6. Dale Jamieson, "Animal Liberation Is an Environmental Ethic," *Environmental Values* 7 (February 1998): 48.

7. Marti Kheel, "The Liberation of Nature: A Circular Affair," *Environmental Ethics* 7 (Summer 1985): 140.

8. Midgley, *Animals and Why They Matter*, 31, 144.

9. Norton, "Why I Am Not a Nonanthropocentrist," 343.

10. Minteer, "Beyond Considerability," 109.

11. Norton, "Why I Am Not a Nonanthropocentrist," 353.

12. Light, "Methodological Pragmatism," 121. See also Minteer, "Beyond Considerability," 98.

13. Light, "Methodological Pragmatism," 128.

14. Jamieson, "Animal Liberation Is an Environmental Ethic," 41.

15. Steiner, *Animals and the Moral Community*, 125.

16. Paul Taylor, "The Ethic of Respect for Nature," in Hargrove, ed., *The Animal Rights/Environmental Ethics Debate*, 95–96.

17. Taylor, *Respect for Nature*, 55.

18. Taylor, "The Ethic of Respect for Nature," 109, 118.

19. Taylor, *Respect for Nature*, 285, 286.

20. Jamieson, "Animal Liberation Is an Environmental Ethic," 52.

21. Callicott, "Animal Liberation and Environmental Ethics," 249.

22. Ibid., 251.

23. Ibid., 250.

24. Ibid., 255, 256.

25. Ibid., 254.

26. Ibid., 257.

27. Ibid., 256, 259.

28. Ibid., 257–58, 251, 259.

29. *Gaudium et Spes* (Pastoral Constitution on the Church in the Modern World), no. 32; see www.vatican.va/archive/hist_councils/ii_vatican_council/documents/vat-ii_cons_19651207_gaudium-et-spes_en.html.

30. John Howard Yoder, *The Politics of Jesus*, 2d ed. (1994), 134.

31. Jay McDaniel, "Practicing the Presence of God: A Christian Approach to Animals," in Waldau and Patton, eds., *A Communion of Subjects*, 139.

32. Gustafson, *A Sense of the Divine*, 44.

33. James M. Gustafson, *Ethics from a Theocentric Perspective* 1:96.

34. Callicott, *Earth's Insights*, 23.

35. Leopold, "The Land Ethic," 240.

36. Lynn White, Jr., "The Historical Roots of Our Ecologic Crisis," *Science* 155 (1967): 1206.

37. Midgley, *Beast and Man*, xxxiv, xxxv.

38. Ibid., 203, 206, xlii.

39. Donna J. Haraway, "Situated Knowedges," in *Simians, Cyborgs, and Women: The Reinvention of Nature*, 189.

40. Thomas Nagel, "What Is It Like to Be a Bat?" *Philosophical Review* 83 (1974): 435–50.

41. Alexandra Horowitz, *Inside of a Dog: What Dogs See, Smell, and Know*, 242–43.

42. Clifford Geertz, "From the Native's Point of View: On the Nature of Anthropological Understanding," in *Local Knowledge: Further Essays in Interpretive Anthropology*, 57.

43. René Descartes, "Discourse on Method," in *Philosophical Essays: Discourse on Method; Meditations; Rules for the Direction of the Mind*, trans. Laurence J. Lafleur, 42.

44. Descartes, "Discourse on Method," 43.

45. Grandin, with Catherine Johnson, *Animals in Translation*, 255.

46. Alison Gopnik, Andrew N. Meltzoff, and Patricia K. Kuhl, *The Scientist in the Crib: What Early Learning Tells Us About the Mind*, 13.

8. Being Animal

1. Marx, "Theses on Feuerbach," 145.

2. Anja Kollmus and Julian Agyeman, "Mind the Gap: Why Do People Act Environmentally and What Are the Barriers to Pro-environmental Behavior?" *Environmental Education and Research* 8.2 (2003): 241. See also James Blake, "Overcoming the Value-Action Gap in Environmental Policy," *Local Environment* 4.3 (1999): 257–78; and Matthias Finger, "From Knowledge to Action? Exploring the Relationships Between Environmental Experiences, Learning, and Behavior," *Journal of Social Issues* 50.3 (Fall 1994): 141–60.

3. David D. Laitin, "Religion, Political Culture, and the Weberian Tradition," *World Politics* 30.4 (July 1978): 571.

4. Juan Luis Segundo, *The Liberation of Theology*, 8.

5. Segundo, *The Liberation of Theology*, 81, 79.

6. Anthony Weston, "Non-Anthropocentrism in a Thoroughly Anthropocentrized World," *The Trumpeter* 8.3 (1991): 1; see http://trumpeter.athabascau.ca/contents/v8.3/weston.html.

7. Marx, *The German Ideology, Part I*, 154.

8. Karl Marx, "The Economic and Philosophical Manuscripts of 1844," in Tucker, ed., *The Marx-Engels Reader*, 76.

9. Karl Marx, *Capital*, vol. 1, in Tucker, ed., *The Marx-Engels Reader*, 344.

10. The "waggle dance" with which bees communicate the location of pollen sources was first identified by Nobel-winning entomologist Karl von Frisch, *The Dance Language and Orientation of Bees*. For a concise summary (and interesting application to human play), see Daniel A. Herms, "The Honeybee Waggle Dance: An Active Participation, Role Playing Game," *Entomology Note*, no. 22; see http://insects.ummz.lsa.umich.edu/MES/notes/entnote22.html.

11. Benton, *Natural Relations*, 2-3.

12. E. P. Thompson, *The Making of the English Working Class*, 9. See also Ollman, *Alienation*, 27–28.

13. Marx, "Theses on Feuerbach," 145.

14. Marx, "Economic and Philosophical Manuscripts of 1844," in *The Marx-Engels Reader*, 66–125.

15. Paul Tillich, *Love, Power, and Justice: Ontological Analyses and Ethical Applications*, 25.

16. Karl Marx, "Contribution to the Critique of Hegel's Philosophy of Right: Introduction," in Tucker, ed., *The Marx-Engels Reader*, 53.

17. Marx, *The German Ideology: Part I*, 160.

18. Marx, "Contribution to the Critique," 63.

19. Karl Marx, *The Economic and Philosophical Manuscripts of 1844*, ed. Dirk J. Struik (New York: International Publishers, 1964), 84.

20. Marx, "Economic and Philosophic Manuscripts of 1844," in *The Marx-Engels Reader*, 75.

21. Noske, *Beyond Boundaries*, 13.

22. Ibid.

23. Marx, "Contribution to the Critique," 64, 65.

24. Marx, *1844 Manuscripts*, quoted in Ollman, *Alienation*, 82.

25. Ollman, *Alienation*, 82–83, 86.

26. Donna J. Haraway, "Animal Sociology and a Natural Economy of the Body Politic," in *Simians, Cyborgs, and Women: The Reinvention of Nature*, 10.

27. Marx, "Economic and Philosophical Manuscripts of 1844," in *The Marx-Engels Reader*, 74, 76.

28. Ibid., 74.

29. Burghardt, *The Genesis of Animal Play*, 7–73.

30. Dale Jamieson and Marc Bekoff, "On Aims and Methods of Cognitive Ethology," in Bekoff and Jamieson, eds., *Readings in Animal Cognition*, 73–74.

31. See, among many examples, Elisabeth Parker, "Boy Allergic to Peanuts Has Dog to Sniff Out Danger," *Seattle Times* , June 19, 2011, http://seattletimes.nwsource.com/html/health/2015326438_peanuts20.html, and Julie Falconer, "On the Scent of Poachers: Rescued Dogs Help Game Wardens in the War Against Wildlife Criminals," *All Animals* (March–April 2010): 14–22.

32. Haraway, *When Species Meet*, 220.

33. Tuan, *Dominance and Affection*, 2.

34. See Marx, *Capital*, vol. 1, in *The Marx Engels Reader*, 303, and Ollman, *Alienation*, 100.

35. Marx, "Economic and Philosophical Manuscripts of 1844," in *The Marx-Engels Reader*, 103–104.

36. Haraway, *When Species Meet*, 45.

37. Ibid., 45, 46.

38. Marx, "Economic and Philosophical Manuscripts of 1844," in *The Marx-Engels Reader*, 105.

39. Webb, *On God and Dogs*, 81.

40. Haraway, *When Species Meet*, 47.

41. St. Augustine, *The City of God*, cited in L. Shannon Jung, *We Are Home: A Spirituality of the Environment*, 5.

42. Simon P. James, *The Presence of Nature: A Study of Phenomenology and Environmental Philosophy*, 42.

43. Shepard, *The Others*, 320.

44. Singer, *Animal Liberation*, ii.

45. Rudy, *Loving Animals*, 25, 68.

46. Tuan, *Dominance and Affection*, 4.

47. Ibid., 5.

48. Ibid., 4, 176.

49. Noddings wrote a follow-up book, many years later, which argued that personal relationships can and should lead to broader moral commitments. See Noddings, *Starting at Home*.

50. Ruddick, *Maternal Thinking*, 79–80.

51. McDaniel, "Practicing the Presence of God," 134.

52. Webb, *On God and Dogs*, 6.

53. Fudge, *Pets*, 19.

54. Grier, *Pets in America*, 232.

55. Ibid., 13.

56. Roel Sterckx, "'Of a tawny bull we make offering': Animals in Early Chinese Religions," in Waldau and Patton, eds., *A Communion of Subjects*, 263.

57. Ian McIntosh, "'Why Umbulka Killed His Master': Aboriginal Reconciliation and the Australian Wild Dog (*Canis lupus dingo*)," in Waldau and Patton, eds., *A Communion of Subjects*, 361.

58. Kathy Rudy, *Loving Animals*, xi.

59. William Jordan III, *The Sunflower Forest: Ecological Restoration and the New Communion with Nature*, 2–3.

60. Pablo Neruda, "A Dog Has Died," in *Winter Garden*, 61.

61. Webb, *On God and Dogs*, 6.

62. Diane Antonio, "Of Wolves and Women," in Adams and Donovan, eds., *Animals and Women*, 214.

63. "Pit bull" is a type of dog which includes several distinct breeds, including the American pit bull terrier, American Staffordshire terrier, and Staffordshire bull terrier, as well as their mixes and, in many cases, similar-looking dogs such as American bulldogs or bull terriers.

64. Jon Franklin, *The Wolf in the Parlor: The Eternal Connection Between Humans and Dogs*.

65. Karen Delise, *The Pit Bull Placebo: The Media, Myths and Politics of Canine Aggression*, 2.

66. Webb, *On God and Dogs*, 100.

67. Vicki Hearne, *Bandit: Dossier of a Dangerous Dog*, 36.

68. Marx, "Theses on Feuerbach," 145, and *The German Ideology*, 149.

69. Marx, *The German Ideology*, 149.

70. Palmer, *Animal Ethics in Context*, 66.

71. Karl Marx, *The Economic and Philosophical Manuscripts of 1844*, edited by Dirk J. Struik, 107.

72. Erica Fudge, *Animal*, 145.

73. Marx, "Contribution to the Critique," 53.

74. Haraway, *When Species Meet*, 46.

BIBLIOGRAPHY

Abram, David. *Becoming Animal: An Earthly Cosmology.* New York: Pantheon, 2010.
——. *The Spell of the Sensuous: Perception and Language in a More-Than-Human World.* New York: Pantheon, 1996.
Adams, Carol J. "Caring About Suffering: A Feminist Exploration" (1995). In Donovan and Adams, eds., *The Feminist Care Tradition in Animal Ethics,* 198–227.
——. *The Feminist Politics of Meat: A Feminist-Vegetarian Critical Theory.* New York: Continuum, 1990.
——. "The War on Compassion" (2006). In Donovan and Adams, eds., *The Feminist Care Tradition in Animal Ethics,* 21–37.
——. "Woman-Battering and Harm to Animals." In Adams and Donovan, eds., *Animals and Women,* 55–84.
Adams, Carol J. and Josephine Donovan, eds. *Animals and Women: Feminist Theoretical Explorations.* Durham and London: Duke UP, 1995.
Antonio, Diane. "Of Wolves and Women." In Adams and Donovan, eds., *Animals and Women,* 213–30.
Armstrong, Susan J. and Richard G. Botzler, eds. *The Animal Ethics Reader.* 2d ed. London and New York: Routledge, 2008.
Badiner, Allan Hunt, ed. *Dharma Gaia: A Harvest of Essays in Buddhism and Ecology.* Berkeley: Parallax Press, 1990.
Balcombe, Jonathan. *Pleasurable Kingdom: Animals and the Nature of Feeling Good.* London: MacMillan, 2007.
——. *Second Nature: The Inner Lives of Animals.* New York: Palgrave MacMillan, 2010.

Bekoff, Marc. *Animal Passions and Beastly Virtues: Reflections on Redecorating Nature*. With a Foreword by Jane Goodall. Philadelphia: Temple UP, 2006.

Bekoff, Marc and Dale Jamieson, eds. *Readings in Animal Cognition*. Cambridge: MIT Press, 1996.

Bekoff, Marc and Jessica Pierce. *Wild Justice: The Moral Lives of Animals*. Chicago: U of Chicago P, 2009.

Benson, Simon. "Man and Canine a Top Team," *Daily Telegraph*, March 25, 2002.

Bentham, Jeremy. *Anarchical Fallacies*. In *The Works of Jeremy Bentham*, vol. 2. Edinburgh: William Tatt, 1843.

——. *Introduction to the Principles of Morals and Legislation*, 2d ed. (1823); see www.econlib .org/library/Bentham/bnthPML18.html.

Benton, Ted. "Humanism = Speciesism: Marx on Humans and Animals," *Radical Philosophy* 50.3 (Autumn 1988): 4–18.

——. "Marxism and the Moral Status of Animals," *Society & Animals* 11.1 (2003): 73–79.

——. *Natural Relations: Ecology, Animal Rights and Social Justice*. London and New York: Verso, 1993.

Bergman, Charles. "Making Animals Matter." *Chronicle of Higher Education*, March 23, 2001, B15; see http://chronicle.com/article/Making-Animals-Matter/1807/.

Berry, Thomas. *The Dream of the Earth*. San Francisco: Sierra Club Books, 1990.

Berry, Wendell. *Home Economics*. New York: Farrar, Strauss and Giroux, 1980.

Beston, Henry. *The Outermost House: A Year of Life on the Great Beach of Cape Cod* (1929). Rpt., New York: Viking, 1962.

Birke, Lynda. *Feminism, Animals and Science: The Naming of the Shrew*. London and Buckingham, PA: Open UP, 1994.

Blake, James. "Overcoming the Value-Action Gap in Environmental Policy." *Local Environment* 4.3 (1999): 257–78.

Boks, Ed. "Analysis of Feral Cat Solutions"; see www.edboks.com/uploads/Analysis_of_Feral_Cat_Solutions.pdf.

Bowden, Peta. *Caring: Gender-sensitive Ethics*. London and New York: Routledge, 1997.

Budiansky, Stephen. The Covenant of the Wild: Why Animals Chose Domestication. New York: William Morrow, 1992.

Bulliet, Richard W. *Hunters, Herders, and Hamburgers: The Past and Future of Human-Animal Relationships*. New York: Columbia UP, 2005.

Burghardt, Gordon M. *The Genesis of Animal Play: Testing the Limits*. Cambridge: MIT Press, 2005.

Callicott, J. Baird. "Animal Liberation: A Triangular Affair" (1980). In Hargrove, ed., *The Animal Rights/Environmental Ethics Debate*, 37–70.

——. "Animal Liberation and Environmental Ethics: Back Together Again" (1989). In Hargrove, ed., *The Animal Rights/Environmental Ethics Debate*, 249–62.

——. "The Conceptual Foundations of the Land Ethic." In *In Defense of the Land Ethic*, 75–100.

——. *Earth's Insights: A Multicultural Survey of Ecological Ethics from the Mediterranean Basin to the Australian Outback*. Berkeley: U of California P, 1994.

——. *In Defense of the Land Ethic: Essays in Environmental Philosophy.* Albany: SUNY Press, 1989.

——. "The Metaphysical Implications of Ecology." In J. Baird Callicott and Roger Ames, eds., *Nature in Asian Traditions of Thought*, 51–66. Albany: SUNY Press, 1989.

——. Review of Tom Regan, *The Case for Animal Rights.* In *In Defense of the Land Ethic*, 39–48.

Callicott, J. Baird and Michael P. Nelson. *American Indian Environmental Ethics: An Ojibwa Case Study.* Upper Saddle River, NJ: Pearson Prentice Hall, 2004.

Caras, Roger. *A Perfect Harmony: The Intertwining Lives of Animals and Humans Throughout History.* New York: Simon and Schuster, 1997.

Chapple, Christopher Key. "Animals and Environment in the Buddhist Birth Stories." In Tucker and Williams, eds., *Buddhism and Ecology*, 131–48.

——. "Inherent Value without Nostalgia: Animals and the Jaini Tradition." In Waldau and Patton, eds., *A Communion of Subjects*, 241–50.

Cheney, Dorothy L. and Robert M. Seyfarth. *How Monkeys See the World: Inside the Mind of Another Species.* Chicago: U of Chicago P, 1990.

Cheney, Jim. "Eco Feminism and Deep Ecology." *Environmental Ethics* 9.2 (Summer 1987): 115–45.

——. "Postmodern Environmental Ethics: Ethics as Bioregional Narrative." *Environmental Ethics* 11.2 (Summer 1989): 117–34.

Cheney, Jim and Anthony Weston. "Environmental Ethics as Environmental Etiquette." *Environmental Ethics* 21.2 (Summer 1999): 115–34.

Clark, Stephen R. L. *The Moral Status of Animals.* Oxford: Clarenden Press, 1977.

——. *The Nature of the Beast: Are Animals Moral?* Oxford: Oxford UP, 1984.

Clement, Grace. "The Ethics of Care and the Problem of Wild Animals" (2003). In Donovan and Adams, eds., *The Feminist Care Tradition in Animal Ethics*, 301–315.

Daly, Mary. *Gyn/Ecology: The Meta-ethics of Radical Feminism.* Boston: Beacon Press, 1978.

Damasio, Antonio. *Descartes' Error: Emotion, Reason, and the Human Brain.* New York: Avon, 1994.

Darwin, Charles. *The Origin of Species by Means of Natural Selection, or the Preservation of Favoured Races in the Struggle for Life.* New York: Penguin Books, 1968 (first published by John Murray, 1859).

Dawkins, Marian Stamp. *Through Our Eyes Only? The Search for Animal Consciousness.* Oxford: Oxford UP, 1998.

Delise, Karen. *The Pit Bull Placebo: The Media, Myths and Politics of Canine Aggression.* Ramsey, NJ: Anubis, 2007.

Derr, Mark. *Dog's Best Friend: Annals of the Dog-Human Relationship.* New York: Henry Holt, 1997.

Derr, Patrick G. and Edward M. McNamara. *Case Studies in Environmental Ethics.* Lanham, MD: Rowman and Littlefield, 2003.

Descartes, René. "Discourse on Method" (1637). In *Philosophical Essays: Discourse on Method; Meditations; Rules for the Direction of the Mind.* Trans. Laurence J. Lafleur. Indianapolis: Bobbs-Merrill, 1964.

De-Shalit, Avner. *Why Posterity Matters: Environmental Policies and Future Generations.* London: Routledge, 1995.

Des Jardins, Joseph. *Environmental Ethics: An Introduction to Environmental Philosophy.* Wadsworth, 2005.

De Waal, Frans. *Good Natured: The Origins of Right and Wrong in Humans and Other Animals.* Cambridge: Harvard UP, 1996.

Dizard, Jan. *Going Wild: Hunting, Animals Rights, and the Contested Meaning of Nature.* Amherst: U of Massachusetts P, 1999.

Donovan, Josephine. "Attention to Suffering: Sympathy as a Basis for Ethical Treatment of Animals" (1994). In Donovan and Adams, eds., *The Feminist Care Tradition in Animal Ethics,* 174–97.

Donovan, Josephine and Carol J. Adams, eds., *The Feminist Care Tradition in Animal Ethics.* New York: Columbia UP, 2007.

Dunayer, Joan. *Animal Equality: Language and Liberation.* Derwood, MD: Ryce Books, 2001.

——. *Speciesism.* Derwood, MD: Ryce Books, 2004.

Eldridge, J. J. and J. P. Gluck. "Gender Differences in Attitudes Toward Animal Research." *Ethics and Behavior* 6.3 (1996): 239–56.

Falconer, Julie. "On the Scent of Poachers: Rescued Dogs Help Game Wardens in the War Against Wildlife Criminals." *All Animals* (March–April 2010): 14–22.

Finger, Matthias. "From Knowledge to Action? Exploring the Relationships Between Environmental Experiences, Learning, and Behavior." *Journal of Social Issues* 50.3 (Fall 1994): 141–60.

Fischer, Frank and Maarten A. Hajer. "Introduction: Beyond Global Discourse: The Rediscovery of Culture in Environmental Politics." In F. Fischer and M. Hajer, eds., *Living with Nature: Environmental Politics as Cultural Discourse,* 1–20. Oxford: Oxford UP, 1999.

Foster, John Bellamy. *Marx's Ecology: Materialism and Nature.* New York: Monthly Review Press, 2000.

Francione, Gary L. *Animals, Property, and the Law.* With a foreword by William M. Kunstler. Philadelphia: Temple UP, 1995.

Franklin, Jon. *The Wolf in the Parlor: The Eternal Connection Between Humans and Dogs.* New York: Henry Holt, 2009.

Fudge, Erica. *Animal.* London: Reaktion Books, 2002.

——. *Pets.* Stocksfield, Eng.: Acumen, 2008.

Galef, Bennett, G., Jr., "The Making of a Science." In Houck and Drickamer, eds., *Foundations of Animal Behavior,* 5–12.

Garbarino, James. "Protecting Children and Animals from Abuse: A Trans-Species Concept of Caring" (1998). In Donovan and Adams, eds., *The Feminist Care Tradition in Animal Ethics,* 250–58.

Geertz, Clifford. "From the Native's Point of View: On the Nature of Anthropological Understanding." In *Local Knowledge: Further Essays in Interpretive Anthropology,* 55–72. New York: Basic Books, 1983.

Gilligan, Carol. *In a Different Voice: Psychological Theory and Women's Development*. Cambridge: Harvard UP, 1982.

——. "Moral Orientation and Moral Development." In Eve Feder Kittay and Diana T. Meyers, eds., *Women and Moral Theory*. New York: Rowman and Littlefield, 1987.

Goodall, Jane. *In The Shadow of Man*. Boston: Houghton Mifflin, 1971; rpt., San Diego: San Diego State UP, 1988.

Gopnik, Alison, Andrew N. Meltzoff, and Patricia K. Kuhl. *The Scientist in the Crib: What Early Learning Tells Us About the Mind*. New York: HarperCollins, 1999.

Grandin, Temple and Catherine Johnson. *Animals Make Us Human: Creating the Best Life for Animals*. New York: Mariner Books, 2009.

Grandin, Temple, with Catherine Johnson. *Animals in Translation: Using the Mysteries of Autism to Decode Animal Behavior*. New York: Simon and Schuster, 2005.

Grier, Katherine C. *Pets in America: A History*. Orlando: Harcourt, 2007.

Griffin, Donald. *Animal Thinking*. Cambridge: Harvard UP, 1984.

Griffin, Susan. *Woman and Nature: The Roaring Inside Her*. New York: Harper, 1978.

Gruen, Lori. "Dismantling Oppression: An Analysis of the Connection Between Women and Animals." In Greta Gaard, ed., *Ecofeminism: Women, Animals, Nature*. Philadelphia: Temple UP, 1993.

Gustafson, James. *Ethics from a Theocentric Perspective*, vol. 1. Chicago: U of Chicago P, 1981.

——. *A Sense of the Divine: The Natural Environment from a Theocentric Perspective*. Cleveland, OH: Pilgrim Press, 1994.

Guttilla, Darcee and Paul Stapp. "Effects of Sterilization on Movements of Feral Cats at a Wildland–Urban Interface." *Journal of Mammalogy* 91.2 (April 2010): 482–89; see www2.allenpress.com/pdf/mamm-91-02-482-489.pdf.

Hall, Lee. *On Their Own Terms: Bringing Animal-Rights Philosophy Down to Earth*. Darien, CT: Nectar Bat Press, 2010.

Hamilton, William. "The Genetical Evolution of Social Behaviour," parts 1 and 2. *Journal of Theoretical Biology* 7 (1964): 1–52; reprinted in Houck and Drickamer, eds., *Foundations of Animal Behavior*, 764–80.

Haraway, Donna J. "Animal Sociology and a Natural Economy of the Body Politic." In *Simians, Cyborgs, and Women: The Reinvention of Nature*, 7–20. New York: Routledge, 1991.

——. *The Companion Species Manifesto: Dogs, People, and Significant Otherness*. Chicago: Prickly Paradigm Press, 2003.

——. "Situated Knowledges." In *Simians, Cyborg, and Women: The Reinvention of Nature*, 183–202. New York: Routledge, 1991.

——. *When Species Meet*. Minneapolis: U of Minnesota P, 2008.

Hargrove, Eugene C. *Foundations of Environmental Ethics*. Denton, TX: Environmental Ethics Books, 1989.

——. "Preface: Animal Welfare Ethics 'versus' Environmental Ethics: The Problem of Sentient Life." In Hargrove, ed., *The Animal Rights/Environmental Ethics Debate*, ix–xxvi.

Hargrove, Eugene C., ed. *The Animal Rights/Environmental Ethics Debate: The Environmental Perspective.* Albany: SUNY Press, 1992.

Harrod, Howard. *The Animals Came Dancing: Native American Sacred Ecology and Animal Kinship.* Tucson: U of Arizona P, 2000.

Hatkoff, Isabella, Craig Hatkoff, and Paula Kahumbu, *Owen and Mzee: The True Story of a Remarkable Friendship.* New York: Scholastic Books, 2006.

Hawkins, Cole C., William E. Grant, and Michael T. Longnecker. "Effect of House Cats Being Fed in Parks on California Birds and Rodents." *Proceedings of the 4th International Urban Wildlife Symposium* (2004), 168; see http://cals.arizona.edu/pubs/adjunct/snr0704/snr07042l.pdf.

Hearne, Vicki. *Adam's Task: Calling Animals by Name.* New York: Harper Perennial, 1994.

——. *Animal Happiness.* New York: HarperCollins, 1994.

——. *Bandit: Dossier of a Dangerous Dog.* New York: HarperCollins, 1991.

Held, Virginia. "Feminist Moral Inquiry and the Feminist Future." In Held, ed., *Justice and Care.*

Held, Virginia, ed. *Justice and Care: Essential Readings in Feminist Ethics.* Boulder: Westview, 1995.

Herms, Daniel A. "The Honeybee Waggle Dance: An Active Participation, Role Playing Game," *Entomology Note*, no. 22. Lansing, MI: Michigan Entomology Society, 1990; see http://insects.ummz.lsa.umich.edu/MES/notes/entnote22.html.

Herzog, Hal. *Some We Love, Some We Hate, Some We Eat: Why It's So Hard to Think Straight About Animals.* New York: HarperCollins, 2010.

Hobgood-Oster, Laura. *The Friends We Keep: Unleashing Christianity's Compassion for Animals.* Waco, TX: Baylor UP, 2010.

Horowitz, Alexandra. *Inside of a Dog: What Dogs See, Smell, and Know.* New York: Scribner, 2009.

Houck, Lynne D. and Lee C. Drickamer, eds. *Foundations of Animal Behavior: Classic Papers with Commentaries.* Chicago: U of Chicago P, 1996.

Howard, Jennifer. "Presses, Journals, and Meetings Buzz with Animal Studies." *Chronicle of Higher Education*, October 18, 2009; see http://chronicle.com/article/Presses-Journals-and/48805/.

Irvine, Leslie. *If You Tame Me: Understanding Our Connection with Animals.* Philadelphia: Temple UP, 2004.

James, Simon P. *The Presence of Nature: A Study of Phenomenology and Environmental Philosophy.* Palgrave MacMillan. 2009.

Jamieson, Dale. "Animal Liberation Is an Environmental Ethic." *Environmental Values* 7 (February 1998): 41–57.

Jamieson, Dale and Marc Bekoff. "On Aims and Methods of Cognitive Ethology." In Bekoff and Jamieson, eds., *Readings in Animal Cognition*, 65–78.

Johnson, Lawrence E. *A Morally Deep World: An Essay on Moral Significance and Environmental Ethics.* Cambridge: Cambridge UP, 1991.

Johnson, Norman H., DVM. *The Complete Puppy and Dog Book: The Standard Work*. Rev. ed. New York: Atheneum: 1977.

Jordan, William III. *The Sunflower Forest: Ecological Restoration and the New Communion with Nature*. Berkeley: U of California P, 2003.

Jung, L. Shannon. *We Are Home: A Spirituality of the Environment*. New York: Paulist Press, 1993.

Kant, Immanuel. *Foundations of the Metaphysics of Morals*. Trans. L. W. Beck. Indianapolis: Bobbs-Merrill, 1969.

Kappeler, Susanne. "Speciesism, Racism, Nationalism . . . or the Power of Scientific Subjectivity." In Adams and Donovan, eds., *Animals and Women*, 320–52.

Katcher, Aaron. "Animals in Therapeutic Education: Guides into the Liminal State." In Peter H. Kahn, Jr., and Stephen R. Kellert, eds., *Children and Nature: Psychological, Sociocultural, and Evolutionary Investigations*, 179–98. Cambridge: MIT Press, 2002.

Katz, Eric. *Nature as Subject: Human Obligation and Natural Community*. Lanham, MD: Rowman and Littlefield, 1997.

Katz, Jon. *The New Work of Dogs: Tending to Life, Love, Family*. New York: Villard, 2003.

Kempton, Willett, James S. Boster, and Jennifer A. Hartley. *Environmental Values in American Culture*. Cambridge: MIT Press, 1995.

Kheel, Marti. "From Heroic to Holistic Ethics: The Ecofeminist Challenge." In Greta Gaard, ed., *Ecofeminism: Women, Animals, Nature*, 243–71. Philadelphia: Temple UP, 1993.

——. "The Liberation of Nature: A Circular Affair." *Environmental Ethics* 7 (Summer 1985): 135–49.

——. "License to Kill: An Ecofeminist Critique of Hunters' Discourse." In Adams and Donovan, eds., *Animals and Women*, 85–125.

——. *Nature Ethics: An Ecofeminist Perspective*. Lanham, MD: Rowman and Littlefield, 2008.

King, Barbara J. *Being with Animals: Why We are Obsessed with the Furry, Scaly, Feathered Creatures Who Populate Our World*. New York: Doubleday, 2010.

King, Roger. "Feral Animals and the Restoration of Nature." *Between the Species* 9 (August 2009): 1–27; see http://digitalcommons.calpoly.edu/bts/vol13/iss9/1.

Klein, Naomi. "After the Oil Spill." *The Nation*, January 31, 2011, 11–18.

Knapp, Caroline. *Pack of Two*. New York: Dial Press, 1998.

Kollmus, Anja and Julian Agyeman. "Mind the Gap: Why Do People Act Environmentally and What Are the Barriers to Pro-environmental Behavior?" *Environmental Education and Research* 8.2 (2003): 239 – 60.

Laitin, David D. "Religion, Political Culture, and the Weberian Tradition." *World Politics* 30.4 (July 1978): 563–92.

Leopold, Aldo. "Game and Wild Life Conservation" (1932). In Armstrong and Botzler, eds., *The Animal Ethics Reader*, 451–53.

——. "The Land Ethic." In *A Sand County Almanac* (1970 ed.), 237–64.

——. *A Sand County Almanac; with Essays on Conservation from Round River*. New York and Oxford: Oxford UP, 1949; rpt., San Francisco and New York: Sierra Club/Ballantine, 1970.

——. "Thinking Like a Mountain." In *A Sand County Almanac* (1970 ed.), 137–41.

——. "Wilderness." In *A Sand County Almanac* (1970 ed.), 264–80.

Lévi-Strauss, Claude. *The Savage Mind*. Chicago: U of Chicago P, 1968.

Light, Andrew. "Methodological Pragmatism, Animal Welfare, and Hunting." In McKenna and Light, eds., *Animal Pragmatism*, 119–39.

Linden, Eugene. *Apes, Men, and Language*. New York: Penguin; rev. ed., 1981.

Linzey, Andrew. *Christianity and the Rights of Animals*. New York: Crossroad, 1987.

——. *Creatures of the Same God: Explorations in Animal Theology*. New York: Lantern Books, 2009.

Lorenz, Konrad Z. *The Foundations of Ethology*. Trans. by Konrad Z. Lorenz and Robert Warren Kickert. New York and Vienna: Springer-Verlag, 1981.

Louv, Ricard. *Last Child in the Woods: Saving Our Children from Nature-Deficit Disorder*. Chapel Hill, NC: Algonquin Books, 2005.

Macy, Joanna. "The Greening of the Self." In Badiner, ed., *Dharma Gaia*, 53–63.

Manes, Christopher [Miss Ann Thropy]. "Population and AIDS." *Earth First* 7.5 (1987): n.p.

——. "Technology and Mortality." *Earth First* 7.1 (1986): n.p.

Marietta, Don E., Jr. *For People and the Planet: Holism and Humanism in Environmental Ethics*. Philadelphia: Temple UP, 1995.

Marx, Karl. *Capital*, vol. 1. In Robert Tucker, ed., *The Marx-Engels Reader*.

——. "Contribution to the Critique of Hegel's Philosophy of Right: Introduction." In Robert Tucker, ed., *The Marx-Engels Reader*, 16–25.

——. "The Economic and Philosophical Manuscripts of 1844." In Robert Tucker, ed., *The Marx-Engels Reader*, 66–125.

——. *The Economic and Philosophical Manuscripts of 1844*. Edited by Dirk J. Struik. New York: International Publishers, 1964.

——. *The German Ideology, Part 1*. In Robert Tucker, ed., *The Marx-Engels Reader*, 146–200.

——. "Theses on Feuerbach." In Robert Tucker, ed., *The Marx-Engels Reader*, 143–45.

McDaniel, Jay. "Practicing the Presence of God: A Christian Approach to Animals." In Waldau and Patton, eds., *A Communion of Subjects*, 132–48.

McIntosh, Ian. "'Why Umbulka Killed His Master': Aboriginal Reconciliation and the Australian Wild Dog (*Canis lupus dingo*)." In Waldau and Patton, eds., *A Communion of Subjects*, 360–70.

McKenna, Erin and Andrew Light, eds. *Animal Pragmatism: Rethinking Human-Nonhuman Relationships*. Bloomington: Indiana UP, 2004.

McKenzie-Mohr, Doug and William Smith. *Fostering Sustainable Behavior: An Introduction to Community-Based Social Marketing*. Gabriola Island, B.C.: New Society, 1999.

McKibben, Bill. *The End of Nature*. New York: Random House, 1989.

Melson, Gail F. *Why the Wild Things Are: Animals in the Lives of Children*. Cambridge: Harvard UP, 2001.

Merchant, Carolyn. *The Death of Nature: Women, Ecology, and the Scientific Revolution.* New York: Harper, 1980.

Midgley, Mary. *Animals and Why They Matter.* Athens: U of Georgia P, 1983.

——. *Beast and Man: The Roots of Human Nature* (orig. 1978, Cornell U P). Rpt., London and New York: Routledge, 1995.

Mill, John Stuart. *Utilitarianism.* In *On Liberty and Other Essays.* Edited by John Gray. Oxford: Oxford UP, 1998.

Minteer, Ben A. "Beyond Considerability: A Deweyan View of the Animal Rights–Environmental Ethics Debate." In McKenna and Light, eds., *Animal Pragmatism,* 97–118.

——. *The Landscape of Reform: Civic Pragmatism and Environmental Thought in America.* Cambridge: MIT Press, 2006.

Morris, Desmond. *Dogs: A Dictionary of Dog Breeds.* North Pomfret, VT: Trafalgar Square, 2002.

Nabhan, Gary P. and Stephen Trimble. *The Geography of Childhood: Why Children Need Wild Places.* Boston: Beacon, 1995.

Naess, Arne. *Ecology, Community and Lifestyle.* Translated and edited by David Rothenberg. Cambridge: Cambridge UP, 1989.

——. "The Shallow and the Deep, Long-Range Ecology Movement." *Inquiry* 16 (1973): 95–100; see www.ecology.ethz.ch/education/Readings_stuff/ Naess_1973.pdf.

Nagel, Thomas. "What Is It Like to Be a Bat?" *Philosophical Review* 83 (1974): 435–50.

Nash, Roderick Frazier. *The Rights of Nature: A History of Environmental Ethics.* Madison: U of Wisconsin P, 1989.

Nelson, Richard. *Heart and Blood: Living with Deer in America.* New York: Vintage, 1998.

——. *Make Prayers to the Raven: A Koyukon View of the Northern Forest.* Chicago: U of Chicago P, 1983.

Neruda, Pablo. *Winter Garden.* Port Townsend, WA: Copper Canyon Press, 1986.

Noddings, Nel. *Caring: A Feminine Approach to Ethics and Moral Education.* Berkeley: U of California P, 1984.

——. *Starting at Home: Caring and Social Policy.* Berkeley: U of California P, 2002.

Norton, Bryan G. "Environmental Ethics and Nonhuman Rights." In Hargrove, ed., *The Animal Rights/Environmental Ethics Debate,* 71–94.

——. "Why I Am Not a Nonanthropocentrist: Callicott and the Failure of Monistic Inherentism." *Environmental Ethics* 17.4 (Winter 1995): 341–58.

Noske, Barbara. *Beyond Boundaries: Humans and Animals.* Montreal: Black Rose Books, 1997.

Nussbaum, Martha. *Frontiers of Justice: Disability, Nationality, Species Membership.* Cambridge, MA: Harvard UP, 2006.

Oelschlaeger, Max. *Caring for Creation: An Ecumenical Approach to the Environmental Crisis.* New Haven: Yale UP, 1994.

Ollman, Bertell. *Alienation: Marx's Conception of Man in Capitalist Society.* Cambridge: Cambridge UP, 1971.

Olmert, Meg Daley. *Made for Each Other: The Biology of the Human-Animal Bond.* Cambridge, MA: Da Capo, 2009.

Orr, David. *Ecological Literacy: Education and the Transition to a Postmodern World.* Albany: SUNY Press, 1992.

Palmer, Clare. *Animal Ethics in Context.* New York: Columbia UP, 2010.

Parelli, Pat, with Kathy Swan. *Natural Horse*Man*Ship.* Colorado Springs, CO: Western Horseman, 1993.

Parker, Elizabeth. "Boy Allergic to Peanuts Has Dog to Sniff Out Danger," *Seattle Times* , June 19, 2011; see http://seattletimes.nwsource.com/html/health/2015326438_peanuts20.html.

Patton, Kimberley. "Animal Sacrifice: Metaphysics of the Sublimated Victim." In Waldau and Patton, eds., *A Communion of Subjects,* 391–405.

——. "'Caught with Ourselves in the Net of Life and Time': Traditional Views of Animals in Religion." In Waldau and Patton, eds., *A Communion of Subjects,* 27–39.

Perlo, Katherine. "Marxism and the Underdog." *Society & Animals* 10.3 (2002): 303–318.

Perry, Melissa. "Michael Vick, Racial History, and Animal Rights." *The Nation* blog (December 30, 2010); see www.thenation.com/blog/157372/michael-vick-racial-history-and-animal-rights.

Petersen, David, ed. *A Hunter's Heart: Honest Essays on Blood Sport.* New York: Holt, 1997.

Peterson, Anna L. *Being Human: Ethics, Environment, and Our Place in the World.* Berkeley: U of California P, 2001.

——. *Everyday Ethics and Social Change: The Education of Desire.* New York: Columbia UP, 2009.

——. "Toward a Materialist Environmental Ethic." *Environmental Ethics* 28.4 (Winter 2006): 375–93.

Pinches, Charles and Jay B. McDaniel, eds. *Good News for Animals: Christian Approaches to Animal Well-Being.* Maryknoll, NY: Orbis, 1993.

Plumwood, Val. *Feminism and the Mastery of Nature.* London and New York: Routledge, 1993.

——. "Nature, Self, and Gender: Feminism, Environmental Philosophy, and the Critique of Rationalism." *Hypatia* 6.1 (Spring 1991): 3–27.

Popper, Ilona. "Field Work." *Bark* (November–December 2009): 52–56.

Price, Edward O. "Domestication and Behavior." In Marc Bekoff, ed., *The Encyclopedia of Animal Behavior* 3:510–14. Westport, CT, and London: Greenwood Press, 2004.

Princen, Thomas, Michael Maniates, and Ken Conca, eds. *Confronting Consumption.* Cambridge: MIT Press, 2002.

Radner, Daisie and Michael Radner. *Animal Consciousness.* Buffalo: Prometheus Books, 1989.

Raglon, Rebecca and Marian Scholtmeijer. "Shifting Ground: Metanarratives, Epistemology, and the Stories of Nature." *Environmental Ethics* 18.1 (Spring 1996): 19–38.

Regan, Tom. *The Case for Animal Rights* (1983). Updated with a new Preface. Berkeley: U of California P, 2004.

Roberts, Elizabeth. "Gaian Buddhism." In Badiner, ed., *Dharma Gaia*, 147–54.

Rodd, Rosemary. *Biology, Ethics and Animals*. Oxford: Oxford UP, 1990.

Rollin, Bernard. *Animal Rights and Human Morality*. Buffalo: Prometheus Books, 1981.

Rolston, Holmes III. *Environmental Ethics: Duties to and Values in the Natural World*. Philadelphia: Temple UP, 1988.

Ruddick, Sara. "Maternal Thinking." *Feminist Studies* 6.2 (Summer 1980): 342–67.

——. *Maternal Thinking: Toward a Politics of Peace*. Boston: Beacon Press, 1995.

Rudy, Kathy. *Loving Animals: Toward a New Animal Advocacy*. Minneapolis: U of Minnesota P, 2011.

Sagoff, Mark. "Animal Liberation and Environmental Ethics: Bad Marriage, Quick Divorce," *Osgoode Hall Law Journal* 22.2 (1984): 297–307; reprinted in Michael E. Zimmerman et al., eds., *Environmental Philosophy*, (1993 ed).

Sanbonmatsu, John. "Listen, Ecological Marxist! (Yes, I said *Animals!*)." *Capitalism, Nature, Socialism* 16.2 (2005): 107–114.

Sandilands, Catriona. *The Good-Natured Feminist: Ecofeminism and the Quest for Democracy*. Minneapolis: U of Minnesota P, 1999.

Sandler, Ronald and Philip Cafaro, eds. *Environmental Virtue Ethics*. Lanham, MD: Rowman and Littlefield, 2005.

Schorsch, Ismar. "Learning to Live with Less: A Jewish Perspective." In Stephen Rockefeller and John C. Elder, eds., *Spirit and Nature: Why the Environment Is a Religious Issue*. Boston: Beacon Press, 1992. Pp. 25–38.

Schwartz, Marion. *A History of Dogs in the Early Americas*. New Haven and London: Yale UP, 1997.

Segundo, Juan Luis. *The Liberation of Theology*. Maryknoll, NY: Orbis, 1976.

Shelton, Jo-Ann. "Killing Animals That Don't Fit In: Moral Dimensions of Habitat Restoration." *Between the Species* 4 (2004): 1–21; see http://digitalcommons.calpoly.edu/bts/vol13/iss4/3.

Shepard, Paul. *Coming Home to the Pleistocene*. Washington, D.C.: Island Press, 1998.

——. *The Others: How Animals Made Us Human*. Washington, D.C.: Island Press, 1996.

Sideris, Lisa H. *Environmental Ethics, Ecological Theology, and Natural Selection*. New York: Columbia UP, 2003.

Simonds, Shelly. "Theory Suggests Greater Role for Man's Best Friend." *ANU Reporter* 29.1; see http://info.anu.edu.au/mac/Newsletters_and_Journals/ANU_Reporter/_pdf/vol_29_no_01/dogs.html.

Singer, Peter. *Animal Liberation* (1975). New rev. ed. New York: Avon, 1990.

Slobodchikoff, Con. "Cognition and Communication in Prairie Dogs." In Marc Bekoff, Colin Allen, and Gordon Burghardt, eds., *The Cognitive Animal: Empirical and Theoretical Perspectives on Animal Cognition*, 257–64. Cambridge: MIT Press, 2002.

Snyder, Gary. "Nets of Beads, Webs of Cells." In *A Place in Space: Ethics, Aesthetics, and Watersheds. New and Selected Prose*, 65–73. Washington, D.C.: Counterpoint, 1995.

Snyder, Samuel. "The Rodman Standoff: A Dam Critique of Bioregionalist Politics of Place." Paper presented at the First International Conference on Religion and Nature, Gainesville, Florida, April 7, 2006.

Soulé, Michael E. and Gary Lease, eds. *Reinventing Nature? Responses to Postmodern Deconstruction*. Washington, D.C.: Island Press, 1995.

Steiner, Gary. *Animals and the Moral Community: Mental Life, Moral Status, and Kinship*. New York: Columbia UP, 2008.

——. *Anthropocentrism and Its Discontents: The Moral Status of Animals in the History of Western Philosophy*. Pittsburgh: U of Pittsburgh P, 2005.

Sterckx, Roel. "'Of a tawny bull we make offering': Animals in Early Chinese Religions." In Waldau and Patton, eds., *A Communion of Subjects*, 259–74.

Strange, Mary Zeiss. *Woman the Hunter*. Boston: Beacon Press, 1998.

Swan, James, ed. *The Sacred Art of Hunting: Myths, Legends, and the Modern Mythos*. Minocqua, WI: Willow Creek Press, 2000.

Taylor, Angus. *Animals and Ethics: An Overview of the Philosophical Debate* (1997). 2d ed. Peterborough, Ontario: Broadview, 2009.

Taylor, Paul. "The Ethic of Respect for Nature." In Hargrove, ed., *The Animal Rights/Environmental Ethics Debate*, 95–120.

——. *Respect for Nature: A Theory of Environmental Ethics*. Princeton, NJ: Princeton UP, 1986.

Tester, Keith. *Animals and Society: The Humanity of Animal Rights*. London and New York: Routledge, 1991.

Thiele, Leslie Paul. "Evolutionary Narratives and Ecological Ethics." *Political Theory* 27.1 (1999): 6–38.

Thompson, E. P. *The Making of the English Working Class*. New York: Vintage, 1966.

——. *William Morris: Romantic to Revolutionary*. Stanford, CA: Stanford UP, 1981.

Thu, Kendall M. and E. Paul Durrenberger, eds. *Pigs, Profits, and Rural Communities*. Albany: SUNY Press, 1998.

Tillich, Paul. *Love, Power, and Justice: Ontological Analyses and Ethical Applications*. New York: Oxford UP, 1960.

Trivers, Robert L. "The Evolution of Reciprocal Altruism." *Quarterly Review of Biology* 46 (1971): 35–46.

——. "Parental Investment and Sexual Selection." In B. Campbell, ed., *Sexual Selection and the Descent of Man, 1871–1971* (Chicago: Aldine, 1972); reprinted in Houck and Drickamer, eds., *Foundations of Animal Behavior*, 795–838.

Tronto, Joan. "Women and Caring: What Can Feminists Learn About Morality from Caring?" In Held, ed., *Justice and Care*.

Tuan, Yi-Fu. *Dominance and Affection: The Making of Pets*. New Haven and London: Yale UP, 1984.

Tucker, Mary Evelyn and Duncan Ryuken Williams, eds. *Buddhism and Ecology: The Interconnection of Dharma and Deeds*. Cambridge: Harvard UP, 1997.

Tucker, Robert, ed. *The Marx-Engels Reader*. New York: Norton, 1978.

Varner, Gary. *In Nature's Interests? Interests, Animal Rights, and Environmental Ethics*. New York and Oxford: Oxford UP, 1998.

Von Frisch, Karl. *The Dance Language and Orientation of Bees*. Cambridge, MA: Belknap Press of Harvard UP, 1967).

Waldau, Paul. "Pushing Environmental Justice to a Natural Limit." In Waldau and Patton, eds., *A Communion of Subjects*, 629–44.

Waldau, Paul and Kimberley Patton, eds. *A Communion of Subjects: Animals in Religion, Science, and Ethics*. New York: Columbia UP, 2006.

Walker, Stephen. *Animal Thought*. London: Routledge and Kegan Paul, 1983.

Warren, Karen. "The Power and Promise of Ecological Feminism." *Environmental Ethics* 12.2 (Summer 1990): 125–46.

Warren, Mary Anne. "The Rights of the Nonhuman World." In Hargrove, ed., *The Animal Rights/Environmental Ethics Debate*, 185–210.

Watson, Richard. "Self-Consciousness and the Rights of Nonhuman Animals and Nature." In Hargrove, ed., *The Animal Rights/Environmental Ethics Debate*, 1–36.

Wayne, Rorbert K. et al. "Multiple and Ancient Origins of the Domestic Dog." *Science* 276.13 (June 1997): 1687–89.

Webb, Stephen H. *On God and Dogs: A Christian Theology of Compassion for Animals*. New York: Oxford, 1998.

Weiner, Jonathan. *The Beak of the Finch: A Story of Evolution in Our Time*. New York: Knopf, 1994.

Welch, Sharon. *A Feminist Ethic of Risk*. Minneapolis: Fortress Press, 1988.

Weston, Anthony. *Back to Earth: Tomorrow's Environmentalism*. Philadelphia: Temple UP, 1994.

——. "Non-Anthropocentrism in a Thoroughly Anthropocentrized World." *The Trumpeter* 8.3 (1991); see http://trumpeter.athabascau.ca/contents/v8.3/weston.html.

White, Lynn, Jr. "The Historical Roots of Our Ecologic Crisis." *Science* 155 (1967): 1203–1207.

Woolf, Virginia. *Flush: A Biography*. New York: Harcourt, 1933.

Working Dogs for Conservation; see www.workingdogsforconservation.org.

Worster, Donald. *Nature's Economy: A History of Ecological Ideas*. 2d ed. Cambridge: Cambridge UP, 1994.

Xenopohon. *The Art of Horsemanship*. Edited and translated by Morris H. Morgan. Mineola, NY: Dover, 2006.

Yoder, John Howard. *The Politics of Jesus*. 2d ed. Grand Rapids, MI: Eerdmans, 1994.

Zimmerman, Michael. "Ecofascism: An Enduring Temptation." In Michael Zimmerman et al., eds., *Environmental Philosophy* (4th ed., 2004). Cited from version available online at www.colorado.edu/philosophy/paper_zimmerman_ecofascism.pdf.

Zimmerman, Michael E., J. Baird Callicott, George Sessions, Karen J. Warren, and John Clark, eds. *Environmental Philosophy: From Animal Rights to Radical Ecology* (1993). 4th ed. Englewood Cliffs, NJ: Prentice-Hall, 2004.

Zirin, Dave. "The Reality of Vick's Return." *The Nation*, August 3, 2009; see www.thenation.com/article/reality-vicks-return.

INDEX

Theocentrism, 40, 52, 154
Tuan, Yi-Fu, 111, 174–75

Utilitarianism, 44–47, 50, 123

Value, encounter, 171–72
Value, exchange, 170–71
Value, instrumental, 101
Value, intrinsic, 21–23, 25, 31–32, 34, 36–37, 43, 48, 70, 151
Value, use, 170–71
Vegetarianism, 46, 54, 134

Weston, Anthony, 162
Wild animals. *See* Animals, wild
Wilderness, 14–15, 18, 71
Wildness, 65–66, 68
Wolves, 92–93, 95–95, 129, 179–80
Women (and animals/nature), 38, 59
Work. *See* Labor

Zimmerman, Marc, 122–24
Zoos, 11, 74, 100, 102